DAMN
LUCKY

DAMN
LUCKY

One Man's Courage During the Bloodiest Military

Campaign in Aviation History

KEVIN
MAURER

ST. MARTIN'S PRESS
NEW YORK

First published in the United States by St. Martin's Press, an imprint of St. Martin's Publishing Group

www.stmartins.com

Designed by Omar Chapa

Endpaper design by Rob Grom
Endpaper art: bomb group © 100th BG Association Archives; image repair and colorization-Nathan Howland-HowdiColour; John Luckadoo photo courtesy of John Luckadoo; clouds © Praew stock / Shutterstock.com; texture © MM_photos / Shutterstock.com; map © Nastasic / Getty Images; B-17 bomber © PF-(aircraft) / Alamy; smaller bombers © Granger

Library of Congress Cataloging-in-Publication Data

Names: Maurer, Kevin, author.
Title: Damn Lucky : one man's courage during the bloodiest military campaign in aviation history / Kevin Maurer.
Other titles: One man's courage during the bloodiest military campaign in aviation history
Description: New York : St. Martin's Press, 2022. | Includes index.
Identifiers: LCCN 2021051080 | ISBN 9781250274380 (hardcover) | ISBN 9781250274397 (ebook)
Subjects: LCSH: Luckadoo, John, 1922- | United States. Army Air Forces. Bomb Group, 100th. | United States. Army Air Forces—Biography. | World War, 1939-1945—Aerial operations, American. | World War, 1939-1945—Campaigns—Western Front. | United States. Army Air Forces—Officers—Biography. | Bomber pilots—United States—Biography.
Classification: LCC D790.253 100th .M38 2022 | DDC 940.54/4973—dc23/eng/20211102
LC record available at https://lccn.loc.gov/2021051080

First Edition: 2022

10 9 8 7 6 5 4 3 2 1

To Lucky, thanks for trusting me with your story

CONTENTS

1. Mission #22 —————————————————— 1

2. Answering the Call —————————————— 11

3. Solo ——————————————————————— 23

4. "You're All Going to Be Killed and You
   Might as Well Accept It" ——————————— 35

5. Station 139 ————————————————————— 59

6. The Professionals ———————————————— 71

7. Tail Gunner————————————————————— 83

8. Five Miles Above ———————————————— 99

9. "A Good Type American"————————————— 113

10. Dye's Last Mission ——————————————— 123

11. *King Bee* —————————————————————— 139

12. Twelve O'Clock High ——————————————— 153

13. Bombs Away ———————————————————— 167

14. Three and a Half Engines and a Prayer————— 183

15. Black Week ——————————————————— 201

16. Friendly Invasion ——————————————— 213

17. Last Post —————————————————————— 227

18. Big B ——————————————237

19. His Best Day ——————————249

20. Home ——————————————261

21. Last Flight ————————————277

Afterword ——————————————285

A Note on Sources ————————291

Acknowledgments —————————293

Index ————————————————295

DAMN
LUCKY

1

MISSION #22

OCTOBER 1943

His nickname was Lucky, but Second Lieutenant John Luckadoo felt anything but.

He was on his twenty-second mission flying B-17 bombers into occupied Europe against the Luftwaffe, meaning he was on someone else's borrowed time. Most bomber crew members only made it to ten missions before they either got wounded, captured after being shot down, or lost their lives altogether.

Lucky stowed his gear near the hatch at the front of the olive-green B-17 bomber and walked around the aircraft looking for anything out of place. He was tall and skinny with a boyish grin. He spoke with a soft voice that had just a hint of an accent with elongated, slow, and drawn-out words like the Tennessee River that ran through his hometown of Chattanooga. His face had an innocence, a kind of aww shucks, easygoing look, that masked what he'd seen over the skies of Nazi Germany.

Lucky ran his hands along the fuselage and wings and worked the ailerons with his hands up and down to make sure the mechanism was smooth. He checked the connection points on the antenna wire that stretched from the top of the tail to the radio hatch just behind the wings.

As he got to the front of the aircraft, he stopped and looked at the ship. The Flying Fortress looked formidable perched on her front landing gears, her nose peering skyward. The bomber's four massive Wright R-1820-97 Cyclone turbo supercharged radial engines towered over him on the 103-foot wings and eleven .50-caliber machine guns poked out of the top, side, and cheeks of the bomber.

The preflight walk was routine before a mission, but not without focus. Lucky knew how important it was because the bomber was the single most important part of the mission. It delivered the bombs, but more importantly acted as a body for the ten-man crew. Each man—from two pilots in the cockpit to the single gunner in the tail—was tethered to the four-engine bomber and relied on the machine for air and warmth.

Confident the ship—nicknamed *King Bee*—was airworthy, he returned to the nose, where a small door was open leading into the cockpit area. No one climbed into a B-17 confident they were coming home. As the war progressed, Lucky realized he was facing not one enemy but four.

Fear of never returning home.

Fighters that attacked with more experienced pilots and better equipment as they aggressively protected their homeland.

Flak from the Nazi antiaircraft guns, which hit American bombers with deadly accuracy.

And freezing temperatures, an unseen enemy in the unpressurized and unheated airplanes that seriously impeded the aircrews' ability to function.

All four factors had a devastating effect on the aircrews' mind and body. There was no way the aircrews could contend with the pressures of combat day after day and remain the same people. Lucky and others had become indifferent to death. They expected it and were surprised when it didn't come. Mustering the courage to get back into the airplane day after frightful day eroded the will of the aircrews. Some withered under the onslaught and refused to continue to do so. Others, like Lucky, found the stamina to remain focused on the job at hand and carried on. But this mission felt different. This time, Lucky was flying with a brand-new crew.

Replacements.

Almost a month earlier, Lucky's original crew completed twenty-five missions and rotated home. For bomber crews in 1943, twenty-five was the magic number. Complete that many missions and you got to board a slow boat back to the United States.

That left Lucky to finish his last four missions with various crews. The crew for this mission, led by Second Lieutenant Maurice Beatty, were strangers. Beatty had been certified for combat by Lucky the month before on a short check ride over the English countryside. His crew had only been with the 100th Bomb Group for a few weeks. They'd flown half a dozen missions—short hops to the French or German coasts.

Milk runs, essentially. They'd only once flown into the teeth of the Luftwaffe defenses over central Germany.

It was early October in 1943, and the mission was a day-time raid on the German industrial town of Bremen. It kicked off a weeklong blitz to cripple the Nazi war machine. Lucky was command pilot leading three bombers in the second element of the low squadron—or Purple Heart Corner, as it was nicknamed—because the low squadron was closest to the massive arsenal of antiaircraft guns defending the target.

Nothing about the mission was comforting. It started with a six-hour slog through frigid cold at twenty-five thousand feet, followed by nerve-destroying antiaircraft fire and relentless Luftwaffe fighter attacks before finally dropping on the target. Then the race back to England, likely in a damaged bomber, and landing safely with shattered nerves.

That was success.

Better odds stood he'd get picked off by fighters either before he reached the target or after being knocked from the formation by antiaircraft fire that shredded his engines and smashed up the fuselage. Free of the formation's protection, the Luftwaffe aces would run them down, ending the mission in either a fiery wreck or—if he bailed out safely—in a German prisoner-of-war camp.

Three outcomes: return home, get shot down and become a prisoner, or death. A one-in-three chance of success. No one had to say it. But that made getting into the aircraft the hardest part of any mission.

In front of Lucky, the bombardier and navigator were climbing into the nose compartment door. Waiting his turn, he felt his anxiety rising. Everyone flying bombers had their own way of dealing with it. Small rituals like carrying a rabbit's foot or a brief prayer that quickly became a survival mantra.

Lucky had acquired two charms.

The first was tucked in his flight suit. He patted his chest and felt the bound pages of a Bible tucked into the inside pocket. His fingers lingered over a crease in the cover caused by a chunk of Nazi shrapnel. An antiaircraft shell exploded near his bomber on a previous mission, peppering the cockpit with shrapnel. A shard punched through the thin metal skin of the fuselage and dug a trench-like groove down the middle of the leather cover. The metal would have killed him had it not been slowed by distance and the skin of the aircraft before stopping against the thick pages of God's word.

Luck?

Divine intervention?

Did it matter?

All Lucky knew was his mother wasn't getting a letter from his commander explaining how shrapnel killed him. After that mission, his Bible became essential equipment, no different from the oxygen mask he used to breathe at twenty-five thousand feet.

Next, his hand went to his neck. His fingers searched under the collar of his leather flight jacket and coveralls for a thin piece of silk stocking. He felt the fabric against his warm skin. The stocking was from a girlfriend left behind in South Carolina. They'd met when Lucky was in flight school. She'd offered it to him, and he tied it around his neck for luck then and now. After giving the stocking a tug, he paused to gather up his courage.

Staring at the nose of *King Bee,* Lucky couldn't help but smirk back at the smiling bumblebee with a crown painted under the cockpit window. He hoped he could put up the kind of fight the bee promised. It was finally Lucky's turn. He felt fear grip his chest as he approached the open hatch. He'd faced the Luftwaffe and flak over Germany and survived, he told himself.

Trust your skills, he told himself. He wasn't going to be the poor son of a bitch who worried about it. He got himself into the war, and now he had to see it through.

The viselike grip slackened, and he grabbed the top of the hatch under the pilot's window and swung his long legs into the bomber. Kneeling in a small passageway underneath the cockpit, he crawled forward, emerging behind the pilot and copilot seats. A thick armor plate fanned out behind each seat. The only armor on the whole Fortress.

The cockpit—nicknamed "the office" by the pilots—was cramped for Lucky's six-foot, two-inch frame. Lucky worked his way over to the right seat. He ducked his head and slid out the copilot seat so he could climb in. After Lucky sat down, he adjusted the copilot seat for leg room.

The B-17's cockpit was one of the most modern in World War II. Each pilot had a control column called a yoke that resembled a car steering wheel with the top cut off. The throttles sat between the pilots' seats, and a half-circle bank of gauges that tracked everything from oil pressure to airspeed sat under a two-pane plexiglass windshield. Both pilots had a side window, and the panes in the roof of the cockpit were transparent. The bombers flew in tight formations, making it imperative the pilots could see above them.

Lucky removed a checklist from a pocket hanging below his side window. He was the command pilot on the mission, but as the copilot on the crew, it was his job to read the pre-flight and takeoff checklist so Beatty—who was also settling in—could execute the commands. Beatty, a Midwesterner from Ohio, pulled on his headphones and started turning knobs and switches to start the bomber.

If Lucky was scared climbing in, he was relaxed now. His mind could no longer live in the what-if. There was a comfort to the checklist. It brought order, but it also locked Lucky into his job. He had a singular focus: Get the aircraft airborne.

"Controls and seats," Lucky said, reading off the checklist.

Both Lucky and Beatty grabbed the yokes to make sure they responded.

"Check," Beatty said.

Lucky knew the checklist by heart, but still read each line from the book. That way it was impossible to miss a step. The pilots worked through seventeen items before it was time to start the engines.

"Clear right," Lucky said, making sure the fire guard, a member of the ground crew with a fire extinguisher stationed near the right engines, was clear of the props.

Beatty cleared the left side.

"Master switch?"

Beatty flicked it to the on position.

"On," he said.

They checked the brakes, generators, and fuel before Beatty started the engines. The number one engine—the first engine on the left wing—had a guttural cough and then started to spin the prop. Lucky felt the vibration of the engine in the fuselage. The cough and sputtering quickly faded into a muscular roar pushing out over a thousand horses. As the engine fell into a gentle purr, Beatty and Lucky started the number two engine. Soon, the black propellers on the left side were churning. They repeated the steps on the right side until all four engines churned with a steady drone.

Beatty released the brakes, and *King Bee* left its hardstand for the end of the runway at Thorpe Abbotts, one of the scores of American bases northeast of London on the bulging part of eastern England that sticks out toward the North Sea. As *King Bee* taxied into position, Lucky scanned the taxiway ahead. The English fog had burned off to reveal Carolina-blue skies. It was a welcome change to the usual thick gray fog that socked in the airfield before most missions.

Up ahead, a long line of olive-green bombers, each with a block capital *D* stenciled on the tail—the letter signified the bomber was part of the 100th Bomb Group—sat in a line waiting for takeoff. This was a max-effort mission. Twenty-one planes with 210 men from the group were headed to Bremen.

Takeoff was just before noon. The planes waited for the signal. Anticipation built as the hum of almost one hundred engines droned across the English countryside. Staff officers assembled on the balcony of the control tower and ground crewmen stood nearby to watch the air armada take off. The tension wasn't reserved for just the aircrews. Lucky knew once they were gone, the guys would congregate around the tower to listen to the radio updates and sweat out the mission.

Lucky looked down at his watch. The seconds ticked by. When the minute hand hit 11:43 a.m., he saw a flash in his windshield as flares shot out of the control tower. Before the flare reached its zenith, the first bomber took off.

Major John "Jack" Kidd, the 100th's operations officer, and Captain Everett Blakely, a lead pilot with the 418th Squadron, led the way in *Just-a-Snappin'*. As they climbed into the blue, the other B-17s thundered into the sky. Every thirty seconds, another plane took off.

Soon, *King Bee* was at the head of the line. Lucky slid the cockpit window shut. Beatty taxied *King Bee* to the end of the concrete runway and turned so it was in position for takeoff. With the checklist still in his hands, Lucky called out the final commands.

"Tail wheel?" he said into the interphone, the bomber's internal intercom between the crew members.

Beatty checked it.

"Locked," he said.

Lucky read the next line.

"Gyro."

"Set," Beatty said.

"Generators."

Beatty checked the panel.

"On."

Beatty and Lucky locked the brakes and throttled the engines up to full power. Luckadoo looked over at the pilot and nodded. Both men waited for the flare, the signal for him to take off. Outside, the four engines roared. The whole aircraft seemed to sway back and forth with pent-up energy. All four engines begging the pilots to let off the brakes so they could fly. Just when it felt like the plane couldn't wait any longer, the flare near the control tower shot into the air.

Lucky and Beatty let off the brakes, and *King Bee* raced down the runway. The bomber drifted to the left, forcing Beatty to make a slight correction to keep the aircraft on the center line as it picked up speed. Lucky felt the tail wheel lift. Then he felt the weight come off the main landing gears under the wings and the once heavy and menacing Fortress lifted off the ground.

King Bee was airborne.

Lucky and Beatty climbed toward the wisps of white clouds high in the sky and then banked to get into the pattern. Each aircraft flew a rectangular pattern around the airfield as it climbed. With hundreds of planes overhead, getting into the pattern and then forming up was like merging into moving traffic. A slight mistake and two planes might collide. Thankfully, there was no fog, which turned takeoff into a white-knuckle, sphincter-clinching affair.

In an hour, the sky over northeastern England was filled with American bombers in arrowhead-shaped formations thundering onward into harm's way.

2

ANSWERING THE CALL

JUNE 1940

It was December 7, 1941, and Lucky—a nineteen-year-old freshman at the University of Chattanooga—was behind the wheel of his neighbor's big black Buick, joyriding around the streets listening to the radio, this time with an occasional Christmas standard thrown into the mix.

Since it was the holiday season, the houses were dressed in Christmas red. Trees were trimmed and lit in the windows, and big green wreaths with flashy red bows hung on the doors.

Most of the houses in the upper-class subdivision of Shepherd Hills in Chattanooga, where Lucky's family moved after the stock market crash in the 1920s, still had two cars. Lucky's father wouldn't let him drive the family car, but their neighbors—who had two cars—used to let him borrow one of theirs, and he used it any chance he could get to drive downtown to meet friends, go to the movies, or attend socials at his fraternity.

But on Sundays, Lucky played chauffeur for the neighborhood kids, who climbed into the car as he circled the neighborhood. The car was like a moving clubhouse. Big band music on the radio poured out of the windows. Younger kids were in the backseat roughhousing and laughing as Lucky wound his way past the houses with immaculate green lawns.

While growing up, Lucky's family lived in a two-story colonial house on a ridge overlooking the small subdivision east of downtown Chattanooga. The house had a massive porch across the front with a swing. Lucky's sister and older brother had their own rooms. He shared a room on the second floor with his brother Bob. At the end of their street was their garage and a small pasture for his father's horses.

Everyone was talking about the holidays and a new year when the music was interrupted by breaking news. A grave voice came over the airwaves. Lucky hushed the kids in the back seat and turned up the radio.

Dateline: Washington.

President Roosevelt said in a statement today that the Japanese had attacked Pearl Harbor, Hawaii, from the air.

Details were sketchy, but it was clear America was under attack. President Franklin Roosevelt confirmed the Japanese attacked Pearl Harbor just before eight o'clock in the morning with hundreds of planes, catching the U.S. Navy by surprise and sinking several ships. Lucky stopped the car and just stared at the radio in disbelief. The holiday spirit was gone. When the report ended, he put the car back in gear and drove in silence, waiting for the next update. The boys in the back stopped wrestling, and everyone hung on the words of the newscaster each time he came on with new details.

Twenty ships—including eight battleships—destroyed.

Three hundred airplanes.

Almost twenty-five hundred dead—including civilians—and more than a thousand wounded.

A pit grew in Lucky's stomach. He'd had no idea there was a Pearl Harbor, let alone where it was. The Japanese threat was something of a surprise to him too. He'd spent months following the Nazi advance across Europe and thinking about Leroy "Sully" Sullivan, his best friend, who had joined the Royal Canadian Air Force almost a year before. They both dreamed of being fighter pilots. His plan to follow Sully to Canada was dashed, but now with America in the war, his dream of being a fighter pilot was again in play. He didn't have to wait to follow Sully—who was in North Africa fighting the Germans—any longer.

It was America's war now, and he was ready to answer the call to defend his country.

Ever since Lucky was in grade school, he'd dreamed of being a soldier marching into battle. He daydreamed about the rifle and cannon fire of Civil War battles as he gazed out of the window of his grade school, where he could see the larger-than-life statues, stacked cannonballs, and cannons in the commemorative memorial park nearby. The park was dedicated to the November 25, 1863, Battle of Missionary Ridge. At recess, Lucky and his friends climbed the five-story steel observation tower—Bragg Tower in honor of the Confederate commander General Braxton Bragg—perched on the crest of the ridge, pretending to fight the battle all over again.

The battle was a turning point of the Civil War. After a disastrous defeat at the Battle of Chickamauga, the Union Army of the Cumberland under Major General William Rosecrans retreated to Chattanooga. Confederate General Braxton Bragg's Army of Tennessee besieged the city and established themselves on Missionary Ridge and Lookout Mountain. Major General Ulysses S. Grant, riding a wave of success after Vicksburg, arrived to break the siege.

Lucky studied the large tablets at the battlefield that explained the movements of the armies. Sweeping attacks. Staunch defenses. Lucky imagined commanding soldiers making critical decisions in the heat of combat and basking in the glory of victory.

In the summers after elementary school, Lucky got a taste of real soldiering riding the old nags and learning how to care for them during two weeks of training at Fort Oglethorpe, which at the time was the headquarters of the Third Cavalry Division. The training was part of the Citizens' Military Training Camps program of the United States. Started in 1921 and held annually until 1940, the camps allowed male citizens to get basic military training without fear of being called up for active duty.

After a long week of basic training, Lucky looked forward to Sundays and the polo match. His favorite riders were all West Pointers—graduates of the United States Military Academy in New York. Even as second lieutenants, they were quite heroic looking with polished boots and brass. Plus, they had an entire stable of polo ponies at their disposal. Lucky's father, LV, raised Arabian horses. Horses were LV's first love.

People called LV "Colonel," not because of his military service but because he was an honorary Kentucky Colonel. Every year, LV and a bunch of his horse cronies used to travel to the Kentucky Derby at Churchill Downs in Louisville. They hired a Pullman car and parked it on the railroad tracks right outside of the racetrack. LV and his friends would spend the week gambling on horses, playing poker, and drinking mint juleps as well as going to the races. And when he would come home, Lucky's mother, Rowena Angeline Sauls, a beautiful, petite woman who was nicknamed "Winks" by the family, would always greet him at the door and ask how he did.

"Well, I just made expenses," LV told her every time.

Lucky and the family never knew how he really did. The only time Lucky knew his father lost was on October 29, 1929, the stock market crash signaling the start of the Great Depression. LV made his fortune in stock trading, including shares of the parent company of Coca-Cola, and built a small fortune—enough to own two cars and Arabian horses. All of LV's holdings were in stocks, so when the market collapsed, so did his fortune. He left for the office a wealthy man and returned home broke. Lucky was seven years old and remembered his father's chin down on his chest and tears in his eyes when he came through the front door. No stock answers this time. No hiding his misfortune.

As the price of stocks tumbled, and family fortunes evaporated that day, one of LV's friends, Carter Lynch, jumped to his death from the eighth story of the Maclellan Building, home office for Provident Life and Accident Insurance Company, on Broad Street in downtown Chattanooga.

But LV held on. After the crash, he sold one car and the horses and the barn. He clawed his way back, rebuilding the family's fortune.

Lucky wanted to be an officer too, in part because when the West Point officers weren't on the polo grounds, they were riding around in convertibles with the prettiest girls.

But Lucky was not going to serve on the back of a horse. His "horse" would take him into the clouds.

In the early 1940s, a pilot was one of that generation's heroic, dashing figures, finding its place in the imaginations of boys and girls across America. Lucky set his sights on flying fighters, dueling with the enemy in the skies above. Being a pilot was far more appealing than slogging through the trenches or living in the field.

Lucky's best friend, Leroy "Sully" Sullivan, shared the fighter pilot's dream. The boys were inseparable. Both were tall and lean with shaggy brown hair and boyish good looks. Both were popular in high school and held command positions in the school's ROTC unit. After high school, both enrolled as freshmen at the University of Chattanooga, where they became Delta Chi fraternity brothers.

Between classes, Sully worked as an usher at the Tivoli Theatre and watched Nazi Germany's rise on newsreels. He and Lucky pored over the papers they delivered, keeping track as the Germans bombed London in preparation for an invasion and later turned east to take on the Soviets. It was clear to both it was only a matter of time before the United States got dragged into it.

Sully and Lucky were eligible for military service and figured chances were likely that they were going to have to serve in some capacity. So, the two friends made a pact. They'd rather choose than be drafted, and they wanted to be fighter pilots, but they couldn't apply to the Army Air Corps unless they had two years in college.

But Sully found out the Royal Canadian Air Force was recruiting pilots in the United States. Sully washed airplanes at Buck's Flying Service and saw a flyer seeking American volunteers.

Canada needed pilots.

Recruiting Americans was against United States law, but that didn't stop the Canadians, who enlisted Clayton Knight, an American who had flown with a British fighter squadron during World War I, to develop an organization to locate American pilots and assist them in coming to Canada on the sly.

This organization became known as the Clayton Knight Committee. Knight rented a suite in the Waldorf-Astoria Hotel in New York City and used word-of-mouth references and brochures sent to aviation schools and airports to recruit.

What piqued Sully's and Lucky's interest was the Canadians didn't require two years of college. They took any able-bodied candidate. Sully and Lucky wrote to get information. At that time, the American government authorized its citizens to join the Royal Canadian Air Force by treating the enlistment as part of the Lend-Lease aid policy. Americans who chose to fly with the Royal Canadian Air Force were exempt from the American military draft. Sully and Lucky figured when the United States eventually joined the Allies, they could transfer and fight in the United States Army Air Corps.

A few weeks after requesting applications, Lucky and Sully got letters back from Canada. Inside the envelopes were application packets. Both men filled them out, tracking down teachers to write recommendations and providing medical information to ensure they were able-bodied. At the end of the application was a waiver for candidates under twenty-one years of age. Since both were only eighteen years old, they needed parental consent.

The first stop was Sully's house. He was raised by his single mother, Nell Louise Sullivan, after his father was exposed to German mustard gas during World War I and later died of blood poisoning months before Sully's birth.

Mrs. Sullivan flipped through the brochure and Sully's application. She thumbed through his letters of recommendation, smiling as she read the accolades about her only son. Across from her, Sully and Lucky sat on the couch. Lucky listened as Sully laid out a persuasive argument for intervention. The Nazis were on the march. England was putting up a valiant fight, but needed help. Sully felt the call to come to England's aid and stem the tide of fascism.

But Lucky also knew both he and Sully were itching to get into the fight. War seemed glorious. They wanted to test their mettle and prove that they could keep their wits and lead their men to victory, just like the men they studied in history books. There was no way they were going to miss the chance to take part in such a historic event.

Mrs. Sullivan listened patiently, folding her hands over the application as her son spoke with passion. The decision wasn't easy. It was clear to Lucky she was wrestling with her emotions. No parent wants to send their son—especially their only child—to war to fight the same enemy as his father. But she knew Sully. Her son was the most popular kid in the freshman class. A natural leader and raconteur, he lived life with passion and conviction. Mrs. Sullivan asked only one question when her son was done.

"Do you think this is the thing that you ought to do?" Mrs. Sullivan said.

Sully nodded. "I do."

"Then you have my blessing," Mrs. Sullivan said and signed the release.

Outside, Sully was excited. He was going to be a fighter pilot. He knew it in his gut. Now it was Lucky's turn. They went over the speech that Sully had just used to win his mother over. Lucky figured his parents, like Sully's mother, would recognize his conviction and sign the waiver and he would be packing his bags in a few weeks and following Sully north. They agreed to meet the next day and mail back their applications together.

When Lucky got home, his father was still at the office. He cornered his mother as she prepared dinner and gave her the speech.

Winks listened quietly as she went about her work. At the end of the speech, Lucky added that Mrs. Sullivan had already approved Sully's application.

Winks paused to face her son.

"I certainly hate to see you do this," Winks said to Lucky. "But if you think you should, you have my permission."

Winks's support was step one, but only his father could put pen to paper. LV would be a tougher sell. After supper, Lucky sat at the table with his father, a tall, broad-chested man with a head of stark-white hair, and pitched him his plan to join the Royal Canadian Air Force, using Sully's speech as a guide. Lucky's father, with one ear on the radio updating the latest news and his eyes on his newspaper, listened for a few minutes to his middle son make an argument. As Lucky talked about answering the call to serve, LV cut him off. He'd worked too hard to let his son go fight someone else's war.

"You idiot," he said, lowering his newspaper so he could see his son. "This isn't your war. You're not involved in any way. You get back in school. I wouldn't give you consent over my dead body."

Winks listened to the conversation from the kitchen. She gave her son a knowing look to not belabor the issue and returned to the sink of dirty dishes. She and Lucky knew from experience LV wasn't going to change his mind.

A few weeks later, Sully went to Canada alone.

Lucky went back to school with plans to study chemical engineering. The goal was to earn a degree and get a job at the same company as his older brother, who'd graduated a few years ahead of him and joined a national chemical company. But that was before he and Sully had dreams of being a pilot. Then Pearl Harbor put a whole generation's plans on hold. After the Japanese surprise attack, Lucky's plans only included him in a cockpit fighting for his country. It was a welcome change, if he were being honest. The chemistry and engineering classes were difficult. Lucky was failing.

President Roosevelt declared war first on Japan and then Germany, and now so did Lucky.

Military leaders scrambled to mobilize the American military in the wake of the Japanese attack. They had a long list of needs—guns, tanks, ships. But people topped the list. The U.S. Army in 1939 had less than 175,000 soldiers, but after the attack on Pearl Harbor, planners knew they'd need millions to fight a two-theater world war.

The ranks swelled with young Americans to answer the nation's call to arms. Less than half of the new recruits volunteered. Most were drafted after the age range for the Selective Training and Service Act in 1940 expanded from eighteen to sixty-five years of age, bringing in more than ten million recruits.

Lucky didn't wait for the draft. After the new year, he joined some of his Delta Chi fraternity brothers from the University of Chattanooga at the recruiting station. Recruiters mobbed him and his friends, luring them to be Marines or sail with the Navy. But Lucky ignored the recruiters and made a beeline to the Army recruiting office. When he sat down in front of the recruiting sergeant, he had one demand. Lucky wanted to be a pilot.

After Pearl Harbor, the Army Air Corps dropped the

two-year college requirement. They dropped the age requirement, and they dropped the non-marriage requirement. There was nothing blocking him from his dream of being a pilot.

The recruiter was happy to oblige and started the paperwork. Over the course of the day, Lucky shuffled from classrooms to waiting rooms as he filled out paperwork and took the entrance exam. When it was all over, the recruiting sergeant assured Lucky he'd hear soon about his application. A couple of weeks or so later, Lucky got a letter from the Army. Slicing it open, he unfolded it and started to read. He had passed the flight exams, and the Army offered him an aviation cadet slot. One signature and Lucky was going to be a pilot.

Lucky was nineteen, and this time, the only signature he needed was his own.

3

SOLO

Lucky had dreamed of being a pilot since his college days in Tennessee.

But as Lucky stared down the runway of an auxiliary airfield in South Carolina, his dream was turning into a nightmare.

It was October 1942, and Lucky was in the second of three phases of flight training. After accepting his aviation cadet slot in early 1942, Lucky was forced to do the most Army thing in the world.

Hurry up and wait.

Instead of shipping immediately to training, Lucky went back to college and waited for his flight school slot to open up. While he was physically in Chattanooga, his mind was in the clouds daydreaming of being in the cockpit. School was wasted on him at this point. With the prospect of flight school on the horizon, college held little allure except for the social aspects. He was counting down the days, chasing girls, and socializing with his fraternity brothers until he got the call to report for training.

The call finally came in March 1942. Lucky got orders to report to preflight training at Maxwell Field in Montgomery, Alabama, in May. He was selected as Wing Adjutant—second in command—of the four thousand cadets, not because he was a great student or breezed through ground school and calisthenics and radio work but because he had the best voice and could scream "Pass in review!" louder than anybody else on the parade ground.

That came from his hog-calling days in Tennessee, he joked.

From Montgomery, he went to Avon Park, Florida, for the first phase of flight training as part of class 43-B. He mastered the basics of takeoff and landing in the PT-17, a biplane designed to be easy to fly. It became a crop duster and recreation plane after the war.

But at Shaw Field in Sumter, South Carolina, Lucky transitioned to a Vultee BT-13 Valiant for the second phase of flight training. The single-engine Vultee had flat wings and a massive engine with a long glass canopy that accommodated the student pilot and the instructor. Dual controls allowed the instructor to take over in case of emergency.

New pilots often had trouble transitioning from one type of airplane to another. It was up to the student to grasp the instruction and learn the techniques. But there was no time to adjust to a new plane. Recruits were getting funneled through training as the American military tried to answer the call after Pearl Harbor.

If the PT-17 was basic math, the Vultee was algebra.

It required the pilot to do more than just fly. Lucky now had to operate a two-way radio with the ground tower. The plane's engine was also more powerful and had a two-position Hamilton Standard controllable-pitch propeller. The advanced propeller allowed a pilot to adjust the blade's pitch—like changing gears in a car—to provide the best performance at different airspeeds.

On takeoff, the pilot chose a lower pitch to make the blade spin faster and provide maximum power. In flight, the pilot switched to a higher pitch to make the blade spin slower and conserve fuel. Nicknamed the "Vibrator," the Vultee shook when it neared stall speed. The canopy also vibrated constantly. So did the propeller in the high pitch position.

From the start, Lucky struggled to control the Vultee's massive engine. He'd failed most of his flights and was one unsuccessful solo flight away from following the line of failed pilots who didn't make it through the ten-week second phase. He'd end up in bombardier or navigation school, riding instead of flying. Lucky didn't want to be a navigator or a bombardier. He wanted to be a pilot or nothing.

But since arriving in South Carolina, he'd been anything but.

Lucky's instructor also didn't do him any favors. He was an Army second lieutenant who'd graduated from West Point. At a glance, the West Pointer appeared to be a squared-away young officer and aviator with a bright future. His uniform was perfect. His hair cut precisely the way he was instructed at West Point and his class ring signaled to other officers that he was a class above.

In the cockpit, he was just as rigid. Instead of adjusting his lessons, he taught from the flight manual, like a robot spitting out facts. Lucky was baffled by the instruction he received. The West Pointer couldn't coach him through the procedures during a stall. He had no advice for how to prioritize flying and working the radio. The West Pointer was teaching a half dozen students, all failing. For Lucky, struggling to handle the Vultee introduced something worse than death.

Doubt.

So much of flying was feel and confidence, two lessons not found in a manual. Lucky and his classmates were nervous handling the new plane. The BT-13 was bigger, faster, and more powerful than anything they'd flown to date, and they weren't confident. They were thinking instead of reacting to the plane and the situation. It took hours in the cockpit for a pilot to turn that fear into the conviction to fly the airplane. The West Pointer did nothing to foster that kind of confidence.

Lucky had reason to be scared. More than fifteen thousand pilots and crew died in training accidents in the U.S. during the war, which is ten times the number of American deaths during the invasion of Normandy. Aviation was still in its infancy. New aircraft were rushed into production without proper testing. Companies that made consumer goods were now making aircraft engines. Engine failures and onboard fires were common. More planes were lost due to pilot error or mechanical failure than were shot down by the enemy. It helped that Lucky was still a teenager and foolhardy enough to ignore the danger. He was still invincible in his mind. The key, Lucky found, was getting over the fear.

As he had in the past because of his love of flying.

Being in the cockpit was exhilarating. Lucky never got tired of feeling the engine vibrations in the control column as he thundered down the runway. It was euphoria each time the wings started to lift and the wheels left the ground. The whole world slipped away as he climbed into the blue skies. He felt weightless. It was peaceful to be in control of a machine that responded to even his slightest movements. The whole exercise was enormously appealing to Lucky, but his days were numbered if he continued to fail his training flights.

Lucky was doing so poorly that during an instructor's meeting early in his second phase of training, the West Pointer failed Lucky after he botched his landings and struggled to respond correctly after a controlled stall.

The West Pointer declared Lucky a washout and wanted to send him on his way to navigator or bombardier school until a civilian instructor named Blackman—"Blackie" to both students and instructors—pointed out they couldn't just wash him out of the class. After all, he was the class cadet captain, appointed to lead the student pilots. That gave the instructors pause.

"If we wash out the captain of the class, it's going to be a pretty bad morale factor for the rest of the kids, the rest of the cadets," Blackie said.

He had another solution.

"You give him to me for thirty minutes, and if I can't qual-ify him, then you can wash him out."

Blackie—a short, portly man in his forties with a thick brown mustache—didn't cut the same kind of dashing figure as the military pilots. But he had more than six thousand flying hours in the Vultee and could fly circles around the other instructors. So, when he spoke up for Lucky, the other instructors agreed to give him one more chance.

After the meeting, a runner found Lucky in the barracks and told him to meet Blackie at the flight line. When Blackie strolled up next to the parked Vultee, Lucky broke out in a cold sweat despite the tropical weather in South Carolina. He knew this was his last chance.

Blackie didn't say anything. Instead, he motioned toward the waiting Vultee, painted royal blue with yellow wings. Lucky climbed into the front, Blackie in the back.

Before takeoff, Lucky placed his hand on the thirty-three controls and switches as Blackie called them out. Blackie then ordered him to take off.

It was time to fly.

Lucky started the engine and taxied the plane to the end of the runway.

He radioed the tower and, when authorized, took off. As they circled the airfield, Blackie gave Lucky some tips on how to handle the plane. For the first time, Lucky was starting to feel comfortable in the plane's cockpit.

Blackie took the controls and started climbing until the Vultee reached an angle where the wings could no longer pro-duce enough lift to stay aloft. Lucky felt the plane shake and shudder. Then it paused a beat like it was trying to decide if it wanted to fight to climb higher or dive. It chose to dive. The engine stalled, and the Vultee fell off to the left. Blackie worked the stick and rudder as the plane started to spin like a corkscrew toward the bright green South Carolina countryside. The whole time, Blackie was in Lucky's ear explaining every move. Blackie explained how it was a matter of coordinating the stick between the pilot's knees and the rudder pedals at his feet. The stick controlled the ailerons, and the rudder kept the plane straight. He worked those two actions to maintain control of the plane and fly it smoothly as it gained speed. After a trio of spins, the plane picked up enough speed to stop the stall, and Blackie leveled it off.

The ten-minute lesson was better than the eleven hours he'd received to that point.

"You've got the controls," Blackie said. "Your turn."

Pulling back on the stick, Lucky climbed until the plane couldn't go any farther. It felt like being perched on the top of the first hill of a roller coaster. Lucky could feel it in his stomach. For a second, everything felt weightless, and then gravity took hold and the Vultee fell toward the left wing. With the engine pointed toward the green fields of South Carolina again, the Vultee started to spin.

Lucky took a few deep breaths and counted the spins.

One.

Two.

Three.

With the third rotation, he pushed the stick to the right and kicked the rudder to the left. The spinning stopped, and now the Vultee was in a dive. Lucky pushed the nose down and watched the gauge spin as the plane picked up airspeed. He felt lift return under the wings and leveled off. Lucky did it two more times to Blackie's satisfaction.

Test one passed.

It was a revelation. He'd had trouble so many times pulling off that same maneuver with the West Pointer, but now, with Blackie in the back, he felt like he was flying the plane instead of the other way around. The confidence flowed back.

The next test was solo touch-and-go landings.

"Let's go out to the auxiliary field," Blackie said over the interphone.

Lucky flew to the landing strip south of Shaw Field, which sat about ten miles west-northwest of downtown Sumter. The auxiliary airfield was just a landing strip surrounded by open farmland near the main base. Used to practice takeoffs and landings, it was far enough from Sumter and other towns just in case one of the student pilots had an accident. A crash wouldn't take out a neighborhood.

Lucky landed the plane and taxied to the end of the strip.

Blackie keyed his mic. "I'm going to go over and sit under that tree and smoke a cigarette, and if you can take this airplane up, take it around the pattern, and land it three times without killing yourself, I'll pass you."

Lucky gave a thumbs-up. Blackie unplugged his headset and climbed out of the plane. Once he cleared the wing, he pointed toward the tree near the landing strip. Lucky watched him stroll over. When he got to the tree, Blackie took off his leather helmet and tossed it in the grass. He then plopped down at the tree's base. Reaching into the breast pocket of his blue work shirt, he fished out a cigarette and flicked open his Zippo. Lucky powered up the Vultee's engine as Blackie exhaled a stream of smoke into the air. By Blackie's second drag, Lucky was at the end of the runway. He paused for a second to steady his nerves.

Three landings.

That was all he needed to stay.

Lucky felt more comfortable than ever in the cockpit, but that was with Blackie. Now it was just him. The fear that he shook earlier filled Blackie's rear seat. It was joined by a little self-doubt. But this time, the fear wasn't just of failure.

He was scared of killing himself.

But Lucky assured himself with one fact. He'd put himself in this situation and had no choice. No one was going to take off and land the plane for him. He wanted to be a pilot. Here was his chance.

Lucky gripped the stick and throttled up the engine. The Vultee started down the strip. Lucky's eyes tracked from the windshield to his instruments. Takeoff was made with full throttle using thirty-six inches of manifold pressure and more than two thousand rpms. The plane thundered into the air at seventy miles per hour, its propeller tips surpassing the speed of sound. As Lucky climbed, his airspeed reached ninety miles an hour.

Once airborne, Lucky leveled out and then jumped into the racetrack-shaped pattern around the airfield to line up

the landing. He cranked the flaps down to forty degrees—
the flaps can go to sixty degrees for landing, but that made
touch-and-go landings difficult because of the enormous
drag.

Lucky had the Vultee lined up on the runway's center line.
The strip grew bigger and bigger in his windshield. Lucky's
breathing was shallow. His mouth was dry. He wrestled with
the stick and the rudder, working to keep the plane straight.
The runway was getting closer and closer when he heard the
screech of the wheels as the plane touched down.

One down. Two more and he could stay in flight school.

Lucky didn't even slow down. After the wheels screeched
on the ground, Lucky gunned the engine and adjusted the
flaps. The plane climbed again into the clear blue sky. He
banked to the left and raced back around for another landing. This time, his apprehension was replaced by a little more
confidence. The wings stayed straight. The plane glided down
and landed smoothly.

Touch-and-go.

It didn't take very long for him to get back into the
air. The last landing was his best, and Lucky taxied over
to the tree where Blackie was smoking and waited. Blackie
crushed the cherry of his cigarette into the dirt and picked
up his helmet. Lucky thought he spotted Blackie smile as he
walked back to the plane.

"Well, fly back to the base and land," Blackie said after
climbing in and plugging in his headset and mic.

Lucky taxied to the end of the runway and took off. He
didn't think. Everything was muscle movement. They flew

back in silence. But inside, Lucky felt different. He'd broken through. No more thinking. He was just flying. The movements to fly and land felt more instinctive. But most of all, the fear was replaced by confidence. He was flying the plane. It was no longer flying him.

Lucky made his fourth landing of the day and taxied back to the ramp. He shut down the engine and climbed down off the wing behind Blackie.

From the corner of his eye, he saw Blackie pull off his helmet as he walked back toward the hangars and instructor offices. Lucky wasn't sure what to do. He and the plane had survived all three landings, but Blackie had given no indication if he'd passed.

Lucky gathered his leather flight helmet, headset, and flight logs and turned to follow Blackie, who was almost to the door of the instructor offices. Before Blackie entered, he turned back to face Lucky and shot him a sign.

Thumbs-up.

The rest of training went smoothly. So did his love life. Lucky spotted Eleanor across the dance floor. She was tall and thin with brunette hair. But it was her smile when he introduced himself that sealed it.

It was just before Christmas 1942, and some local girls were at the base for a dance. Bing Crosby's "White Christmas" was playing when Lucky asked Eleanor to dance. That's all it took. They were inseparable after that. The Christmas classic became their theme song. Before long, Lucky and Stinky—his pet name for Eleanor—were seen about town. Lucky had dinner at her home, and they attended all the dances together.

Eleanor came from a prominent family. Her father was a doctor who'd passed away when she was a little girl. She lived with her mother and sister. They had Lucky over for the holidays. The whirlwind romance lasted until graduation.

When it was time for Lucky to ship out to the next phase at Moody Field in Valdosta, Georgia, they went on one last date. Eleanor promised to write every day, and they made vague plans to meet when he returned from the war.

Before they parted, Eleanor gave Lucky a gift. A single white silk stocking. Lucky took it out of the box and felt the silk on his fingers. It was smooth, warm, and smelled of her.

A perfect memento to remember his love.

4

"YOU'RE ALL GOING TO BE KILLED AND YOU MIGHT AS WELL ACCEPT IT"

JUNE 1943

A heavy fog set in around the airfield at Gander Lake, Newfoundland, as Lucky and his crew were waiting for a favorable tailwind to attempt the twelve-hour flight across the North Atlantic to join the war.

They'd come to Newfoundland with the rest of their group, but their departure was on hold after the lead pilot on Lucky's crew—First Lieutenant Glenn W. Dye—slept with a member of the British Women's Auxiliary Air Force (WAAF) and contracted gonorrhea. The WAAF were more than 180,000 women recruited to the war effort. They served on bases packing parachutes, forecasting weather, and working on aircraft, among other duties.

The 100th Bomb Group finally got the call to join the dozens of heavy bomber groups heading east to make up for crews waging a losing battle against the Luftwaffe over the Fatherland. But now all Lucky—the crew's copilot—could do was watch the rest of the group take off because Dye was receiving sulfa treatments at the base hospital. He was too weak to fly. With the last of the 100th Bomb Group crews gone, it was only Dye's crew left in Newfoundland. Lucky and the rest retreated to the barracks to play cards and read.

And wait for Dye to recover.

For Lucky, it was his first break since getting out of flight training.

After almost washing out in South Carolina, Lucky didn't have any further difficulty and transitioned to twin-engine aircraft and completed his training. Nearly everybody who learns to fly in the military aspires to be a fighter pilot. Lucky joined the Air Corps dreaming of being a fighter ace too, but when he got assigned to a twin-engine aircraft for advanced flight training, he knew that dream was gone. If he were being honest, Lucky didn't feel he could be a fighter pilot anyway. He was too tall to fit in the cockpit.

Plus, the Air Corps needed bomber pilots.

Now, Lucky was determined to be a great bomber pilot. For nine weeks, he mastered the art of flying a multi-engine plane in formation and using instruments to fly at night. At graduation, Lucky had seventy hours in an AT-10.

When it came time to pick the aircraft he wanted to fly, Lucky chose the A-20, B-25, or B-26. Considered a light bomber, the A-20's mission was more for low-altitude ground support. B-25s and B-26s were medium bombers used for strafing airfields and mid-altitude bombing. While the military might ask what a new pilot wants, their answer is just a suggestion. When Lucky's finger landed on his name, B-17s were listed as his aircraft.

Heavy bombers.

The B-17 Flying Fortress dropped bombs from high altitude, and that brought a heavy emphasis on formation and instrument flying, handling four engines instead of two, and leading a crew of ten instead of a crew of three or five. Lucky had his work cut out for him, seeing that he'd never flown anything with more than two engines and never with a crew.

With his newly pinned wings came orders to Kearney, Nebraska. He was going to learn on the job as a copilot with the 100th Bomb Group. The news shocked him and his classmates. They'd never set foot in a B-17, and now, from the jump, they were expected to learn to fly one and act as second in command of a crew of ten. Plus, rumors around the Air Corps was the 100th Bomb Group and its commander, Colonel Darr Alkire, were jinxed.

The 100th Bomb Group was made up of four bomb squadrons—the 349th, 350th, 351st, and 418th—along with administrative, operations, engineering, and ground support personnel. The 100th started training to deploy to England in Walla Walla, Washington, and Wendover, Utah, and then finished in Sioux City, Iowa, where the crews focused on formation flying and navigation.

In February 1943, the group's deployment was delayed when the 100th fliers got assigned as instructors. The group's ground crews went to Kearney, Nebraska. While in limbo, the group's piloting skills regressed. In April, just before they were supposed to head overseas, Colonel Alkire, who took command of the group in November 1942, brought the squadrons back together for a 1,300-mile training and certification flight from Kearney to Hamilton Field in California.

Twenty-one planes took off in Nebraska. Seventeen landed in California. Three, including Alkire's, landed in Las Vegas, and one landed in Lucky's home state of Tennessee. The mission was a disaster. Alkire lost his command, and the group was sent for refresher training. There were rumors the whole group was getting scrapped and the crews would be parceled out as replacements to other groups.

Morale cratered.

To compound the 100th's problems, the Army Air Corps headquarters looked at the crews' flight hours and realized the copilots were accruing more time in the cockpit than some of the first pilots. The solution: Transfer the copilots to other squadrons in need of experienced pilots and bring in recent twin-engine pilot school graduates—namely, nearly forty members of flight school class 43-B at Moody Field in Valdosta, Georgia.

Lucky arrived in Kearney, Nebraska, in early March 1943 and was assigned to the 351st Bombardment Squadron. He became part of the crew commanded by First Lieutenant Glenn Dye, from Ohio, who was a short, thicker man with a thin mustache. At twenty-four years old, he was an old man compared to the twenty-year-old officers and teenage gunners on his crew. Because of his age, Dye caught a nickname: "Pop" or "Dad."

Lucky's first meeting with Dye was all business. A firm handshake. A welcome aboard. Nothing more. They had a practice mission the next day, and Lucky did his best to prepare, poking around the grounded B-17 and trying to get acclimated to the half-moon panel of gauges in front of him. He was a long way from South Carolina and the patience of Blackie. The only training he was going to get now was on the job from Dye.

The next morning, Dye taught Lucky how to take off and land the B-17. Dye was a good pilot. His movements were efficient and confident. His personality carried over to the controls. Nothing was hurried. It didn't matter what was going on—from engine trouble to fighter attacks over Germany—Dye was calm. Lucky did his best to sponge up as much knowledge as he could, but the B-17 was massive and took two men to fly efficiently. So not only did he need to learn how to handle it, Lucky had to learn how to work with Dye so their movements complemented one another's. That came with hours in the cockpit, starting with that first flight.

But on the ground, the learning was much harder.

Some of the crews—Lucky's included—took a pretty dim view of replacing seasoned copilots, who'd trained for months with the crew, with newly graduated shavetails. All the crews were tight and saw that bond as their best chance of surviving combat. Adding a new guy hurt their chances, in their minds. Replacing the copilots, who were better pilots and had built a bond with their crewmates, was an off-the-wall decision for the men who'd been working closely together for months, which created a rift among some of the crews. Lucky was likely considered a jinx. Changing anything on a crew was looked at as a bad omen. But an order was an order. Some crews embraced the new guy and trained him up, knowing he'd have to perform for the crew to survive.

Not Dye's crew.

Lucky never met the guy he replaced. Only knew him by his last name: Townsend. But what Lucky did know was Dye's crew very much liked him and didn't like the idea of Lucky taking his seat. He heard them talk about Townsend and grousing about the decision to replace him.

"What in the world caused this?" Second Lieutenant Timothy J. Cavanaugh, the navigator, said soon after Lucky joined the crew. "They didn't go through our training. I don't have any confidence in somebody that is totally inexperienced and is suddenly just thrust into that position."

Instead of trying to train Lucky, Cavanaugh and Second Lieutenant Francis C. Chaney, the bombardier, hazed or ignored him. They short-sheeted his bed by folding and tucking in the top sheet so that it simulated both the top and bottom sheets. When Lucky got into bed, his legs were obstructed by the fold.

Late one night, Lucky felt someone shake him awake. They were flying the next day, and Lucky had turned in early to make sure he was rested. He was still trying to master the B-17 and wanted to be sharp.

"Hey, you need to go to headquarters because they're looking for you," said Cavanaugh, who was lanky but wore a cocky expression.

From the corner of his eye, Lucky spotted Chaney, a short, slight man, watching.

"Ah, OK," Lucky said. "What do they want?"

Cavanaugh looked over at Chaney and smirked. He then looked back at Lucky and shrugged. "Don't know. Just said they wanted you. Something about an order."

Lucky was skeptical. His gut told him it was bullshit, but the only way he'd be sure was if he checked it out himself. He climbed out of bed and put his uniform back on. He grabbed his cover and headed for the headquarters building. It took a few minutes to walk from the barracks to the headquarters. It was early spring in Nebraska, and Lucky could see his breath as he shivered his way down the sidewalk and into the building. When he got inside, a sergeant working the night shift at the desk was baffled when Lucky reported.

"We don't know why you're here."

Lucky cursed and headed back into the cold night, his hands thrust angrily in his jacket pockets. Back at the barracks, Lucky wanted to confront his crewmates, but they were asleep, or at least pretending to be. He got undressed and tried to climb into bed, but of course it was short-sheeted.

The next morning, Cavanaugh and Chaney had trouble hiding their amusement as they got ready for the day's training. Lucky knew they were having a ball. Lucky was thrust into an impossible learning curve of training to fly the massive B-17 while watching his six o'clock for pranks. Cavanaugh and Chaney were always waiting in the wings with a sharp comment, while Dye mostly kept to himself or pretended not to notice. When Dye spoke, it was to give direction. He might offer a chuckle at a good joke, but overall, Lucky found him distant and cold. Dye looked the other way and never intervened. As the leader of the crew, he either told Cavanaugh and Chaney to do it or condoned it.

While the crew was required to work in concert in the air, they were like two different teams on the ground. The officers stayed in their huddle. They had their own barracks and chow halls. They played cards in the officers' club. The rest of the crew hung together in the enlisted barracks. They had their own card games.

While the officers resisted Lucky, the gunners accepted him right off the bat. They didn't really have a choice, and since they were segregated from the officers on the ground, they had no idea Chaney and Cavanaugh were antagonizing Lucky.

Technical Sergeant Victor Combs was the senior non-commissioned officer on board and manned the top twin .50-caliber turret. As the crew chief, Combs knew more about the actual systems of the aircraft and handed out instructions to the rest of the crew. He also showed Lucky around the bomber, educating him on the workings of the Fortress.

Staff Sergeant Richard Cooke was picked to man the ball turret because he could fit into the small plexiglass sphere that hung like a single testicle underneath the fuselage of the ship. Sparks—the nickname for Technical Sergeant George Flanagan—operated the radio. Most radio operators were called "sparks." Flanagan was tall and thin like Lucky, and Lucky got along well with Flanagan, who was a skilled radio operator and took a liking to his new officer. They'd share a kind word or a quick joke before preflight, but they didn't mix or mingle any other time.

Staff Sergeants Elder Dickerson and Leroy Baker were the

waist gunners. Baker was short and a few years older. He was seasoned and street savvy and used to give the others a lot of guff. Lucky learned from Flanagan that Baker was a felon. He'd been imprisoned and released so he could join the Air Corps, where he found himself behind a .50 caliber in the open window of a B-17.

Donald Ellis was the tail gunner and youngest at eighteen years old. He followed the other gunners around like a little brother, and they treated him as such. When they weren't flying, he became a gofer, running errands for the crew.

After the first few weeks, the operations tempo started to take its toll. The 100th crews wanted to get overseas, so the stress level was high as they worked to complete all the checks. Things came to a head in Walla Walla, Washington. The trip was the last stop before they shipped out to England. Each squadron in the group was sent to a separate base to do additional training. Calibrating compasses. Flying mock missions. Lucky was learning his job and got his first opportunity to fly. But overall the weather was miserable. Wetter than a dishrag, so the crews played cards to pass the time.

One night, Lucky joined eight guys from different crews around a poker table at the base's officers' club. Major Robert White—part of the group's permanent party—was across from Lucky. Cavanaugh, Chaney, and Dye were also at the table. A haze hung over the game as the cards slid across the table and the pilots blew clouds of smoke into the air. Lucky found his way to the table naturally. He was still new and was trying his best to go along with the flow. He was sure when Cavanaugh and Chaney asked him to join the game that they had him pegged as a patsy.

But Lucky was a pretty good card player.

It wasn't long before he had a few stacks in front of him and a good handle on the other players, particularly Major White. He was a terrible player who telegraphed his hand by betting light with the slump of his shoulders or heavy when he had a gleam in his eye.

At first, the chatter around the table was cordial. It ping-ponged from girls, to flying stories—each one more daring than the last—to the regular ribbing between men with healthy egos. But soon the chatter became increasingly pointed toward Lucky. He was the junior officer, and he wasn't expected to be coming out on top. His job was to shut up and lose.

After a few hours, Lucky amassed the biggest stack at the table. His crewmates couldn't believe it. Neither could Major White. He started to taunt Lucky. Riding him about his age. His lack of experience. How he'd taken Townsend's seat on Dye's crew. Anything to throw him off his game.

Lucky ignored the taunts and focused on his cards. It wasn't long before he'd cleaned the major out. Seeing his money in front of Lucky enraged White. He was losing to a junior officer with no experience. But worse, he lost to the man who stole a seat from a friend and veteran of the 100th.

Out of money, White got up from the table and walked around to where Lucky was sitting. Lucky didn't pay him any attention except to shield his cards with his body, thinking White was trying to peek and signal Cavanaugh and Chaney. White watched the hand in silence, seething behind Lucky's chair. When it was Lucky's turn to bet, he placed his cards facedown on the table and grabbed a few chips. He started to count out his bet when he felt hands on the back of his chair, and then he was weightless.

For a second, Lucky seemed to hang in the air. He reached out for anything solid, but his hand just flopped on the table, sending chips flying as he crashed onto the hardwood floor. Pain shot up his tailbone and lower back. The room was spinning. Lucky looked up to see White glaring at him from above. No one stepped up to defend Lucky. Dye, Chaney, and Cavanaugh all sat in their chairs in silence.

Lucky was enraged. He popped to his feet. Fury welled up in his chest, threatening to boil over. It wasn't just at White, who'd set him off, but Chaney and Cavanaugh. The clowns had poked and teased Lucky since he arrived. He'd had enough.

But then reason kicked in.

Lucky's eyes tracked from White's smirk to the gold oak leaf on his collar and then back to White as he started to berate him.

It was a trap.

White was looking for any reason to charge Lucky with insubordination. Lucky took a deep breath and sidestepped the major. He swept his winnings into his hat and turned on his heels and headed for the door. He didn't even look back at Chaney and Cavanaugh as he walked out of the club.

The next day, Chaney and Cavanaugh acted as if nothing happened. These were the men Lucky had to live with and work with and maybe die with. But it was a bitter experience to learn that the officers that he was flying with, whom he had to depend on and they on him, treated Lucky in such a disgraceful way. Since Lucky arrived, Dye let the devil take the hindmost.

But lapses in judgment were not unexpected with Dye.

Before he even caught a venereal disease on his way to war, he almost lost a bomber when he made an unauthorized flight to Ohio to visit his wife.

It was May 1943. The crew was set for a training flight, but no one knew where they were going. Dye didn't consult the crew. After preflight, they taxied their bomber to the end of the runway at Kearney and took off heading eastward.

They flew for hours until they reached Steubenville, Ohio, just west of Pittsburgh, Pennsylvania. The crew had no idea why they'd flown to Ohio until Dye circled his house and then headed for a green pasture near New Philadelphia, where Dye had received his pilot's training.

Dye buzzed the field to check on its condition. Lucky surveyed Harry Clever Field from his window. The grass strip was surrounded by trees. If Dye wanted to land there, it was going to be a tight fit. A small trainer was one thing, but they were flying a four-engine, thirty-ton bomber. Dye ignored Lucky's questions, telling him they'd be fine. He knew the field well.

Dye steered the bomber into the pattern and adjusted the flaps. Lucky fell into his duties as a copilot, going through the landing checklist as Dye lined the bomber up on the grass strip. He cleared the trees at the far end and brought the bomber down for a landing.

Lucky and Dye stood on the brakes to slow the bomber as the tree line at the end of the strip got bigger and bigger. The bomber finally slowed with a few yards to spare, just enough to turn it around. Lucky and Dye turned their yokes to pivot the bomber so it was pointing down the runway. Just as it was lined up, the nose dipped slightly.

Not a good sign.

Lucky and Dye shut down the engines and followed the crew out of the hatch. Lucky's boots sank into the mud. The whole field was saturated. He could hear the men's soggy boots slosh in the mud as Victor Combs inspected the landing gears. The wheels were sunk to the hubcaps in the soft ground, he reported.

They were stuck.

Lucky heard the enlisted crew members grumbling behind him as everyone looked at Dye for guidance. It wasn't part of his personality to be a leader and take the crew into his confidence to explain why he was doing something. There was no mistaking Dye's selfishness. His stubbornness had put the whole crew in jeopardy, but he was in command of the crew, and they were stuck with him. But the whole crew knew this was going to be difficult to explain when they got back, if they got back to Kearney.

Before the crew could come up with a plan, they saw cars coming from all directions. The sound of the bomber landing created a stir. Airport employees and bystanders swarmed the bomber. Dye's wife and son were in the crowd. He greeted them with hugs and kisses before pulling a town official at the head of the crowd off to the side. Lucky watched Dye gesture at the tires stuck in the mud. The official nodded and then disappeared.

The rest of the crew stood off to the side and smoked as Dye visited with his son and wife. Lucky watched with amusement as kids climbed in and out of the hatches. But a sense of dread hung over the whole affair. Lucky had no idea how they were going to get off the field. He figured they'd have to spend the night and hope the pasture dried out by morning.

Soon, he heard the rumble of engines. It grew louder as a convoy of tractors, backhoes, trucks, and wreckers for miles around arrived at the field. They surrounded the plane and started to unload tow bars and ropes. Volunteers, nearby naval air cadets, and state troopers with shovels started to dig around the landing gear. The locals worked three hours with the bomber crew to extricate the plane out of the mud.

When it was free, Combs supervised the rest of the gunners as they hooked towlines to the plane. When everything was secure, a New Philadelphia city grader and truck revved their engines. The towlines strained, but the bomber didn't budge. Combs waved to the drivers to stop. He huddled with Dye for a minute before waving a Weaver Motor Company wrecker over. They added one more towline from the truck's winch. Combs gave the order, and the wrecker crew flipped the switch. The winch started to drag in the towline. The mud held fast initially, but then, slowly, the bomber started to rise from the muck until it was on solid ground.

The volunteers laid wooden planks in front of the wheels so the bomber wouldn't sink again on takeoff. The planks were a start, but Lucky wasn't sure they would still have enough momentum to keep going if they sank. He was skeptical they'd be able to take off as he and the crew climbed into the bomber to leave. Dye got in last after he kissed his wife and son goodbye. Lucky took his seat in the cockpit and led Dye through the checklist.

It was around 12:30 a.m. when the engines started.

The townspeople, who came to see the bomber, lined up their cars along the sides of the field. The headlights shone on the grass strip.

It was time to go.

Lucky and Dye ran the engines up to full power. Combs stood behind the pilots, watching the gauges and, by the look on his face, praying they'd make it down the runway and clear the trees at the end.

With the propellers at full speed, Dye cut the brakes. The B-17 thundered down the muddy field toward a wall of trees at the far end. The bomber bounced up and down on the planks as it tried to lift off. Lucky put down quarter flaps, hoping to generate lift. As the trees got closer and closer, Lucky finally felt the wheels lift off. He and Dye pulled the yoke to their stomachs as the bomber responded with a steep climb. The tops of the trees filled the cockpit windows, and then Lucky saw the stars.

The bomber cleared the tree line—just barely. The sound of snapping branches broke through the drone of the engines. Lucky hoped it wasn't worse than a few twigs in the landing gear because they couldn't land if the bomber's tires were flat or the landing gear was still in Ohio.

The crew flew home in silence.

Dye was even more distant, likely reliving his last visit with his family before he left for England. The rest of the crew was just angry Dye had put them in harm's way for something so selfish.

When the bomber landed back at Kearney, it had tree branches in its landing gear. Dye told the headquarters they were on a cross-country training flight when they asked why he'd returned so late, and to Lucky's knowledge, no one said anything about the branches from Ohio. Dye never apologized or made amends with the crew.

The training mission to Ohio was soon forgotten because the 100th Bomb Group was called back together in Nebraska. Earlier that week, they'd gotten new airplanes—Dye named his *Sunny* after his son—and orders to head overseas. The deployment order came earlier than expected. Heavy bomber groups were needed in England urgently. Casualty rates were spiking. The statistical chances for a heavy bomber crew in Europe to be lost on a mission were one in ten. In a single 376-plane raid in August 1943, 60 B-17s were shot down. That was a 16 percent loss rate and meant six hundred empty bunks in England that evening.

Colonel Howard Turner, who replaced Alkire as commander, gathered the crews in formation a few days before debarkation. This was the last time the whole group would be together before heading east to England. Since learning they were headed overseas, Lucky and the others packed and studied the flight plan that took them from Nebraska to Bangor, Maine, to Gander Lake, Newfoundland, to Prestwick, Scotland.

The whole dress-right-dress formation was a formality. After coming to attention, Turner ordered the men to stand at ease as he addressed them. The speech was full of platitudes and talk of duty and service. But what stuck out to Lucky was how frank Turner was about the danger they faced in the skies over Germany.

At this point, Lucky had no firsthand knowledge of what the Germans were. He was cognizant of what a prominent place they occupied in world news and that it would fall on his shoulders to defend his ideals and his values against them in combat. But he had no idea what that meant in reality. Turner laid it out in starker terms.

"The need is so great in England, in Europe for us to support the English that we're likely to be killed anyway, so we're being sent to England," Turner said. "Look at the man on either side of you. Only one of you will be coming back. You're all going to be killed and you might as well accept it."

It's unlikely there was a dourer pep talk by a commander to troops in history. It's a miracle the men climbed into their bombers to fly overseas at all.

Back at Gander Lake, the tailwind Lucky was waiting for arrived two weeks after the rest of the group left, and if he and the rest of the crew were going to make it overseas, now was the time.

Lucky and Chaney went to the base hospital and loaded Dye into a jeep. His gear was already stowed away on board *Sunny*. At the hardstand, they loaded him into the plane. Dye couldn't stand up, and Lucky and Chaney helped him fall into his pilot seat in a heap. His head slumped down like he had spaghetti for a neck. After Lucky and Combs strapped him in, Dye slowly picked his head up and rested it against the window, exhausted.

Lucky was in shock. All Dye had done was get on board.

"Well, Lucky, you're going to have to fly it, because I can't," Dye said in a raspy, weak voice.

Lucky shrugged. There was no checklist for a deadbeat pilot. He was on his own and couldn't hold back his sarcasm.

"Well, obviously," he said.

Lucky tried to play it off, but he was nervous. He barely had sixty hours in the aircraft, and the trip across the Atlantic wasn't a cakewalk. It was a twelve-hour marathon flight. Beneath him, German submarine wolf packs patrolled the frigid waters, sinking Liberty ships bringing supplies to the Allies. They also broadcast false signals to direct bombers off course, forcing them to ditch in the ocean after running out of fuel.

With Dye in the cockpit, Lucky climbed out to check the aircraft. He walked around the bomber, inspecting the flaps and antennas. As he approached the plexiglass nose, he signaled to Combs and the others to get on board. He then corralled Cavanaugh and Chaney as they loaded the last of their gear.

"Dye is out," he said, grabbing the rest of his gear. "Now, you guys have made my life hell, but you've got to depend on me to get us to Scotland."

Cavanaugh and Chaney exchanged a look of dread. All the hazing had come home to roost. Their lives were in the jinx's hands now. Before he climbed back into the bomber,

Lucky turned to Cavanaugh, who had been the chief antag-onist. Success rested in large part on him since he was the navigator.

"Tim, you hit that landfall on the nose or I will person-ally throw your ass out of the airplane without a parachute," Lucky said.

Cavanaugh chuckled to break the tension. But it was clear Lucky wasn't kidding.

In the cockpit, Lucky worked through the checklist with Dye helping when he could. Staring into the fog at the end of the runway, Lucky's chest hurt because his heart was beating so hard. When it was time to take off, Lucky shot a glance over to Dye, who was catatonic in the pilot seat.

Lucky knew the plane was heavy with the extra fuel on board to enable them to extend their range sufficiently to make it across the North Atlantic. Lucky prayed the tailwind at altitude was gusting hard enough to get them across the Atlantic.

Lucky scanned the gauges one more time, throttled up all four engines, and let off the brakes. The B-17 started down the runway. Everything was running smoothly, but it felt like the plane was struggling to get lift. He checked the gauges. Noth-ing was amiss. But up ahead, he was running out of runway. He pushed the throttles forward, but they were maxed. There was no stopping now. Lucky had no choice but to continue forward.

The runway quickly slipped away when he felt the wheels come off the tarmac, but instead of raising up, the bomber sank down as the runway ended.

For a split second, Lucky thought they might be crashing. Then he remembered how his squadron mates' planes lumbered down the runway and never seemed to climb into the sky, instead skirting above the waves until they were out of sight.

Lucky looked out of his window. The bomber seemed to fly just out of reach of the whitecaps as they headed east.

Lucky keyed his interphone.

"Copilot to navigator," he said. "What is our heading?"

Cavanaugh checked his plot and gave Lucky a bearing. Lucky put the ship on course and watched the fuel gauges. The fog was thick, and there was nothing to look at. Over the next several hours, Lucky stair-stepped his way to a higher altitude. Finally, after hours of flying, they'd burned off enough fuel to start to climb out of the gray overcast.

At ten thousand feet, *Sunny* broke through the cloud bank. It felt like Lucky exhaled for the first time. The tension of flying in blinding grayness melted away as his windshield filled with stars. On the horizon, he saw swirling green and yellows. The aurora borealis—the northern lights—danced and shimmered. For a few minutes, Lucky was mesmerized. He couldn't pull his eyes away.

At this altitude, the world seemed foreign. He could no longer see the sea. It was just darkness and the lights. It was easy, in front of that kind of beauty, to forget he was flying to war.

For the rest of the crew, it was twelve hours of drudgery. Between checking their bearing and monitoring the engines and fuel, Lucky kept an eye on Dye. He was just hanging on.

It took everything he had to stay in the seat. Lucky didn't know Dye well, but he sensed his commander was ashamed. He'd let the crew down again.

At dawn, Lucky heard Cavanaugh in his headset.

"Navigator to copilot," he said. "We should be making landfall soon."

Both men scanned the darkness ahead, Lucky from the copilot seat and Cavanaugh from the plexiglass bubble in the nose. Then, from out of the clouds, they spotted a line of darkness—absent of any stars. As the sun came up, the dark line became the green of Scotland on the horizon.

They'd made it.

As soon as they crossed the coast, Lucky got landing instructions from a field outside of Prestwick in Ayr, a small town south of Glasgow. Lucky set *Sunny* down without incident. He was exhausted and hungry and cold. When he slipped out of the forward hatch, his legs felt rubbery as he tried to walk the circulation back into them.

An American staff officer took the officers to a barracks where they could ground their gear. It would be a short layover before flying south to their new home in England. No one wanted to sleep, despite the long flight. They'd made it and wanted to celebrate their first victory. Everyone except Dye, who crashed in the transit quarters, hit the pub just outside the gate. After exchanging some dollars for pounds, they caught a ride to Ayr. At the bar, Lucky ordered bourbon. He was from Tennessee, after all. The bartender looked at him with a cocked eye and offered him scotch.

"Well what kind of scotch do you have?" Lucky said.

"We've got Vat 33."

"Well, I'm sorry, but I never heard of Vat 33. I've heard of Vat 69."

That was a popular blended scotch in the United States. But after the long flight and arriving safely, Lucky didn't care if it was 33 or 69. He wanted a drink.

"Well, I'll have some of your Vat 33," he said. "I'll give it a try."

The bartender handed him a shot glass with a few fingers of scotch neat. Lucky took a sip and coughed. The bartender smiled. But the taste was familiar. Another few sips and Lucky put his finger on it. Vat 33 tasted like Vat 69 watered down.

Lucky joined Cavanaugh and Chaney at a table. Having delivered them safely to Scotland, he had earned their respect. A détente had set in between the men. They were not friends but no longer enemies. It was an armed truce because they had a common enemy, and the Luftwaffe was all they could handle. There was little time or energy for hazing.

When Lucky came back for another round, a Scottish sea captain was at the bar. Lucky nodded to him and raised his glass. The man was wearing a uniform and had a cap pushed all the way back on his head. A white beard covered his cheeks.

"Can I buy you a drink?"

"Well, laddie, I don't care if you do."

Lucky got another round and started talking to the captain. The man commanded a submarine, but Lucky was having trouble making out much else through his thick brogue. When the drinks came, Lucky fished out his pounds. To him, it looked like play money. Crowns. Half crowns. Pounds. Shillings and pennies. All different colors unlike the drab-green dollars. He had no idea what the value of the coins were, so he just held out his hand with the pile of coins in his palm to the bartender. The captain looked at Lucky in horror. How could Lucky be so naive as to let the bartender take what was owed.

"My God, laddie, you never, ever offer a bartender to take what he wants," the sea captain said, taking a few coins from Lucky's hand and paying the tab.

"Thanks," Lucky said.

It was just money. Lucky knew where he was going, and his days were likely numbered.

5

STATION 139

From the right seat, England was an endless sea of green.

Unlike flying over the United States, Lucky noticed the English horizon was dotted with massive barrage balloons near major cities to ward off Nazi air attacks.

Dye was at the controls, allowing Lucky to take in the scenery. After the long flight from Newfoundland and a few hours of sleep in Scotland, Dye had recovered enough to fly the crew to their new home. The destination was Station 139, or Thorpe Abbotts, a brand-new base cut into South Norfolk farmland in East Anglia near the North Sea.

All over England, American forces were building bases and training areas in anticipation of the invasion of France. The buildup—dubbed the "friendly invasion"—began in 1942. Thorpe Abbotts was part of hundreds of miles of concrete runway laid over farmland. The American arrival transformed the English countryside. Halls that were once the residence of lords turned into military headquarters where generals and planners waged war. Country houses owned by nobles or England's rich families turned into flak houses, where fliers with rattled nerves could rest. American military trucks and jeeps crowded the small country lanes, ferrying supplies through the bases that dotted the countryside.

As they approached Thorpe Abbotts, Lucky got his first view of his new home. It looked like the military had cut an airport out of a tapestry of fields near the village of Diss. The buildings and hardstands were scattered so German bombers couldn't hit multiple targets with one bomb. The runway and taxiways made a concrete capital *A* with the main runway as the east to west cross of the letter. Paddle-shaped hardstands dotted the airfield. As they flew over, Lucky saw bombers from the 100th parked on the concrete pads. All around them were ground crew working to keep the bombers airworthy. Two massive hangars were under construction for larger repair jobs, and another long building was being constructed to house the long table used by riggers to pack the aircrews' parachutes. As they came around to land, Lucky spotted the armory where the bombs were stored on the southwestern corner of the base.

Dye lined up *Sunny* and put the bomber down with barely a jolt. Lucky helped Dye taxi to their hardstand, where they shut down the bomber and climbed out. The hardstand was a circular parking ramp for a B-17 connected to the taxiway. Each ship in the squadron had its own hardstand. Between missions, the ground crew performed maintenance and repairs there. A-frames used to lift the planes' heavy engines, tools, and spare parts surrounded the concrete pad. While the aircrews slept, the ground crews spent all night preparing the planes for combat the next day.

All around the runways were Nissen huts used as barracks for the crews, staff, and mechanics. The huts resembled a can split down the middle with its round sides resting on the ground. A door was in the middle of the front end. The huts sat in a row. Inside, bunks lined the outer wall with a walkway down the middle. There were eight beds along each side of an open bay. The men slept on cots with their feet aiming toward the center aisle. When Lucky got out of bed, he had to watch the slope of the wall to keep from hitting his head.

Enlisted soldiers, like the gunners on Lucky's crew, lived on the outskirts of the base away from the headquarters and hardstands. They had to walk across several barnyards, forcing many of them to buy bikes to get to work. The bikes cost about four pounds—about sixty dollars at the time—and were equipped with hand brakes. The American airmen were used to bikes that stopped when the rider pedaled backward, so over the first few months, the airmen crashed regularly.

A sick quarters, barbershop, and a cobbler were also built, making the base self-sufficient. A movie theater was erected a couple of months after Lucky arrived, but the center of the social universe was Silver Wings—the base's officers' club—a dark lounge with a bar, poker tables, bridge games, and a small library in a corner of it. Guys used smoke from a candle to write their names up on the ceiling. It was a place to swap stories, take in some liquid courage, and try to leave the war behind with a few glasses of gin at twenty-five cents apiece.

A traffic light mounted near the fireplace mantel alerted

the crews of pending missions. A red light meant drink away, no one was flying. A yellow light was the same as on the road—caution. A mission could be in the works, but nothing official. Green light meant the next day, crews from the 100th Bomb Group were headed into harm's way.

Crews had to police themselves. Commanders didn't put any limits, but those who over-imbibed paid a very dear price if they were flying the next day. The job was hard enough without a hangover. Once, Lucky went off the base to a local pub in Diss, the nearby village, thinking he wasn't flying. He got the news about the pending mission when he returned and found himself suffering pretty badly. He was on oxygen from the ground up because his head felt bigger than the cockpit. But sucking in 100 percent oxygen was a good antidote for a hangover, and he completed the mission.

The aircrews started arriving at Thorpe Abbotts in June with Lucky and the rest of Crew 25 in the 351st Bomb Squadron arriving two weeks later, with nine airplanes per squadron. The 100th joined the 95th and 390th Bomb Groups to form the 13th Combat Wing of the Eighth Air Force's Third Bombardment Division.

While the base was being finished, the aircrews rehearsed and flew around the area, getting familiar with the aircraft and the conditions. They also practiced formation flying. The standard formation was three squadrons of six ships each for eighteen planes total. A formation would fly with alternates to fill in, in the event a ship aborted. Despite arriving later than the rest, Lucky and his crew quickly got into the operational tempo. The 100th was still settling in, and Lucky's day fell into a rhythm of training missions to get acclimated with the surroundings, additional training, and trips to Silver Wings in his off-duty time.

While Lucky had friends in other crews, once they arrived at Thorpe Abbotts, the men quickly formed tight connections to their own crews and the men they lived with in the barracks. Lucky, like many of the officers, found it easier to just run around with the men in their crew. That way, when other crews went down, they were still strangers and not friends.

It kept the war from getting personal.

But after how Lucky was treated by Dye and his crew, he kept his social circle to just some of the guys from his flight school class—guys like Charlie Via, a lean man with a crooked smile from Clifton Forge, Virginia, and Ed Moffly, from Philadelphia. When they could, which wasn't often, they rode into town and hit the Red Lion, a pub frequented by the aircrews in Diss. They'd get pints of half beer and half ale, play darts, and chase women, but most nights, they were stuck at Silver Wings.

But after enduring the hazing when he first arrived, Lucky kept mostly to himself. Not antisocial but cautious. Being tall and skinny and erect created some animosity in folks because they seemed to think he was arrogant. It never occurred to Lucky, but Via and Moffly pointed it out to him one night at Silver Wings that others believed he thought more highly of himself than he should. It created friction and resentment.

Lucky thanked them for their insight, but inside shook

off the criticism. This wasn't a popularity contest in Lucky's mind. As far as liking and disliking people was concerned, it didn't matter to him. They were fighting a war. Flying was the job that had to be done and the reason he was in England.

Plus, the 100th had enough characters. He wasn't interested in competing for the limelight.

While he was a regular at Silver Wings, Lucky didn't engage in the theatrics of being a pilot. That was the job of Major John "Buck" Egan, commanding officer of the 418th Bomb Squadron, and Major Bucky Cleven, commanding officer of the 350th Bomb Squadron.

Both were flamboyant and boisterous pilots who liked to hold court around the bar. Harry Crosby, the 100th's group navigator, described both as "debonair," who looked like they walked off the screen of a Hollywood movie.

"The men wanted leaders like that," Crosby wrote in his memoir.

Egan was short and skinny, wore his black hair in a pompadour, and sported a pencil-thin mustache. He wore a white fleece-lined jacket and a white scarf tied around his neck.

Cleven was also lean with stooped shoulders who often had a toothpick dangling out of his mouth. A Wyoming native, he worked on an oil-drilling crew before joining the war. Cleven was by far the best storyteller in the outfit. Both wore their hats cocked on their heads, and liked to call young lieutenants over to drink and listen to their stories.

The Buckys—as they were known around the bomb group—had a nickname for everyone. Egan called Omar

Gonzales, a first lieutenant from San Antonio, Texas, "Pancho." Cleven called him "Omar the Tent Maker." Their bravado made Silver Wings fun, but it also served as a morale booster. The swagger kept the younger pilots confident, especially in the face of overwhelming odds that they'd be killed a few missions into their tours.

But Lucky suspected it was really the Buckys' way of keeping their own courage up. He didn't judge a pilot by his skills as a raconteur. A good bomber pilot was a leader. He took care of his crew. Cool under fire. A pilot who maintained formation even when German fighters were doing their best to break up the group or antiaircraft fire was showering the ship with shrapnel. A good bomber pilot believed in himself and trusted in his ability to perform under stress.

The one leader in Lucky's eyes who lived up to that was Major Jack Kidd, the group's operations officer. Lucky met Kidd when he arrived at the squadron and was taken by the man's leadership. A fair and competent leader, he seemed more concerned with his men and his job than his legend. He was the opposite of the Buckys.

Kidd was born in Cleveland in 1919 and graduated Oberlin College and joined the Army Air Corps in 1940. He was inspired to be a pilot by Jimmy Doolittle, a famous American aviator who would go on to bomb Tokyo in 1942 using bombers launched from a Navy aircraft carrier. After Pearl Harbor, Kidd served as a flight instructor before transitioning to the B-17 in May 1942. He commanded Lucky's unit, the 351st Bomb Squadron, until the squadron arrived at Thorpe Abbotts, where he transitioned to the group operations officer—third in the chain of command. His duties were to organize the bombing missions, brief each mission, and oversee training, navigation, and bombing. On bigger missions, he served as command pilot leading the whole formation. Kidd was relieved when he got the group operations job and a promotion to major because he'd suffered enough *Treasure Island* Captain Kidd jokes to last a lifetime.

Kidd was a straight-arrow officer who knew his stuff. Lucky looked up to him and tried to emulate him both in the cockpit and around Thorpe Abbotts.

While the crews prepared to fight the Luftwaffe, the first hurdle was the English weather. Lucky had known many days that were gray and foggy and rainy, especially near the Tennessee River that runs through his hometown of Chattanooga. But English weather was something else. Every day felt like it was wrapped in a moist gray blanket. The dreariness of it weighed on Lucky as he contemplated never seeing the green hills of Chattanooga again.

In addition to being a morale killer, the thick fog forced the pilots to fly instruments until they could climb up through the overcast. Lucky and Dye weren't trained to fly using only instruments, so they devised a way to take off in the thick fog because switching from visual to instruments often caused vertigo. Pilots didn't know whether they were upside down or downside up. A few bombers crashed because of the issue. During takeoff, Lucky kept the plane straight on the runway right down the center line, and Dye watched the instrument panel. Lucky and Dye practiced the technique over and over during training flights until it became second nature, because it wouldn't be long before they'd be part of America's daylight precision bombing campaign.

When Colonel Curtis E. LeMay, commander of the 305th Bomb Group at Grafton Underwood, got to England in September 1942, the bombing campaign was in disarray. There were no tactics, no strategy, and it showed. LeMay admitted later there was no period when American bomber crews arrived in England well trained.

"I don't think we had to make any change in tactics in England; there weren't any tactics there when we started, because there wasn't anybody there who knew anything about it," he told an interviewer. "They didn't even know those basics, much less anything about tactics. Everybody was learning the business from the ground up."

The Army Air Corps was created to support ground forces. They were there to provide reconnaissance, maybe drop a bomb or two, but there was nothing they could do alone to tip the scales toward victory. No one believed airplanes could win a war, or at least that is what the military establishment thought of airplanes. But in the years between the world wars, a small group of airmen at the Air Corps Tactical School at Maxwell Airfield in Montgomery, Alabama, challenged the idea that airplanes couldn't win a war.

These were men with an undying love for planes who knew—in their guts—the platform could transform warfare. Not fighters—which after World War I were considered romantic with aces in leather jackets and helmets and silk scarves dueling in the skies—but bombers. Lots of long-range bombers that could smash America's enemies before they ever reached its shores through the destruction of industrial and military targets deep behind enemy lines.

The strategy was derived from Italian General Giulio Douhet's plan to bomb population centers, an idea the Americans modified. Brigadier General Billy Mitchell and his disciples advocated pinpoint strikes on the enemy's industry, creating minimal casualties and avoiding the trench warfare of World War I.

In April 1939, Major Muir Fairchild presented the plan by imagining an attack on New York City using fewer than twenty bombs. In the scenario, Germany and the United States were fighting in Europe. Germany, in hopes of bringing the war to an end, targets New York. The goal is to cut off the city by destroying its aqueducts, knocking down its bridges, and crippling the power grid, leaving New York dark, without water, and with no easy avenues for relief. The plan called for seventeen bombs total and led to the citizens of the city calling on their leaders to make peace. The idea being the bomber could force a country to quit fighting and spare the world future scenarios where whole generations are slaughtered fighting over no-man's-land.

The plan was met with skepticism. Military planners didn't think airplanes could bring a country to its knees. The aviators—called the "Bomber Mafia"—ignored the criticism and continued to develop their doctrine, which the Army Air Corps adopted in 1940. The strategy centered around a fleet of B-17 and B-24 heavy bombers performing daylight precision bombing raids. Each bomber was armed with a secret weapon: the Norden bombsight.

Up until the 1930s, pilots on a bombing run eyeballed it. Carl Norden, an engineer who worked in a shop on Lafayette Street in downtown Manhattan, changed all of that.

He built a fifty-pound bombsight—the Mark 15—that allowed a bombardier to plug several variables like airspeed, altitude, and wind drift into the device, and it provided a solution allowing him to drop a bomb into a pickle barrel from high altitude, or at least that was the saying. In 1940, Theodore H. Barth, president of Carl L. Norden Inc., said a bombardier flying level on autopilot could hit a fifteen-foot square from four miles up. Perfect conditions, maybe. But none of the crews over Germany ever got perfect conditions.

The U.S. military bought ninety thousand bombsights and declared their existence a national secret. Three guards escorted it onto the bomber, and it was never photographed. An incendiary device inside destroyed the Norden bombsight in the event a bomber was lost over enemy territory.

The myth of the "pickle barrel" led planners into believing daylight precision bombing was not just a goal but a reality. So, after Pearl Harbor, the American plan called for combat groups to carry out a daylight, high-altitude precision bombing campaign against Germany.

When the Eighth Air Force arrived in England in 1942, its methods were at odds with those of the Royal Air Force. Air Chief Marshal Arthur T. Harris, chief of Bomber Command, was leading the night area-bombing campaign. It targeted the German population centers and was supported by Prime

Minister Winston Churchill. The idea was to "dehouse" the German civilians and workforce. Churchill wanted the Americans to join the campaign.

At the Casablanca Conference in January 1943, Major General Ira C. Eaker, commander of the Eighth Air Force, briefed Churchill on the merits of the American daylight plan. Eaker's key point was the value of keeping the Germans under attack around the clock.

But the Germans in 1943 were up to the challenge.

Some of the German pilots had been flying in combat since 1936, honing skills in support of fascists in the Spanish Civil War, and had dozens of aerial victories. Adolf Hitler and Hermann Goering were convinced that the Americans' daylight bombing could never sustain the heavy losses of aircrews and planes the Luftwaffe could inflict.

On June 25, 1943, the streetlight in Silver Wings turned from yellow to green, meaning the 100th was going to fly its first combat mission.

They'd come to fight, and they were finally going to get the chance.

6

THE PROFESSIONALS

JUNE 1943

Lucky saw specks on the horizon as they approached the coast.

It looked like debris on the windshield at first until the specks started to move. For a fleeting second, he hoped the planes were American fighters headed for Le Mans too.

But hope is a shitty plan.

Lucky knew the truth. With each passing second, the specks became more menacing as they grew into gray single-engine Focke-Wulf Fw 190 fighters. When they spotted the American formation, the fighters started to climb to get on top of the incoming bombers.

"Jerry coming," Lucky heard Dye say over the interphone. "Thirty thousand feet. Twelve o'clock high."

It was June 28, 1943, and this was the first time Lucky and the rest of the crew were going to take on the Germans. Two days before, they'd flown mission #1, but didn't drop their bombs because the target was covered by clouds. Instead, they salvoed the payload into the English Channel and re-turned to Thorpe Abbotts disappointed, but relieved they'd gotten through one mission.

Now, on mission #2, they were headed to bomb the sub-marine pens at Saint-Nazaire at the tip of the Brittany penin-sula, which extends out into the Atlantic Ocean.

In 1943, a twenty-five-mission tour of duty was required from every bomber crew member. The U.S. Army Air Corps decided that twenty-five missions while serving in a heavy bomber of the Eighth Army Air Force would constitute a "completed tour of duty" because of the "physical and men-tal strain on the crew." Statistically, there was a less than 25 percent chance of accomplishing that goal. Many crews never made it past their fifth mission. In 1943, the average bomber crew was expected to complete eight to twelve missions before being shot down or disabled.

After arriving two weeks behind the rest of the group, Dye was determined to complete the required twenty-five combat missions and return to the United States as quickly as possible. To accomplish his goal, Dye volunteered his crew for every mission.

There would be no breaks for Crew 25.

Lucky was relieved that morning when they saw the tar-get for their second mission was in France too. The chat-ter around the base was they were headed into Germany, so France felt like a break. The red ribbon on the map at the front of the briefing room ran from their base in East Anglia through southern England and then across the Channel to a port at the tip of the Brittany peninsula. Instead of flying across France, the flight plan took them into the North Atlantic before swinging around at the tip of the peninsula.

"Gentlemen, our target is the submarine pens at Saint-Nazaire," Major Minor Shaw, the group's intelligence officer, told the assembled crews during the morning mission brief. "If we hit it, there will be fewer losses of the ships coming here from America."

Major Jack Kidd, the group's operation officer, replaced Shaw on the small stage. This was one of the first times the 100th was going to tangle with the Luftwaffe. In addition to the long flight and fighters from four bases within fifty miles of the target, there were over one hundred antiaircraft guns surrounding the submarine pens.

Kidd's message was simple. The bombers had to stick together to survive.

"Some of you won't be back unless you fly good formation and keep your gunners alert," Kidd said.

After the briefing, the crews headed for their bombers. Lucky's hands shook and his chest felt tight as they waited to take off. He knew he was about to be shot at, but he didn't know where, when, or how. Lucky couldn't find anyone on the base with any prior combat experience from whom to get advice. He was terrified to face a more experienced and well-equipped enemy in the Luftwaffe. The German aces were determined to prevent Lucky and his squadron mates from destroying their homeland. The Luftwaffe had already been fighting against the Russians, since June 1941, and the British. They were battle-tested professionals—and Lucky and the American crews were just citizen soldiers and amateurs.

Before the flare signaling his group to take off, Lucky said a prayer. He was raised a Christian. He knew the Ten Commandments. He'd been told since he was a child, "Thou shalt not kill," but he'd also been told it was "kill or be killed" up in the cold blue. That reality coming hand in hand with flying a very expensive piece of equipment and knowing the lives of nine others depended on him was very sobering. His prayer was simple. He didn't pray for victory or himself. He asked for the safe return of the crews and for the strength to withstand whatever he faced. Then a flare shot up from the control tower and Dye let off the brakes.

There was no turning back now.

To discourage fighter attacks, the bombers flew in tight—almost claustrophobic—formations in staggered groups. Created by LeMay, the staggered combat box formation allowed the B-17 gunners to protect each other from virtually all angles, increasing the survivability of the entire group. The formation allowed the bombers to put the maximum amount of firepower on incoming fighters—over two hundred .50-caliber machine guns firing six hundred rounds a minute.

The group formation of twenty-one bombers was the basic unit on most missions, but on some missions the whole wing of sixty-three bombers or a division of multiple wings hit one target. On big missions, the groups followed one another between twenty thousand and twenty-eight thousand feet and covered one thousand feet vertically and about two thousand feet horizontally. The lead squadron in each group flew slightly ahead with one squadron high above and to the right and one squadron beneath and to the left.

The formation stretched six hundred yards long, a mile or so wide, and half a mile deep with one thousand feet between the low and high squadrons. When it was time to drop, each group bombed individually, but came back together afterward to fly back to England.

The 100th bombers took off near dawn on June 28, 1943, and climbed through the thick morning fog until they reached twenty thousand feet. After forming up, the formation flew past London and Stonehenge before it cleared the coast. On the ground, the bombers looked like an air armada of hundreds of planes with contrails stretching out for miles.

Below the cockpit, Cavanaugh plotted their position and updated the pilots regularly while Chaney, the bombardier, manned a "cheek" gun—a .50-caliber machine gun sticking out of the side of the nose at an angle near the Norden bombsight at the front of the plexiglass nose. In the event a crew member was wounded, Chaney would also administer morphine or bandages. If he was incapacitated, it was the responsibility of Flanagan, the radio operator. Everybody else except the pilot and copilot was either looking out for attacking fighters or manning a gun.

Cavanaugh had the same cheek gun as the bombardier on the other side. His duties were to follow the course of the lead navigator as well as keep up with the exact position of the bomber in case they were forced from the formation. He could give the pilot a heading to get back home. The navigator had a constant communication with the pilot and the copilot as to where they were, what direction they were flying in, how many minutes until the next checkpoint, and how much time there was before the initial point to start the bomb run.

Above the nose was the cockpit. The massive four-engine bomber was impossible to fly solo, so the pilots were a team within a team. Most would develop a shorthand. Like a tennis double's team, they knew one another's moves and knew how to fly the ship together. Dye was the airplane commander. He led the crew and flew the plane. Everything that happened was his responsibility.

Lucky, the copilot, was there to assist and to relieve the pilot in flying the plane. He was responsible for maintaining contact with all the other crew members over the interphone. The interphone was the team's only means of communication. In combat, the crew wanted the interphone clear so gunners could call out attacking fighters. Pilots could get updates from the navigator or bombardier or send help if someone was wounded. Lucky was also responsible for monitoring the performance of the airplane and handling all the fuel. He'd transfer fuel from one tank to another to maintain the weight and balance of the airplane.

So far, everything was running well.

As they headed for the target, the bomber crews kept the chatter down on the interphone because the navigator would be calling back to the pilot, giving him headings or telling him where they were. After the last update from Cavanaugh, Lucky reviewed the flight plan. They were just passing Brest and getting close to making the turn inland for Saint-Nazaire, nicknamed "Flak City." The interphone crackled to life. It was Cavanaugh with a heads-up. The formation was about to turn. Ahead, Lucky saw the bombers in the high squadron dip their wings and bank to the left.

When it was the middle squadron's turn, Lucky and Dye banked to the left and followed the high squadron inland. It was there Lucky spotted the German fighters on the horizon. He didn't see just one. He saw wave after wave. Lucky's heart rate picked up. His breathing labored. It felt like something was compressing his rib cage.

As the lead fighter closed, Lucky made out the massive engine and cockpit of a Focke-Wulf Fw 190 A-4. German fighters had one mission. Knock Lucky out of the sky. For a split second, Lucky questioned every choice he'd made from the recruitment office to climbing into the cockpit that morning.

How the hell did I get into a spot like this? Lucky thought as he sat at high altitude as German fighters closed. *What was I thinking?*

The Luftwaffe was quick to come up with ways to down bombers. One of the most lethal was the Focke-Wulf Fw 190 A-4. Deployed in the summer of 1943, it was armed with two 7.9 mm machine guns and four 20 mm cannons. It was built to kill bombers. German bombers also dropped bombs timed to explode when they were at the same altitude as the American formation, or trailed a steel cable through the American formation that fowled props or cut wings off.

But the aces of the Luftwaffe knew if they were going to down bombers, they had to attack them with fighters. German pilots were initially intimidated by the Fortresses' nearly 104-foot wingspan. They marveled at the B-17s speed, ruggedness, and most of all its defensive firepower.

"Against twenty Russians trying to shoot you down or even twenty Spitfires, it can be exciting, even fun," wrote Fips Phillips, an Eastern front ace who commanded a fighter squadron against American bombers over Northern Germany. "But curve in toward forty Fortresses and all your past sins flash before your eyes."

The Germans called the formation the "flying porcupine" or *pulk,* meaning "herd." At first, they weren't sure how to break it. But warfare is a series of moves and countermoves. The Germans quickly learned the box formation worked if the entire group stayed together. If one pilot left the formation for any reason, fighters could pick them off, and the entire formation was now vulnerable until the gap was closed.

The key for the Luftwaffe was to break up the *pulk,* and the only way to do it was head-on. Defended by only four machine guns, the nose of the B-17—and more importantly the cockpit—was vulnerable to a head-on attack.

German fighter ace Egon Mayer successfully tested the head-on attack in November 1942, and by December, it was the preferred tactic against American bombers. To do it, the fighters flew a parallel course out of range of the bombers' guns. When they reached a point about three miles ahead of the formation, the fighters peeled off in groups of three and made high-speed strafing attacks. The angle of attack was ten degrees above the horizontal, or "twelve o'clock high" from the point of view of the B-17 pilots. It put the bombers' oil tanks—inside of the inboard engine housing—and wing fuel tanks—inside the outboard engine housing—directly in the fighter pilot's sights.

The German pilot had seconds to aim, fire, and peel away before careening into the heavy bombers. Over time, the Luftwaffe abandoned the waves, and the whole group attacked, spread out in line abreast. It was a game of chicken.

The tactic stopped the bomber crews in their tracks. Casualties among crews began to mount steadily as B-17s were being blown out of the sky with growing consistency. Commanders and crews started sending messages back to Boeing demanding a way to protect the aircraft's nose.

In response, Boeing came up with the B-17G model, adding a Bendix remotely operated twin .50-caliber chin turret underneath the plexiglass bubble on the nose. The additional guns brought the defensive armament to thirteen .50-caliber machine guns. The first G model arrived in the middle of October 1943. The new models slowly trickled in, meaning the bomber crews flew a mixture of G and F models, which was sufficient to ward off the frontal attacks.

But on Lucky's June 1943 mission, there were no G models.

As the formation crossed the French coastline, Lucky watched the fighters spread out into one line abreast. Luftwaffe Fw 190 fighters raced through the lead B-17 formation, cutting through the bombers and letting loose a stream of fire from their two synchronized MG 131 machine guns mounted in the engine cowling. The guns fired over the top of the engine and through the propeller arc.

The interphone exploded with warnings and gunners calling out fighter locations and headings. Lucky expected to hear panic, but the gunners' voices were heightened, yet calm. Lucky relaxed a bit hearing the gunners find purpose in their jobs. But his mouth was dry as the Fw 190s shot past his windshield in a gray flash. One second, the fighters were in front of him. Then he'd blink and they were gone. As the first fighter shot past *Sunny,* Lucky ducked. It was instinctive because the planes were flying so close. Each pass raised Lucky's heart rate, but each beat confirmed he was still alive.

Soon, fighters were cutting through the contrails left in the wake of the bombers as they climbed above the formation for another pass. A few exited from the bottom of the formation, disappearing underneath the planes. None of the bombers were damaged or fell out of formation, which buoyed Lucky's spirits. But there was little time to dwell on his first encounter with the Luftwaffe as the fighters disappeared only to be replaced by tufts of black smoke.

Flak.

The B-17 bucked as shrapnel from the antiaircraft shells smashed into the bomber's fuselage and wings. They'd reached the initial point, or IP. This was the spot where the bombardier took control and guided the plane to the target using the bombsight.

"Pilot, bombardier," Chaney said over the interphone. "I've got control."

Dye flicked on the autopilot. He and Lucky had nothing to do now but wait as Chaney—using the Norden bombsight—completed the bombing run. Lucky folded his hands and focused on the instruments in a vain attempt to ignore the maelstrom of flak exploding around them. As they neared the submarine pen, Lucky peeked up ahead and saw the lead plane's bombs tumble out of the bomb bay. Seconds later, his own plane shot up in the air as the bombs dropped from the bay.

Dye and Lucky instinctively reached for the controls.

Up ahead, the lead ship fired an orange flare signaling the formation to come back together for the flight home. The formation was intact. Flying almost wingtip to wingtip, the bombers packed together and headed for the Atlantic and safety. Clearing the coast, they turned north for England. Hours later, the 100th bomber crews returned from their first successful mission. They'd dropped bombs on an enemy target and all returned.

For Lucky, it was a sobering experience. Patriotism got Lucky into the copilot seat the first time, but he learned quickly it couldn't save him from the Luftwaffe.

There was no other branch in the Army where soldiers were learning on the job in combat. Even new infantrymen qualified on their rifles and completed exercises before going into combat the first time. Lucky had never flown a B-17 before he joined Crew 25. Dye taught him as they prepared to deploy to England. No wonder the crew hated him. They thought he was a jinx. A harbinger of misfortune and death.

As Lucky climbed out of the bomber—exhausted and rattled after hours airborne in the elements, dodging shrapnel and veteran enemy fighter pilots—his swagger was replaced with a determination not to finish twenty-five missions as much as survive them.

7

TAIL GUNNER

JULY 1943

Technical Sergeant Donald O. Ellis and Lucky climbed into the cramped tail gun position and went over the basics.

"This is how you aim," Ellis said, showing Lucky a small circular bull's-eye sight perched over the twin guns. Ellis pointed to the tail gun's butterfly triggers.

"This is how you fire."

Lucky nodded and then took a quick survey of the cramped tail compartment before he crawled out with a pit in his stomach. Ellis stayed behind and finished mounting and loading the pair of .50-caliber machine guns that he'd just cleaned because Lucky wasn't trained to do either.

What the hell am I doing? Lucky thought.

The 100th was on its tenth mission and had already lost sixty men. Lucky's crew had flown half of the 100th's missions and he was just getting the handle on being the copilot when he was ordered to man the tail guns after Crew 25 was designated a lead crew.

Lead crews were usually the most experienced airmen in the organization. The lead of the group was rotated among the 100th's four squadrons. There were several lead crews selected in each squadron, and the operations officer designated who flew which mission.

The morning of July 26, 1943, Lucky learned his crew was going to lead the mission to bomb Hanover's rubber works and rail yards. Major Ollie Turner, the squadron commander, would be the command pilot, moving Lucky into the tail gun as the formation control officer. The revelation surprised the hell out of Lucky when he'd been told after the briefing.

Ride in the back. What the hell for?

Lucky was barely comfortable in the cockpit. He'd never even fired the .50 caliber machine guns, and the tail gunner was one of the most important defenders on the B-17. The position protected the rear of the aircraft. Luftwaffe pilots gained a healthy respect for the tail guns, which forced German pilots to rethink their tactics, leading them to attack into formations head-on at twelve o'clock high.

Lucky protested after the briefing, asking Dye to explain the logic behind the move.

"By putting a pilot in the tail of the lead ship, you can see everything that is attacking the formation from the rear," Dye told him as they walked toward the equipment shack to get their gear. "You can see where the bombs hit. Report on stragglers lagging behind the formation and count chutes if we lose anyone."

All of that made sense on paper. It was all valuable information coveted by debriefers after a mission. But it made no sense when you factored in Lucky's level of training.

"I've never fired the guns," Lucky said. "Never."

Dye just patted Lucky on the shoulder and shrugged. "Just aim and shoot, right?"

Lucky got the message. It was an order. Plus, Dye wasn't all that concerned about logic. He just wanted to notch one more mission. Each time he flew was one step closer to getting back to his wife and his son. At the hardstand, Lucky waited near the nose with Dye, Chaney, and Cavanaugh as Ellis finished with the guns in the tail. It was an old habit. Plus, he really didn't want to be down at the other end of the plane. He belonged in the cockpit.

When it was time to go, Lucky watched as Dye and Turner climbed into the door underneath the cockpit. Ellis, now finished, climbed out of the B-17 and gave Lucky a thumbs-up before retreating to the crew jeep that would take him back to the barracks, where he would sweat out the mission.

Lucky was still staring at the open nose hatch when he felt a tap on the shoulder.

"You're with us, sir," Tech Sergeant George Flanagan said, flashing a crooked smile.

Lucky shook off his stupor and followed Flanagan, the crew's radio operator, toward a hatch between the tail gunner's compartment and the waist gunner's position.

"OK, Sparks," Lucky said as the radioman climbed through the door.

Once inside, they weaved their way up to the radio room

behind the bomb bay—the strongest part of the aircraft, where the wings intersect with the fuselage.

Lucky wedged himself into the corner of the already cramped compartment with Staff Sergeant Leroy Baker and Staff Sergeant Elder Dickerson—the waist gunners—and Staff Sergeant Richard Cooke—the ball turret gunner. The radio room was one of the only places where crew could congregate in the cramped bomber. It also put the weight forward in the fuselage, which was better because it was closer to the center of gravity of the airplane.

As the plane started to taxi, Lucky braced himself against the other gunners because there were no seats or any way to strap in. It was a strange sensation for Lucky, who was used to being in control of the plane. Riding in the back felt alien. It was dark, and the prospect of crawling back to the tail and doing a job he wasn't trained for was looming over his head. The stress was so much that he couldn't participate in the banter between the gunners as they waited for takeoff. Instead, Lucky sat quietly trapped in his own nerves. He understood how each position on the crew was integral. It was clear to the other gunners he was a weak link. In the back of their heads, they had to be thinking about how they could cover the rear, because even if Lucky got the guns firing, there was no guarantee he could hit anything.

It took a little while until the bomber got to altitude. Lucky saw Flanagan, who was monitoring the radio, nod to the group and gave the gunners the signal to man their positions. Lucky followed Baker and Dickerson and Cooke out a small door at the rear of the radio room that led toward the aircraft's waist. The group traveled aft, peeling off as they reached their positions.

Cooke arrived at his position first. The ball turret was a claustrophobic plexiglass sphere with dual .50-caliber machine guns. He slipped off the hatch and climbed inside. He looked like an unborn baby in the womb with his knees jacked up to his ears. Cooke would spend the rest of the flight protecting the bomber's belly. Lucky was grateful he didn't have to man that position. At six feet two inches tall, it would be impossible to fold his lanky body into the ball turret.

Lucky followed Baker and Dickerson to the next compartment. As soon as they opened the door, a blast of frigid air hit them. It was like standing in a wind tunnel. Both men seemed unfazed as they took their positions behind .50-caliber machine guns mounted in the open windows in the waist area behind the wings. They plugged in their interphones, heated suits, and oxygen masks and then loaded their weapons.

The roar of wind was deafening as Lucky pushed past and made his way down the narrow passageway toward the tail. He passed a generator and breaker box before crawling around the retracted tail wheel and passing through a small door in the bulkhead that separated it from the tail gunner's station. He made note of the small hatch along the left side of the fuselage. If he had to bail out, that was his exit.

Lucky climbed behind the guns and tucked his legs under the narrow bike seat, pushing the parachute strapped to his back into position behind him. He hooked up his oxygen mask first, then plugged in his heated suit and radio cable.

A canvas boot surrounded the guns and was the only thing keeping Lucky's legs out of the wind.

It didn't take long before both Lucky's arms and legs were tight and sore. He was losing feeling in his feet because he was forced to fold them under his body weight. The tail gunner compartment was the second tightest on the ship, beaten only by the ball turret. The fit was considerably tighter for Lucky.

The temperature dropped as the plane got up to bombing altitude. Lucky peered through the little windshield, clearing the windows of frost with his leather glove. Lucky peered up and down, marveling at the sight. Bombers in tight formation thundered along behind him with contrails coming off the wings and tails. It was like staring into the wake of the Greek fleet heading for Troy. Down below, he knew the Germans could see them coming for miles.

On the interphone, he heard the normal cascade of check-ins and observations. Usually he was at the center of the action, managing the crew and the aircraft. But back in the tail, he felt isolated. It felt like he was eavesdropping on the action from a secret perch. Cavanaugh, the navigator, updated the ship's position and course. A few feet behind him, Baker and Dickerson reported the waist guns were manned and ready.

Once over the water, Dye keyed his mic. "Pilot. All gunners. Test guns."

Lucky paused for a second. He pressed his face against the windows and made sure the tail was clear before sliding his thumbs onto the triggers. There was a small circular metal sight used to aim the twin .50-caliber machine guns. Cables connected the guns to the ring and bead sight. Lucky swung the guns around in a ninety-degree arc, making sure he knew the left and right limits before slowly pressing down on the triggers. The burst startled him, and he pulled his hands off the guns almost instantly. His heart was beating so hard he could feel it through his leather flight jacket.

He'd never been that close to guns firing before. The roar. The vibration as six hundred bullets a minute exploded out of the barrel. Firing the guns seemed to tap into something primal. There was something powerful about wielding a weapon capable of knocking an airplane out of the sky. It was embarrassing, but few things were as exhilarating as firing a machine gun, let alone two.

Lucky looked through the sight again and pressed the trigger. A few tracer rounds flickered in the sky. Every fifth round in the belt had an incendiary so the gunner could see the trajectory of the bullets.

"Don't use the tracers to aim," Ellis told Lucky as he was installing the guns in the tail section. "A bullet has a different trajectory. Just use 'em to see where you're shooting and adjust from there."

Lucky peered through the sight as the plane bobbed up and down. He wasn't confident that he could hit a streaking German fighter. Plus, being in the rear, he didn't want to miss and hit a B-17 in formation. Maybe he wouldn't even need to fire, he hoped. But Lucky knew that was unlikely.

As the formation approached the coast, Lucky heard Turner on the interphone. German fighters were on the horizon. As they crossed the Dutch coast, Lucky spotted some planes in the distance behind the formation. They were Me 110s, dual-engine fighter-bombers with a long glass canopy and a split tail. The Luftwaffe aircraft kept their distance, staying out of range of the B-17s' guns.

The Luftwaffe sent up the Me 110s equipped with rockets. They would fly abreast behind a bomber formation and fire 210 mm, tube-launched, spin-stabilized rockets employed with eighty-pound warheads at the B-17s' gas tanks on the wings.

From the cockpit, Lucky had had to watch the Luftwaffe attack from twelve o'clock high, line abreast with their guns lighting up as they peppered the bombers. He'd blink and they'd be gone. Everything happened pretty darn fast. But in the tail, it was like slow motion.

The 110s seemed to hang motionless behind them. It was like being stalked by a turtle. Finally, Lucky saw small flashes. The 110s' 37 mm cannon had enough reach to hit the bombers outside of the .50-caliber's range. Then, Lucky saw smoke stream out from under the 110s' wings as a salvo of rockets arced toward the formation.

"Tail gunner to pilot. Rockets inbound," Lucky said, willing his voice to stay even and calm.

In the tail gun position, Lucky gripped the gun handles. There was no way he could shoot the rockets, but he didn't know what else to do. A wall of smoke built up behind the rockets as they closed on the bombers. Lucky held his breath as the salvo arrived. Some fell short, falling through the contrails trailing the bombers. Others whistled past. Lucky couldn't tell if any bombers were damaged up ahead, but the rockets missed the ships he could see. Nothing came over the radio. Lucky figured that was probably a good sign.

After the 110s fired, they banked to the right and turned for home. Lucky saw a few tracers from either nervous gunners or opportunists hoping for a lucky hit. But the bullets fell well short. None of the German bombers ventured close enough to come under fire from the formation's gunners.

The Me 109 fighters came next.

"Copilot to gunners," Turner said over the interphone. "Enemy fighters. Stay alert."

Lucky's heart started pounding again. While the 110s peppered the formation with rockets, Lucky still felt safe because the Germans had kept their distance. Plus, there was nothing he could do to defend against rockets. But fighters—Me 109s—meant he'd have to fight them off. Lucky swiveled the guns to the left and right to make sure everything was operational, and set his thumbs on the triggers. He was ready. Maybe he'd live up to his nickname and hit one.

"Fighter passing on the right," Dickerson said. "Three o'clock level."

Lucky swiveled the gun to the left and waited for the gray fighter to come into view. It arrived in a gray blur. Lucky tracked the blur to the left, trying to keep up, and pressed the triggers. He wasn't really aiming, just firing bullets downrange, hoping to hit something.

The bark of the .50-caliber machine guns cut through the howl of the wind and left his ears ringing as Lucky kept the triggers depressed. The burst lasted a few seconds and then stopped. In his interphone, he could hear the other gunners calling out fighters followed by a short burst of fire—mostly coming from the waist gunners.

Lucky saw another fighter shoot past and pressed the triggers again.

Nothing.

He checked the ammo cannisters. Full. Lucky ran his hands over the belts that went from the ammunition canisters to the twin machine guns, making sure there were not kinks or obstructions. All clear. He tried the triggers again.

Nothing.

Lucky started to panic. He didn't know why the guns wouldn't fire. There was ammunition. The rounds were getting to the chamber. This is what he feared. Lucky had no training on how to troubleshoot the problem. Then he remembered hearing the gunners talking about how you could burn out the barrels if you weren't careful. When subjected to two hundred rounds of continuous fire, a .50-caliber will overheat. The manual—had Lucky been given it to read or trained in it—mandated six- to nine-second bursts. But when Lucky saw the fighter, he'd just pressed the triggers and let the twin guns eat. No break. To add insult, the fighter was likely out of range seconds after passing him, meaning he had no chance of hitting it. He'd busted his guns on an impossible target to hit. The rear of the bomber was now undefended. Lucky keyed the interphone.

"Tail gunner to pilot. Guns have seized."

He didn't want to imagine Dye's and Turner's reactions in the cockpit. It made him sick to make the call because the last thing he wanted to do was let down his crew.

"Roger, tail gunner," Dye said over the interphone. "We'll notify the formation. Keep us informed of what you see."

Dye then alerted Cooke in the ball turret and Tech Sergeant Victor Combs in the top turret to protect the bomber's flanks. Lucky scanned the sky behind the plane. He watched as the other bombers fought off German attacks. Lucky continued to relay updates on the condition of the formation, but he felt pretty doggone useless sitting in the back of the plane, freezing his ass off, with nothing to do but get shot at by the passing fighters.

It was embarrassing.

Finally, Lucky heard Chaney take over at the initial point. That meant they were on the bomb run. Lucky heard a rumble that sounded like thunder, but he knew better. Flak. He peered out of the window and spotted the flashes of anti-aircraft batteries as they sent a new shell aloft. Twenty-five seconds later, it reached altitude and exploded.

Lucky's heart was in his mouth as the shells exploded, throwing shrapnel in all directions. For all the talk about being a fortress, B-17s had little armor. Bullets and shrapnel cut through the bomber's fuselage like tissue paper. What little armor the plane did have was focused on protecting vital areas. A firewall was formed by half-inch-thick armor plates behind the pilot and copilot positions. There was no armor to protect him in the tail gun. Hell, only a canvas boot covered his feet. It wouldn't stop an angry German grandmother with a knife, let alone exploding shrapnel from 88 mm shells.

The bomber shook and rattled as the shells and shrapnel exploded all around him. The barrage lasted until they reached the target. Finally, Lucky heard the two sweetest words to a bomber crew.

"Bombs away."

The plane lurched upward as the bombs left the bomb bay. Lucky watched as the rest of the formation's bombs started to fall. He'd never seen a mission from this vantage point. Hundreds of bombers dropping thousands of bombs. The gray factory complex below disappeared in smoke and fire. Lucky saw the orange and red fire blooms flashing in the dark black smoke. It looked like lightning flashing in a storm cloud. A pillar of black smoke climbed into the sky behind him, providing a dark, ominous background for the rest of the formation.

Lucky felt the plane bank. The other bombers followed as they headed for the rally point and then home to Thorpe Abbotts. They were a few minutes into the return leg when he heard the bombardier over the interphone.

"We missed," Chaney said.

As the lead crew, Chaney was directing the bomb drop, and he'd miscalculated. Lucky didn't know if Chaney misidentified the target or whether they dropped the load from that altitude and the wind currents diverted the bombs so they fell harmlessly nine miles away.

It didn't matter.

They'd missed, meaning that at some point they'd have to come back. God willing, not with Lucky in the tail gun position. As they passed the target, Lucky peered down and saw the Hanover rubber works still standing. The bombs landed all around. The smoke and fire were tremendous, but not where it needed to be. Lucky was crestfallen. The mission was a failure, and so was his stint in the tail gun.

He sat idle in the back as the formation battled back to the coast and then out over the North Sea and finally the safety of England. As they got close to home, Lucky negotiated the piles of spent shells in the waist section on his way back to the radio room. He was the last one to arrive. The other gunners nodded as he found a spot on the floor.

They were relieved, having survived another mission. Lucky was less enthusiastic. He was grateful to have another mission done, but was still surly about being in the tail gun position. He'd felt like a passenger for most of the mission. A war tourist, not a member of the crew. Lucky decided whoever dreamed up putting a pilot in a tail gun position ought to be castrated because it was an absolutely ridiculous practice. He was set up to fail by placing him in a job with equipment he wasn't trained to use.

And his misgivings had proven out.

He'd burned through the barrels promptly and not only put himself but more importantly his whole crew in danger. That was his biggest sin. Everyone shared the same risks, but no one wanted to be the one to seal a crew's doom. Not doing your job was the ultimate sin. Bomber crews lived because they all worked together, but Lucky knew he'd let his crew down that day. That's what hurt the most. He'd worked hard to be the best pilot he could and had earned the respect of not only the other gunners but Dye, Chaney, and Cavanaugh.

Now he felt like he was back at square one.

After safely landing at Thorpe Abbotts, Lucky climbed out and made a beeline over to Major Turner, the squadron commander who'd replaced him as copilot on the mission.

He was chatting with Dye near the nose. They were about to climb into the crew jeep when Lucky stopped them.

"Major," Lucky said. "Can I get a word, sir?"

"Sure, Lieutenant," Turner said.

Chaney and Cavanaugh were joking as they loaded their gear in the jeep. Turner stopped taking his gear off and faced Lucky. Dye also stopped to listen.

"I don't understand what I'm supposed to be doing back there, and I have no training for it," Lucky said.

Turner explained he was back there to relay information on the condition of the formation to the pilots, which he did. This helped to coordinate the formation and keep it as tight as possible. Lucky just shook his head. That made sense on paper, but it didn't prove out in practice. Plus, the tail gunner could easily report the same information and man the gun. The issue in Lucky's mind was leaving the rear of the aircraft unguarded because he didn't know how to operate and troubleshoot the guns.

"I've never fired a .50-caliber machine gun before today, and I burned up both barrels in seconds, so they've got to be replaced," Lucky said. "There was no one defending our six o'clock for most of the mission."

Turner tried to rationalize it. Lucky would do better next time, he said.

"Well, you won't make that mistake again," Turner told Lucky.

But right there on the hardstand, Lucky vowed he would never put himself or his crew in harm's way again.

"You can take my wings or court-martial me or do whatever you want to, but I'm not getting in the tail again," Lucky told Turner. "I'm not going to fly back there anymore."

Turner—likely eager to get through debrief—just shrugged.

"Well, I guess you'll have to sit on the ground, then, when your crew leads," he said.

Turner looked at Dye to see if he had anything to add before heading to the jeep. Dye didn't say anything. He just picked up his kit and followed Turner.

"Yes, sir, I'll be glad to do that," Lucky said.

He gathered up his equipment and climbed into the back of the jeep with the other officers.

The next time his crew got tapped to lead, Lucky stayed behind. He watched them take off and waited around the control tower for them to come back. He knew the mission timeline and when the boys were supposed to return. He stood on the balcony overlooking the airfield with the ground crews and staff officers. Sweating out a mission on the ground was grim business. It was almost harder than flying the mission because on the ground he was fighting the unknown. At least in the air with his crew, he not only knew what was happening, but if there was a problem, he could help fix it.

Now, all he could do was wait.

With field glasses in hand, he scanned the horizon and strained his ears to hear the drone of the four-engine bombers. Standing nearby was the operations staff who counted the crews that survived and got a report on what happened to those who did not. But Lucky was really only looking out for his crew and didn't relax until he saw Dye and the boys land.

He was relieved to see his crew return each time, but with every mission they led, Lucky fell further behind in the count.

There was no way he'd complete his twenty-five missions at the same time as the rest of Crew 25.

8

FIVE MILES ABOVE

JULY 1943

Lucky pulled on his oxygen mask as the formation climbed to its cruising altitude of twenty-five thousand feet. He could feel the cold on his face, and his breathing was labored as the altimeter crept higher and higher.

"Copilot to crew, ten thousand feet. Masks on. All check in."

It was July 30, 1943, and he was back in the cockpit next to Dye. They were headed to Kassel, located along the Fulda River in Northern Germany. Kassel had several targets. A Tiger tank factory, a rail works, two engine plants, and the Fieseler aircraft plant, which was the day's target.

Lucky adjusted the rubber mask to make sure it covered both his mouth and nose, and inhaled. His labored breathing faded with each breath as the altimeter crept higher and higher, stopping after the formation reached twenty-five thousand feet.

Almost five miles up. It was like being on top of Mount Everest.

There was no other battlefield in World War II more hostile than the skies over the Third Reich, and it wasn't just the Luftwaffe. For Lucky and the crew, every mission was fought in an alien environment. To survive, the crew needed oxygen pumped through the ship's systems. But maybe the most debilitating part of a mission was the cold. It sapped the energy out of the crew and made even simple tasks treacherous. It was so cold in the waist gun posts that if a gunner removed a glove at altitude, his hands would stick to the metal or be frostbitten. Lucky knew gunners whose fingers were amputated at the nearest knuckle.

As the formation climbed, the mercury fell to subzero temperatures—fifty to sixty degrees below zero. Lucky shivered even though he was cloaked in leather and sheep's wool from head to toe. Each man wore a wool-lined leather jacket and gloves over a thin pair of silk gloves, and underneath that, heated gloves and booties. The heated gloves and boots plugged directly into the plane's electrical system, when it worked. It would often short out or get shot out, so they didn't depend on it to keep them warm.

The crews' faces were covered almost completely by the oxygen mask, but that didn't stop the cold from complicating things. Frozen breath, perspiration, and sweat could cut off the flow of oxygen, so they were always on guard for it, squishing the rubber mask to break up any ice crystals.

Lucky made a point to listen to the updates from the crew and keep a tally of who was talking. Everyone was constantly searching for enemy aircraft. The pilots were focused on keeping the aircraft running at peak efficiency. There was no reason to not answer an interphone call. If a crew member nodded off, it was a sure sign of oxygen deprivation.

Once the bomber reached altitude, even simple things like relieving oneself were tricky. A pilot's only relief was a condom. Body heat allowed the urine to flow, but it didn't take long for the condom to freeze solid. The pilots tossed the urine-filled condoms into their steel helmets so they wouldn't roll around the cockpit. When the bomber got down to lower altitudes, the temperature rose, thawing out the urine-filled condoms. Urine could cause a lot of damage to the switches and controls if moisture got into the panels and froze. Before descending, the pilots would pass the condoms back to one of the gunners, who threw them out the bomb bay. It was a little easier for the gunners. They just pissed out of the bomb bay, but they had to be careful not to hit the bomb shackles, for fear it would freeze and prevent the payload from dropping.

For the unlucky bomber crew member who had to do more than piss, there was no relief. The only option was to hold it for hours or soil their pants. Luckily, it would freeze solid for most of the mission. But at lower attitudes, it would thaw. Lucky saw a few crew members waddle out of a plane with a full payload.

This was mission #11, and Lucky knew what to expect. Crossing the European coast, the formation was met by a mix of Me 109s and Fw 190s. This time, the Germans targeted another group. Dye and Lucky watched the fighters and bombers battle it out up ahead, with an occasional pass by a fighter that was fended off by their gunners.

As the formation reached the initial point and started its bombing run, the blue sky in front of Lucky went from clear to stormy, with antiaircraft shells exploding all around him.

The shock waves battered the bomber, sending it bucking up and down. It was like being in perpetual turbulence. Lucky wasn't sure what was worse: playing chicken with Fw 190s or flying through a maelstrom of explosions and shrapnel.

For the Germans, that was the point.

When the Americans arrived in the spring of 1942, they thought the fighters were the threat. Flak—an abbreviation for the German word *fliegerabwehrkanonen*—was an annoyance.

"The fighters bothered me more than anything else, mainly because I had been in fighters for seven years, and seeing those guns winking at me out there bothered me, whereas the flak didn't," Curtis LeMay, who commanded bombers over Europe before transferring to the Pacific, said after the war.

But what American planners didn't understand was they were playing into the Germans' hands. Antiaircraft fire served two purposes. One, to shoot down bombers or knock them out of formation so fighters could swoop in for the kill. But more often, it was a deterrent meant to force bombers to fly higher or erratically, which decreased bombing accuracy.

Instead of following the RAF strategy of night bombing, they ignored all the lessons learned by the British from the Spanish Civil War to the Battle of Britain and decided on a daylight, high-altitude, precision-bombing campaign. American planners believed their planes, bombsights, and doctrine were superior. For the German gunners, instead of engaging the RAF at night and relying on gun-laying radar to spot unseen planes, the flak defenses finally had daylight targets. The batteries were radar controlled and electronically fired, so they didn't need gunners. The radar calculated the formation's direction and altitude, and Nazi youth loaded the guns. Once the Germans determined the target, they moved the guns into position and filled the skies above with shrapnel.

From the start of the war, Hitler took a keen interest in the Luftwaffe's antiaircraft defenses. The Germans were already producing one of the best antiaircraft guns in the war—the 88 mm—and Hitler knew the guns provided a stiff defense, but more importantly, every boom of an antiaircraft gun was a reminder to the beleaguered German civilians that the Reich was fighting off the bombers.

As the war progressed, the Germans stockpiled ammunition and guns, setting up huge flak fences around potential targets or putting the guns on railcars so they could be transported from target to target. German commanders were also ordered to use all captured guns in the defense of the fatherland. By 1943, almost three hundred captured Russian guns were defending Germany.

The German gunners developed a technique of firing antiaircraft shells in a box barrage formation that completely encompassed the bomber formation. Each shell was fired twenty-five seconds before it got to the bombers' altitude. The explosion had a blast radius of about 100–150 feet. The shrapnel easily punctured the very thin aluminum skin of the bombers.

At first, the bombers did their best to jink and juke to

avoid the shells. Pilots thought if they flew a straight line for more than ten seconds, the German gunners could shoot them down. The crews were spending so much time dodging shells that by the time the bombers got back on the bombing run, the bombardiers only had a few seconds to line up the target and drop.

And they were missing.

When his pilots told LeMay flying straight through the flak was suicide, he did the math. LeMay took a class in artillery when he was at Ohio State. Using data from previous bomber missions, he worked toward a solution. First, he determined how many antiaircraft rounds it took to bring down a B-17 bomber.

Three hundred and seventy.

That's a lot of hits just to bring down one plane. It was unlikely any one bomber would take a sustained barrage. The numbers were on his side.

Next, LeMay figured it was more important to hit the target the first time so they didn't have to come back. The only way to improve accuracy was to give the bombardier a stable platform. That meant flying straight in and level. On the next mission, LeMay ordered his crews to fly through the flak.

"We are going to make a straight-in run from the time we see the target until we drop the bombs off," LeMay said.

He then volunteered to lead the raid. It was November 1942, and LeMay's bombers hit a target in France. They took no evasive action and put twice as many bombs on target.

At the end of the run, LeMay radioed the bombardier. "How did we do?"

"Well, we hit the target, but I would have done better if it wasn't for the clouds," the bombardier said.

There weren't any clouds, just smoke from the exploding flak. And they didn't lose one ship.

For pilots, who were used to controlling risk, flak was maddening because there was nothing the crew could do. The only way to survive flak was to endure it.

Small black puffs of smoke appeared on the horizon as the bombers approached Kassel. Lucky hated flak. He felt like a duck flying past a blind full of hunters.

He pulled on his flak vest with metal plates that covered his chest and a steel helmet to protect his head. None of that was going to stop a direct hit. Soon the shells were exploding all around the plane. Each explosion forced Lucky to brace for it. He heard the shrapnel peppering the bomber's skin like hail until a shell exploded directly in front of them. It felt like the ship took a punch. The hit jarred the bomber up, forcing Lucky and Dye to retake control momentarily to avoid hitting the bomber above them in the formation. It didn't feel like a direct hit, but it was more than just a shrapnel shower. Lucky keyed the interphone and called down to Chaney and Cavanaugh in the nose.

"You guys OK?"

Chaney came on first. "Roger," he said. "We're fine. Flak busted the nose. Got showered by some shrapnel, but we're OK."

A burst of flak punched a hole in the plexiglass nose cone. A frigid jet stream flowed straight into the copilot's side of the cockpit directly on Lucky's feet. They were traveling at about two hundred miles an hour, and the cold blast cut through his leather, fleece-lined booties. He tried to move his feet out of the flow, but couldn't because he needed to use the rudder pedals. There was no way he could avoid the blast of cold air.

Lucky reached over and jiggered the plug to the electrical warmer—which was designed to stave off the cold—hoping it would come back on line and warm his feet. It had failed hours before, and his toes were past cold now. They were getting numb. Lucky wiggled his toes to keep the circulation going, but it was no use. His feet tingled, and pins and needles cascaded up his ankles and calves.

Outside the windshield, flak exploded again, forcing Lucky's concentration off his feet and back to the mission. Another shell exploded nearby followed by the loud *thunk* of metal hitting metal. Lucky peered out of the window and saw thick black smoke shoot out of engine number three. The engine's housing was shredded, exposing the prop's internal mechanism.

"Number three is hit," Lucky said. "But she is still running."

Dye looked across Lucky and out of the window. He could see the smoke. Dye nodded and scanned the gauges.

The B-17 could fly with only three engines, but not as fast as the formation. Falling out of formation—much like being separated from the herd on the Serengeti—was a surefire way to get shot down. Nazi fighters waited for damaged bombers to lag behind the formation before pouncing on them. They needed to keep engine number three running so it didn't drag and then have to make up the airspeed using the trio of working engines.

With Lucky's attention on the gauges and the fuel consumption, Dye adjusted the throttle and fuel mixture to make sure they were getting as much power as possible. To Lucky's relief, their airspeed didn't lag and the ship stayed in formation long enough to drop the bombs.

Turning for home, Lucky had forgotten about the cold over Kassel, but now his feet weren't cold anymore. They were numb with waves of pain followed by pins and needles. It was getting difficult to keep his feet on the rudder pedals. Lucky wasn't sure he could endure hours with his feet in the wind. Plus, he'd need them to work when it was time to land.

"Hey, can you plug that hole?" Lucky asked Chaney or Cavanaugh.

In the nose, Chaney and Cavanaugh were huddled together trying to stay warm. If it was cold on Lucky's feet, it was worse in the crippled bombardier compartment. The wind blew Cavanaugh's charts around and battered the two men in a constant windstorm.

"Negative," Chaney said through chattering teeth. "The hole is too big. We don't have anything to plug it."

Everyone had to endure.

Lucky felt the energy draining from him. His feet were beyond numb. He couldn't feel anything below his ankles. His whole body ached, and his jaw was sore because of the constant chattering of his teeth.

Finally, after clearing the European coast, the formation

started to descend. It took a while to get down from twenty-five thousand feet. By the time the green fields of southern England were in sight, things started to warm up. Lucky's feet were no longer cold. Now they hurt. Approaching Thorpe Abbotts, Lucky pressed the rudder pedals and almost let out a scream. Jolts of sharp pain, like a knife being stabbed into his feet, shot through his leg. Even a little pressure sent a charge of pain up his leg and into his back. It was agony to fly the plane.

Lucky keyed his interphone.

"Are your feet frostbitten?"

Dye looked over at Lucky and shook his head. "They're awful cold, but I don't think they're frostbitten," Dye said.

Lucky took a few deep breaths as he pushed down the pain. He tried to wiggle his toes, but wasn't sure if anything was happening. His feet felt like weights at the end of his legs.

"I can't feel my feet at all," he said over the interphone. "Can't press the rudder pedals."

Both pilots needed to press the brakes during landing, especially with one crippled engine and god knew what other damage. They knew flak had damaged the number three engine, but it may have crippled the landing gear or worse.

"Do what you can," Dye said.

Lucky moved his feet up and down the pedals until he could finally add pressure with his heels. He could apply the brakes, and the pain was bearable. The problem now was every time he got his heels in place, his feet slipped off. Lucky dragged his feet back into position over and over again as they prepared to land. Even if he could apply the brakes, there was no way he could get out of the plane if something happened. He was literally frozen stiff.

Over Thorpe Abbotts, Dye lined the bomber up for landing. Lucky worked to keep his feet on the pedals as the concrete airstrip got closer and closer. Lucky felt the landing gear hit and pushed down on the brakes, but he couldn't muster much strength. The end of the runway was coming up fast. Dye pumped the brakes and slowed the plane enough to turn before the runway ended.

When they got back to the hardstand, Lucky tried to get up, but couldn't put any weight on his feet. A jolt of fear shot through Lucky when it dawned on him he could lose both feet.

Lucky heard Dye call over to medics who had climbed into the cockpit.

"Feet are frozen," Lucky said when they got to him.

The medic patted Lucky on the shoulder and then climbed under his legs to work on his injured feet.

There was no way Lucky could stand. Some of the ground crew lifted him from his seat and eased him out of the plane through the bomb bay. They carried him to an ambulance waiting nearby. Once inside, the ambulance raced to the sick quarters. Medics with a gurney met the ambulance.

Lucky heard one of the medics tell the waiting hospital staff he had frostbite. When the nurses pulled off Lucky's boots, his feet were black and blistered. The doctor ran a stainless steel hammer along the length of his right foot.

"Feel that?" the doctor said.

Lucky shook his head. "No," he said.

He knew the doctor was touching his feet, but he couldn't feel anything below his ankles.

"Hey, Doc, you going to have to amputate my feet?" Lucky said, not really sure if he wanted to hear the answer.

The doctor looked up after the examination and shook his head. "Well, your feet are frostbitten," he said. "Not the worst case I've seen. But it's pretty bad."

A nurse came in with a bowl and some bandages.

"Wrap 'em up and let them thaw," the doctor said to the nurse before turning to Lucky. "You're going to be OK," the doctor said.

The nurses treated his feet by first packing them in ice and then thawed them slowly by immersing them in warm water. Lucky kept his feet in the bath until the skin was a reddish purple and he could feel and move his toes. The nurses repeated the procedure two times a day until his feet started to return to a normal peach color.

After rewarming, the nurses wrapped his feet in bandages to avoid infection. The skin on his feet was delicate with red blisters mixed with pink, new skin as he healed. Unable to walk, he was confined to a hospital bed. For the next several days, the nurses massaged his feet. Keeping circulation in his feet was paramount to warding off gangrene.

Dye and some of the gunners came to check on him a few days later. They'd flown another mission, meaning Lucky was now three behind after losing two missions because he refused to fly in the tail gun position. His crewmates wanted to know if he was still alive and then if he was going to be removed from the crew permanently. Lucky assured them he planned to return to the copilot seat.

A few days into his hospital stay, a ball turret gunner on another crew was wheeled in after getting treatment for frostbite. The gunner pissed his pants during a mission, and the urine froze his butt to the ball turret. Lucky and the gunner laughed about it in the hospital, but it was no laughing matter to the gunner's crew.

They had to fly around after the mission as they tried to thaw him out. When the bomber ran low on gas, the pilot had no choice but to land with him still in the ball turret. Bombers weren't supposed to land with anyone in the turret because it only hangs a foot from the ground. A hard landing would crush the gunner inside. With the gunner still in the turret, the pilot put the bomber down on the grass next to the concrete runway. He figured the man had a better chance to survive over soft ground. The ground crew got him out of the turret and into the ambulance.

Lucky spent eight days in the hospital. Just before he was discharged, a clerk from the personnel section came to tell both men they'd earned a Purple Heart, awarded to American servicemen wounded in combat.

Lucky declined his because he didn't think his injuries warranted it. He knew men who'd been maimed in the line of duty. He'd had a couple of days of pins and needles and a short stay relaxing in a hospital bed. That did not merit an award.

The ball turret gunner also declined to accept the award. When the clerk left, Lucky asked why he'd turned down the award.

"I don't want to explain how I got it," he told Lucky.

9

"A GOOD TYPE AMERICAN"

JULY 1943

Lucky didn't believe it.

When the sergeant from headquarters came to get him at his Quonset hut, he didn't trust he had a phone call at the headquarters. Lucky had fallen for this kind of thing before he deployed to Thorpe Abbotts and spent a cold night tracking down phantom orders as a prank soon after joining Dye's crew in Nebraska. So, when the sergeant came down to tell him he had a phone call, he was skeptical.

Who was calling him?

The sergeant didn't know. It was a man calling from London.

That didn't make any sense to Lucky. No one from home knew where he was, and everyone else he knew in England was at Thorpe Abbotts. He shot a glance at the rest of his crew, but they weren't paying attention to him.

He must really have had a call.

Lucky followed the sergeant back to the headquarters. On

the desk was the black phone receiver. When Lucky picked it up, he heard a familiar voice.

"Hi. I'm in London."

Lucky knew the voice immediately.

It was Lucky's younger brother Bob on the line.

Bob was a midshipman with the Merchant Marines. His Liberty ship was supposedly dodging Nazi submarines as it transported war materials from America's East Coast to England as the Allies built up for the inevitable invasion of Europe. But Bob, after a successful crossing, had taken leave as his ship unloaded and found his older brother at Thorpe Abbotts.

"Bob?" Lucky said.

He was dumbfounded.

"I'm coming to see you," Bob said.

"Bob, you're out of your gourd," Lucky said. "You don't even know where I am. The location is a secret."

Bob laughed. "Yes, I do," he said. "You're at Thorpe Abbotts, near the village of Diss."

Bob had sent letters about his time in the running convoys to England and his duties aboard his ship. Lucky had written back about his own daily duties, but he'd never mentioned the base. His mail was censored anyway. There was no way of knowing the name of the base since it didn't go by Thorpe Abbotts officially. It was Station 139, or APO 139, if you wanted to send a letter there.

"How in the world did you find out?"

Bob told Lucky after making port, he got the train to

London and marched into the headquarters of the Eighth Air Force.

"I told them I was your brother and I wanted to go see you," Bob said. "They told me where you are. I'm getting the next train."

So much for operational security. No wonder the Germans seemed to always know where the formation was headed. But Lucky was excited to see a face from home, especially his younger brother. He hadn't seen Bob since he'd left for flight school. Bob was the youngest of the three brothers. Lucky and Bob had shared a room growing up and were close. Bob and his friends used to go on joyrides with Lucky on Sundays.

Lucky didn't get a lot of letters. Besides his family, only Eleanor wrote him regularly. She wrote almost every day about the home front, her family, and the goings-on around Sumter. The letters were a welcome respite from the horror of his every day. But with each letter from Eleanor, Lucky realized she expected them to marry. She talked of vague plans of a life together upon his return. But he couldn't imagine being a husband any more than he could imagine a future at all. He didn't give himself permission to think beyond the job at hand, be it flying through a flak barrage or nursing a glass of gin at Silver Wings.

His every fiber was focused on surviving.

When he did have time to write back, Lucky didn't address her future plans. Since his letters were censored, he couldn't disclose anything but the mundane and stuck to the food, the weather, and any funny story he could muster.

Eleanor was a constant companion on missions. After arriving in England, he tied her silk stocking around his neck for warmth and then with each successful return to Thorpe Abbotts, for luck.

The next day, Bob arrived as promised. He was dressed in his navy-blue uniform and carried a green seabag over his shoulder. News photographers shot photos of the brothers— one in a Merchant Marines uniform and the other in Army Air Corps pinks and greens with silver wings and crusher cap—shaking hands. The story of the brothers' reunion got all the way back to the papers in Chattanooga. Lucky wasn't flying that day, and the Luckadoo brothers retreated to Silver Wings and enjoyed a few rounds while they caught up.

That night, Lucky set up a cot in the bachelor officers' quarters, and his brother slept, ate, and hung around with the ground crew while Lucky flew missions. At night, after dinner, the brothers drank and played cards in the officers' club. It was a grand visit, but Lucky knew sweating out the missions took a toll on his brother.

Lucky worried about Bob too. Crossing the Atlantic in a slow boat while German submarines stalked the cold waters below was equally unnerving. But far easier since Lucky didn't have to wait for Bob's ship to come in. It wasn't easy for Bob to eat breakfast with his brother, knowing that he might not return that afternoon. Lucky could see the relief on Bob's face when Lucky climbed out of the ship unharmed.

After two days, Bob packed up his seabag and headed for the train. He had a ship to catch, and Lucky had missions to fly. Both men had no idea if this was their last visit. Lucky was aware of how dangerous crossing the Atlantic was for the transport crews. Both Luckadoo brothers were in the war's longest and costliest battles. The brothers embraced a final time and said their goodbyes, reminding one another to write their mother, Winks, at home and to keep safe.

As Bob left to catch the train back to London, Lucky realized Bob was the first person from home he'd seen in months. Since arriving in England, he'd lost track of his other friends from college, including Sully. They hadn't corresponded since he'd left for training, and Lucky only kept up with him through rumors from mutual friends.

Lucky knew Sully had already fought the Germans in Egypt and was back in England, but not that he was stationed only thirty-five miles south of Thorpe Abbotts.

Sully officially enlisted in the Royal Canadian Air Force in January 1941 in Windsor, Ontario. The doctor, after completing his physical, declared him "a good type American. Poor motives. Good coordination. Capable . . . Good satisfactory material."

From Ontario, Sully went to Toronto for flight school and was rated forty-third out of one hundred and thirteen in his class, with an 87 percent average. Recommended for a commission, his instructors said he "should make an excellent pilot."

And Sully was to some degree.

His flight school instructors described him as hardworking and a clear thinker and leader, but he got sloppy at times and had bouts of poor judgment, especially during forced landings. Sully was the classic gray man who stayed in the middle of the pack, but that was enough to earn his flying badge in November 1941, and he deployed to England in December.

Before he left, Sully met his mother in Detroit for a visit. They spent two days visiting the stores and coffee shops on the waterfront. The visit ended with Sully seeing her off— leaving quickly after checking her bags at the station. He felt like hell and didn't want to make things worse with his tears. His mother was the only family he had, and Sully knew where he was headed and what that could mean.

"I love her more than anything in the world," he wrote in his diary. "May never see her again."

Sully arrived in England in December 1941. Trapped on the boat with Christmas coming, Sully and three friends ordered one hundred whiskeys from the ship's bar and poured them into quart beer bottles. Sully also liberated a box of crackers that turned out to be Communion wafers, and the quartet retreated to their cabin to eat and drink the night away. In no time, wafer crumbs covered the cramped transport cabin like snow. The party was so loud, the captain, dressed in yellow silk pajamas, pounded on the door and broke it up, but not before Sully got his fill, stumbling back to his cabin to sleep it off.

A couple of days later, the boat docked in Liverpool. Sully and the others boarded trains for their bases, where he found comfort in some of England's culture—especially teatime.

"Have tea twice daily, and I've already gotten to the stage at which I'm damn well upset if I don't get some tea and crumpets at 10:00 a.m. or 4:00 p.m.," he wrote in a letter to his friend Grady Long.

Between missions, Sully visited London, seeing all the important spots: 10 Downing Street, Trafalgar Square, Piccadilly Circus in London's West End. But the English people impressed him the most after witnessing the destruction wrought by the German bombers. During the Battle of Britain, the Luftwaffe bombed London for fifty-six straight days. More than 40,000 British civilians were killed during the Blitz and almost 140,000 wounded.

"Dear God, but it does give a man inspiration to fight and die for a cause after seeing these things," he wrote to Grady after visiting London. "Talked to endless numbers of people in subways, trams, on the street, and have a good picture of what went on . . . These people have the most remarkable spirit yet. Do you—or could you—guess the headlines on one of today's leading London papers? A savage New Year to the Germans."

But Sully didn't stay in England long. He deployed to Egypt in March 1942, where he helped fend off the Afrika Korps and turn the tide of the war. Dressed in a pith helmet and shorts, Sully toured the region with stops in Eritrea, Palestine, and Abyssinia, writing he felt like he was part of a Canadian Club whiskey advertisement. Despite his travels, he never found anywhere "as dear as old Tennessee."

With the Allies preparing to invade Europe, Sully returned to England in October 1942, eventually ending up with the No. 56 (Punjab) Squadron based at RAF Martlesham Heath. It was commanded by Wing Commander Gordon Leonard

Sinclair, a veteran of Dunkirk and the Battle of Britain who downed more than ten German fighters and bombers. The No. 56 Squadron's role started as low-level defense against Fw 190 and Me 109 fighter-bomber attacks, but under Sinclair's command, it had evolved into becoming fighter-bombers and attacking ground and sea targets. Sinclair led missions against V-1 rocket sites in Pas-de-Calais and German airfields.

While Sully was in the thick of combat, he wrote very little about it in letters to Grady or his diary, instead focusing on the hijinks fueled by the monotony of waiting for the next mission.

Once, after a long night of drinking, Sully and his confederates found a shotgun and proceeded to fire it in his squadron mates' barracks rooms, scattering pellets into the walls and ceilings and scaring the hell out of the occupants with the tremendous boom.

"Consequently, we have a couple of big gaping holes in the ceilings, due, no doubt, to some slight miscalculation!" Sully wrote later.

Sully also kept busy with rounds of bridge and cribbage or drinking and carousing.

"No lie, Grady, the women over here go for my Mom's fair-haired boy in a large way," he wrote to Long. "Not bragging at all. In some instances, it gets me in a few mix-ups, but I suppose I can chalk it all up as experience."

One Polish friend told Sully to marry a wealthy Englishwoman. He'd found one, Peggy. Officially a "Lady," she had a string of polo ponies that took her to New York, India, South Africa, and Australia. When the war broke out, the

British government told her that she had to get back to England or they'd confiscate all her British property for the war effort. She reluctantly returned, but joked she'd pay someone to smuggle her out of England.

How Peggy and Sully fell in together is unclear. He didn't tell friends or his diary, but he told Grady he desperately wanted to follow his Polish friend's advice, but couldn't. She was married.

"Everything that I want is just out of range—Peggy for instance," Sully wrote in his diary.

But that didn't stop him from seeing her as often as possible. Sully wrung every drop of life out of a day, but wrote letters and diary entries like a condemned man, or at least one who recognized his own mortality. The crucible of combat had shaken his faith. He left Tennessee a Christian man, but war brought him to the realization he was an atheist.

"Religious aspect has ceased to worry me," he wrote Grady, after telling his friend in previous letters he was struggling with his faith. "There either is or there ain't, and I'm secretly laying odds that there ain't."

Sully hoped to return to the United States after the war, but how he'd spend his postwar years troubled him. His ambition was gone and he told Grady how content he'd be as a firefighter with a "decent library, some decent records." He'd "be as happy as a small boy."

His mother, never far from his thoughts, was his real worry. He understood the toll that having her only son in harm's way was taking on her health and well-being. Sully planned on paying back that debt.

"The big thing for me will be to take care of mom and really devote myself to making her happy," he wrote to Grady. "The rest doesn't make a helluva lot of difference."

Sully was comfortable with death. Losing squadron mates was painful, but to be expected, and it wasn't out of the question to wonder when death came for you. That thought often crept into his mind while writing home, prompting him to ask Grady to take care of his mother and keep her spirits up. Sully suggested his mother take a vacation to Mexico in hopes of getting her mind off him and the war.

It was a luxury he didn't have in England.

"I shall surely lose my ass or a great part of it before it is all over," Sully wrote to Grady. "And yet what better cause is there for losing a man's ass? None that I can see. I'm not being pessimistic and I know this is contrary to what I've said before, but I don't suppose I'll be back to see either of you."

Sully fell in love with poetry, writing some and rewriting others, including a solemn line from English poet Rupert Brooke's "The Soldier" to make it more personal. His edited line closed a somber letter to Grady.

"If I should die, think only this of me: That there's some corner of a foreign field that is forever Tennessee."

10

DYE'S LAST MISSION

SEPTEMBER 1943

Captain Glen Dye's twenty-fifth mission was a milk run, so far, and that is the way they wanted it.

No matter how much they told themselves this was just another mission, no one, including Dye and the rest of his crew, believed it. Last one. But the fact wasn't lost on the crew that their final mission was the same type of target they missed on their second mission.

Pretty discouraging.

After four months of flying into harm's way, Dye and most of Crew 25 were going home if they could survive one more mission. Dye's goal of finishing his allotted missions in record time was in reach. Only Lucky—four missions behind—and Dickerson, the waist gunner on his twenty-fourth mission, were short of the magic number, but they were still excited for their crewmates.

Early that morning, they'd been woken up with a flashlight

in their face for the mission briefing. Lucky felt like he was being pulled along by Dye and the rest of the crew's exuberance. The day before, they'd flown the twenty-fourth mission to Paris to bomb the Renault aircraft plant and everyone hoped for a target in France, preferably along the coast. Their eagerness to fly faded when the operations sergeant removed the curtain in the briefing room to reveal the map with a long red line pointing at Bordeaux, a port city near the Atlantic Coast along the Garonne River. The secondary target was La Pallice, the sub pens they'd bombed on one of their first missions.

Dye, sitting shoulder to shoulder with Lucky, shrugged, but the rest of the crew slumped in their chairs. Chaney and Cavanaugh started grumbling as the briefers laid out the plan. Lucky took notes. The flight time to the target was a bit longer, and it was better defended than the first raid. The defenses would no doubt be heavier this time, and the flight was long, testing the endurance of the B-17 and the crew.

Lucky smirked. He wasn't surprised.

It was sort of fitting to end on the same type of a target they'd already hit.

Daylight precision bombing was off to a rocky start. Bombing accuracy was terrible. The average circular error in 1943 was 1,200 feet, meaning that only 16 percent of the bombs fell within a thousand feet of the aiming point.

"Rather than dropping bombs into pickle barrels, Eighth Air Force bombardiers were having trouble hitting the broad side of a barn," said historian Stephen L. McFarland.

For Lucky and the crews, the pickle barrel myth was laughable.

Lucky knew damn well it was impossible for the bombardiers to achieve that level of accuracy. He was sure of it because he'd just witnessed it, plus they'd attacked targets multiple times because the previous mission missed. But the aircrews didn't have any choice. They were still sent out day after day after day into the teeth of the Luftwaffe to complete a mission everyone from the crews to the leadership knew really was impossible.

Lucky was living the folly of war.

LeMay, a made man in the Bomber Mafia, went about fixing it. He identified the best bombardiers and made them lead the formation. The idea was all the aircraft dropped their bombs when the lead bombardier did instead of relying on each craft to hit the target independently.

Accuracy improved. The odds of survival didn't.

Losses of thirty or more aircraft—three hundred men— were not uncommon across the bomber groups. For new crews, there was a 400 percent turnover in the first ninety days of combat. Good bomber crews learned in a hurry or they didn't learn at all.

Then, overnight, things improved. LeMay didn't know why until it dawned on him a few months later. The crews could do the math. They saw the toll the Germans were inflicting on their numbers. The crews in the crowded mission briefings rarely returned intact. Flying in the Eighth Air Force "was like holding a ticket to a funeral—your own" became a popular saying.

"The men had concluded, 'We are not going to make it. We might as well get shot down today as tomorrow; let's go,'" LeMay said. "It was that simple."

No one looked forward to a mission any longer. The 100th had taken horrific losses since arriving in England, including several times where it lost a dozen or more aircraft on a single mission. From their first missions, Lucky felt a sense of loss.

He saw bombers go down, but never the results of the crash. Did the crews bail out and survive? Were they alive in a prisoner-of-war camp? On the ground, the horror of war was staring them in the face. But Lucky and the aircrews were never faced with burying the dead. One minute, a crew was at Silver Wings or around the dinner table. The next minute, they were gone, their personal effects packed up and their names removed from the roster.

No memorial service. No closure.

The casualties were too numerous to stop and mourn everyone, leaving those still fighting to continue onward. It had gotten so bad Lucky was numb to it. They faced death every day, and Lucky expected to leave Thorpe Abbotts in the morning and that night see operations orderlies packing up personal effects around empty beds. It was a bigger shock to return from a mission with everyone who left. Crew 25 was fortunate. They hadn't lost anyone, save for a few injuries like Lucky's frostbite.

But no one wanted to go down with one mission left.

After the briefing, Lucky gathered his gear and climbed into the crew truck when it was time to head to the hardstand. As they rode out to the plane, he felt the anxiety building in his chest. It was a familiar feeling that took hold before every mission. Climbing into the plane was like getting into a coffin. At this point, with more than twenty missions completed, he wasn't just on borrowed time. He was on someone else's borrowed time.

Flying into the gloomy English weather time and again, Lucky locked the fear and doubt away with his dreams of a future. His plans of being a chemical engineer or anything other than a survivor were long gone. The thought felt silly. His world was now a single moment lived one at a time. Lucky only thought of what he could touch and feel.

The vibration of the aircraft.

The cold.

Nasty, bitter gin sipped in silence at Silver Wings after a mission.

The relief of another breath.

The trauma of the missions crept into his subconscious. It clouded his mind, not allowing him to plan beyond the next task, the next meal, the next mission. Lucky knew the sand was flowing out of the hourglass of his life, and he was never sure when the last grain would fall. Nor did he care because there was no controlling it. Instead, he found comfort in the process. His normal routine.

A quick prayer.

Check.

The Bible damaged by shrapnel in his jacket pocket.

Check.

Eleanor's silk stocking.

Check.

He was ready.

But this mission seemed to grip harder. He was flying with a crew one mission away from going home. That seemed to only tip the scales on the unlucky side. The fear was, of course, that they'd go down on their last mission and not be able to finish. End up as POWs or worse.

No one wanted to die on the last mission.

Once the 100th formed up, the formation flew low over the English countryside to avoid German radar. Over Wales, they went around instead of over a hill. Like their second mission, the formation swung wide of occupied France, the Brittany peninsula, and heading out to sea before turning to the south to parallel the coast.

Far out to sea, the German fighters weren't a threat. Lucky peeked out of his cockpit window and saw nothing but the gray Atlantic Ocean stretching to the horizon. He knew on the other side of that horizon was home. But that felt so far away. He'd pushed home so deep down that he couldn't reach it anymore. The thought just left him cold, like the dark ocean below or the subzero temperatures of the cockpit.

The interphone was quiet except for Cavanaugh's updates. Being the lead crew meant he was navigating for the ships behind them.

Behind *Sunny II*—the original *Sunny* was shot down by flak thirteen days earlier—Captain Robert Wolff was in *Wild Cargo*.

Arriving after Lucky, Wolff was on his eighth mission. His plane had been flown by another crew the day before and returned damaged. The ground crew worked overnight to get the bomber in fighting shape. By the time Wolff and crew were airborne, the formation had a two-hour head start. Since Wolff was in the tail-end Charlie position, the last and lowest plane in the formation, he had time to catch up. Wolff got into position just as the formation paralleled the French Atlantic coast.

As the formation neared Bordeaux it turned inland and started its bombing run. Lucky's group was farther back, meaning when he arrived over the target, the defenders were alert. Fighters buzzed the formation, and puffs of black smoke dotted the horizon. They were coming in lower this time—seventeen thousand feet—in hopes of hitting the target. The goal was to make this the last time they'd have to attack this target—until Chaney keyed the interphone.

"We're socked in. Cloud cover is too thick. We can't drop."

Lucky looked over at Dye. He'd been stoic when they announced the target and indifferent as they went through preflight, but when they learned the target was covered up, his shoulders slumped. He wanted to be done, but now they'd have to hit the secondary target, meaning more time in harm's way.

"Roger," Lucky said. "Heading for the secondary."

Cavanaugh came on next with a heading for the secondary target, La Pallice. The formation lumbered on, fending off fighters as they went. As they approached La Pallice, Lucky was relieved to see the clouds breaking up. He spotted the massive concrete submarine pens at the head of the peninsula along the Atlantic Ocean. The pens had twelve to sixteen feet of solid concrete protecting them.

Lucky knew the Eighth Air Force didn't have anything in their arsenal that could dent it. Even a direct hit did little more than force the mechanics to put down their wrenches for a few minutes. He figured they were back to work before the drone of the formation's engines faded.

Lucky shook his head. He and his squadron mates were risking their lives again and again for little purpose. The only salvation was adding another mission to his total so he could go home. Chaney took control of the bomber, and Lucky watched as the submarine pens got larger and larger before slipping below the wings. Flak was heavy, and the plane bobbed up and down as shrapnel and shock waves from the explosions battered the fuselage. Just before Lucky couldn't take it anymore, Chaney came over the interphone.

"Bombs away," he said for the last time.

Everything on the bomber felt lighter. The weight of the bombs and the last mission were lifting. Now, all they had to do was get home. Clear of the target, Dye banked to the left and started to turn back for the rendezvous point over the sea.

Wolff was just happy to be in formation. The race to catch up was stressful, but now in place, protected by the others, he could concentrate on his mission. Up ahead, he watched the others drop. The last plane over the target, *Wild Cargo* rocked and shook as the flak gunners took their best shot. The explosions came at Wolff in succession. It was like being in an earthquake as the bomber was pummeled, rocking up and down as every gun around the submarine pen was aiming at him.

Wolff was focused on the airspeed gauge when he heard the crack of an explosion and then a *thunk*. *Wild Cargo*'s airspeed started to fade.

"They got engine three," the copilot said.

Wolff sat up in his seat and peered out of the window on his copilot's right. The engine was smoking. Wolff looked up and saw the rest of the formation pulling away. He immediately started to feather the engine so he could catch up with the formation. The other three engines strained to maintain the bomber's airspeed. With the bombs gone, the aircraft was lighter and he was making up the distance between him and the formation when he heard a loud explosion and felt the stick go to mush followed by machine parts twisting and breaking.

Wolff looked out the window to his left and saw a line of black smoke pouring out of the engine closest to the cockpit. Engine number two was peppered with shrapnel. There was no feathering this one. It was gone. The static propeller had the opposite effect, creating drag and slowing the plane.

But the bigger problem was the mushy controls. The plane seemed to hesitate when Wolff tried to adjust the course. He fought the controls more than guided them. He keyed his mic. "Pilot to top turret. Can you see any damage on the tail?"

The turret gunner spun his guns to the rear. "Roger. We've got a hole in the tail."

That was why the controls were sluggish and turning was a chore. With only two engines in operation and a damaged tail rudder, Wolff could not maintain his spot in the formation. The rest of the bombers were getting smaller in the windshield as he fought to keep up.

They were doomed.

Soon, the interphone exploded with reports of fighters as they cleared the flak screen. The Fw 190s, waiting for the formation to clear, were back to pick on the stragglers.

No longer in formation, *Wild Cargo* was on its own. Wolff shoved the controls forward, pushing the nose of the bomber toward the French countryside. The altimeter spun as *Wild Cargo* picked up speed. When they were only a couple of thousand feet from the deck, Wolff and his copilot pulled up and leveled off. Staying close to the ground meant the fighters couldn't dive on the bomber without risking a crash. But that didn't stop fighters from giving pursuit.

"We've got six Fw 190s six o'clock high," the tail gunner reported.

Wolff heard *Wild Cargo*'s guns open fire. The bursts were sporadic at first, but became more sustained as the fighters closed. Wolff focused on keeping the plane airborne, but monitored the battle in his headphones. His gunners got two right away. One of the Fw 190s started to smoke as it passed into Wolff's peripheral vision. He turned to look just as it crashed behind some trees.

The other four Fw 190s shot past, turning to re-attack. Wolff pushed the nose of the bomber down lower and leveled off around one hundred feet. The French countryside was a green blur. Up ahead, he saw a white church steeple. He pulled up slightly to clear it before dipping back down. A bridge before the town of Rochefort was too low to fly under, forcing Wolff to go over it as well. It flashed underneath his fuselage just as he spotted the gray ocean.

Safety.

Wolff relaxed when they cleared the coast and headed out to sea.

"Fighters are turning back," the tail gunner said as they crossed over the beach.

Three miles out to sea, Wolff heard a pop and then two more. It sounded like cylinder heads.

"Engine three is on fire," the top turret gunner reported.

Wolff saw orange flames shooting out of the engine. He and the copilot scrambled to shut it down, but the flames started to spread, quickly overtaking the right wing.

His luck had run out. *Wild Cargo* couldn't take the abuse. She'd been pushed to the limits escaping the Fw 190s and had nothing more to give. There was no way *Wild Cargo* was going to make it back to Thorpe Abbotts with flames crawling up the wing toward the cockpit. Wolff keyed his mic and told the crew they were ditching.

While the gunners scrambled to the radio room to hunker down, Wolff lowered the flaps. He picked a spot on the smooth water and brought the plane down at a shallow angle. The controls were mush, and he fought to keep the plane level. He didn't want to catch a wing and send the bomber cartwheeling across the waves. Just before the bomber hit the water, he pulled up, and *Wild Cargo* belly flopped into the Atlantic. A wave of green water splashed over his windshield as Wolff unbuckled and followed the crew chief and copilot out of the cockpit.

The water was smooth, and the B-17 stayed afloat long enough for Wolff and his crew to climb into inflatable dinghies.

Before *Wild Cargo* slipped below the water, Wolff spotted the massive hole in his now shark-fin-like tail.

They'd ditched offshore, but not so far that they'd be lost at sea. A ship would spot them sooner or later. Wolff and his crew bobbed out in the water for a while. Everyone was relieved to be out of the wounded B-17, but the uneasy fact of being out in the open ocean was dawning on them. Their only hope was to get picked up by a French fisherman who might be able to smuggle them ashore where they could link up with the Resistance and escape. Worst case, a German patrol boat picked them up.

After about an hour, a boat appeared on the horizon. At first, Wolff thought it might be a German patrol boat. But as it steamed closer, they saw it was a French fishing boat. The crew waved them down, and the fisherman pulled the American fliers on board. They were safe, for now. Sitting on the deck with the boat's catch, Wolff and his crew had some hope they'd be able to evade capture and return to England.

But that thought was dashed when a gray German patrol boat appeared right behind the French fishing vessel. A German sailor trained a machine gun on the soggy bomber crew as the patrol boat's captain directed the French vessel to a dock on a nearby island. Stepping off the fishing boat, Wolff and his crew were surrounded by German soldiers and made prisoners of war.

They'd spend the rest of the war as prisoners.

Back in England, the bombers started to return. The mighty formation from the 100th Bomb Group that had thundered off ten hours before limped back with smoking engines and hundreds of holes in their wings. Dye's squadron came in last. Lucky watched as he brought *Sunny II* down for his last landing at Thorpe Abbotts.

As the propellers slowed, the crew climbed out to a heroes' welcome. The ground crew and command staff—including the squadron commander Major Ollie Turner—met Dye on the circular hardstand for pictures.

From June 25, 1943, to September 16, 1943, the 100th Bomb Group completed more than thirty missions, of which Dye and his crew, with the exception of Lucky and Dickerson, completed twenty-five. They did it in less than eleven weeks, a mark never surpassed in the Eighth Air Force. They didn't know it then, but Dye and his crew might be the only ones out of the original group to complete all twenty-five missions.

Dye made it clear when he arrived in England that they'd be the first and he'd accomplished that goal. The celebration made its way from the hardstand to the debrief to Silver Wings. Lucky joined the crowd and toasted his crewmates. He was glad they survived, and seeing them complete the missions gave him hope that both he and Dickerson could also make it. It was a high-water mark for others to shoot at. But after so many days when he should have died, nothing seemed that important.

When Lucky first arrived in England, he had a pretty good idea of why he volunteered and what he was fighting for. But as the war wore on and the losses began to take their toll, he lost sight of it. It came down to a matter of survival. He wasn't fighting for his ideals as much as he was surviving.

The drinking went on into the early-morning hours.

After the party broke up, the fliers slept off the celebration. No one was flying the next day. A few days later, Dye and the rest of the crew—save for Lucky and Staff Sergeant Elder Dickerson—cleared out of the barracks. He saw his former crew off, but watching them drive away to start their journey home didn't make him sad. They'd become somewhat close since arriving at Thorpe Abbotts, but that was only because of the crucible of combat. If he were being honest, he was happy to be rid of them. His relationship with Dye, Cavanaugh, and Chaney had been a little rocky from the start, and now he was no longer tied to them. Lucky didn't have to worry about being part of a team that never welcomed him.

It didn't take long for his empty barracks bay to fill up with replacement crews. The Eighth Air Force was throwing crews into the fight almost immediately. Americans could replace their losses and increase the number of bombers quickly. When German pilots—especially their aces—were lost, the damage was immediate. They didn't have the manpower or extra resources to train new pilots. Plus, unlike in the United States, the Germans didn't have vast, safe training fields. American crews—most poorly trained like Lucky—could be mass-produced in the safety of the United States.

These men were strangers to Lucky. Some new crews wouldn't even get to unpack because the bomber crews were ordered to put up a maximum effort, and they were so desperately needed to fly that they were being pressed immediately into combat. They'd fly their first missions before they even had been checked out or given any practice missions and not make it back for dinner.

Lucky was hesitant to form really close relationships because if they went down or if they didn't come back from a mission, it was harder to bear if he was close to them. With Dye and the crew gone, Lucky kept to himself. He was far more focused on doing what he thought was a good job and being a good pilot.

This chapter in his tour was over.

The next chapter would cover his last four missions. As Lucky waited for his number to be called, he got checked out as a command pilot and slated to fly missions as the formation lead.

The call to lead finally came in October, when he got word that his first mission as a command pilot was leading the second element in the low squadron to Bremen.

11

KING BEE

OCTOBER 1943

The weather in Silver Wings was overcast from the cigarette smoke. The mounted traffic light was red. Lucky was at the bar sipping a scotch when an orderly from the operations shop walked into the club and headed for the traffic light. His presence cut the chatter. Everyone knew what was going to happen. They just wanted to see what color the light landed on. The orderly flipped the light from red to green and retreated from the collective groan.

With the green light on, Lucky watched as the crews finished drinks and stamped out cigarettes. They were headed back to the barracks to rest. They were flying tomorrow. Lucky stayed at the bar to finish his drink. He was a man without a crew, so he wasn't flying. That was until Captain Al Barker, the 351st Bomb Squadron operations officer, walked over. Lucky knew what was coming before Barker got to him. There was no reason for the operations officer, who was likely flying, to come over otherwise.

"Hey, Lieutenant Luckadoo," Barker said, giving Lucky a reassuring pat on the shoulder. "You're going to fly tomorrow as a command pilot. I got you with a new crew."

"Well, they'll be new to me, at any rate," Lucky said with a smile.

Barker nodded.

"I know, but this one is a replacement crew that's come in. They've only flown a few missions," Barker said. "I'm gonna fly with Tom Murphy in the lead ship."

Barker didn't share any information about the target, but stressed tomorrow's mission was maximum effort, meaning the Eighth Air Force was throwing as many bombers as they could muster at the target. Lucky let out a little whistle. Everyone was going on this one.

"I got you leading the second element of our squadron," he said. "I'll be the command pilot in the ship in front of you, but you'll be flying with this new crew in *King Bee*."

Lucky shrugged. It was not like he had a choice. "Roger," he said. "Well, I guess I will see you tomorrow."

Barker nodded and taxied over to the door.

Lucky was alone at the bar. He watched the stragglers clear out as he polished off the last of his scotch. There was a buzz in the air. To the uninitiated, it was excitement. To the veterans, it was resignation. Another roll of the dice over the skies of Nazi Germany.

Outside, Lucky shoved his hands into his A-2 leather jacket as he walked back to his barracks alone. All around him, small groups of officers speculated on the target. Lucky heard snippets as he walked.

Hamburg. Kassel. Even Berlin.

But Lucky had been in this situation enough to know it didn't matter. He'd know the target in a few hours. What he did know was he would be flying with people he wasn't familiar with over Germany or France, bombing a target in broad daylight.

That was enough to worry about.

A few hours later, an orderly from the operations shop shook Lucky awake and put a flashlight in his face. It felt like he'd only been asleep for a few minutes.

"You're flying today, Lieutenant."

Lucky blinked and threw his legs off the side of the bunk. All around him, he heard the grunts of his squadron mates as they rubbed their eyes or stretched their limbs.

Mission day.

Lucky checked his watch and did a little math. Take-off wasn't until around noon, meaning they'd likely be over the target by midafternoon. Lucky had no idea why they'd changed the schedule. They usually got up well before dawn and were in the air by now.

Grabbing his towel and shaving kit, he headed for a lukewarm shower. With a towel cinched around his waist, he took out his shaving kit and spread shaving cream on his cheeks and neck. Taking his razor, he cleaned off the thin layer of stubble. Lucky didn't have much of a beard, but he shaved every day because even a day's growth of beard irritated the skin around the oxygen mask.

Back at his bunk, he slipped into his long johns, blue

flannel underwear wired so he could plug it into the plane's heating system, olive wool pants and shirt. He sat on his bunk to tie his brown oxford shoes before stepping into his flying coveralls.

Lucky pulled on his A-2 leather jacket and headed for the mess hall. Following a narrow dirt lane, he could see farmers' fences and sheep as he decided where he wanted to eat. He had two choices: the Officers' Mess or the Flying Mess.

The Officers' Mess was a stuffy affair with tablecloths and uniform requirements. The Flying Mess was more relaxed. He could just wear his A-2 jacket and flight suit. Seeing how he was dressed, there wasn't really a choice. When he got to the Flying Mess, it was packed with crews eating before the mission briefing.

Lucky got in line with the rest. The procession moved quickly. Since Lucky was going on the mission, he got better grub. Fresh eggs instead of powdered. Bacon. Fresh orange juice. The mess hall always brought out the best stuff on days the squadron was flying because it might be the crews' last meal. The cooks filled his tray and shooed him along so they could serve the next guy. Balancing his tray as he moved through the crowd, Lucky found a seat at the same table as his new crew.

Second Lieutenant Maurice Beatty, from Portsmouth, Ohio, was huddled at a table near the far wall with Second Lieutenant Grady Moyle, a navigator from Albemarle, North Carolina, and Second Lieutenant Reid E. Griffiths, the bombardier from Salt Lake City, Utah. Griffiths, who had a round, friendly face, worked at a grocery store before joining the Air Corps in 1942.

All three were doing their best to hide signs of nervousness, nodding to Lucky as he sat down. After a quick round of greetings and handshakes, they went back to their breakfast.

Lucky recognized the men as he shook salt and pepper over his eggs. He'd conducted the crew's check flight after they arrived less than a month earlier. Everyone was a little tense. Lucky understood. He still remembered how he'd felt flying his first few missions. Everyone was in shock. They knew about the fighters and the flak, but not to what degree. Was it their squadron in the Germans' sights? No way of knowing until it was too late. Even if flak and fighters were light, there was still the cold blue. High altitude had an impact on an airman's ability to function. At least now the new crews had some veterans to ask, unlike Lucky, who'd flown his first missions with all rookies.

Beatty, Moyle, and Griffiths seemed to move their food around their tray. Lucky's tray was stacked, but he didn't have much of an appetite. He only ate to keep his body and spirits up. It was part of the ritual on his personal preflight checklist.

Finally, Beatty broke the ice. "So, you're *lucky*," he said, ending the statement in a smirk.

"I have been so far, but that's no guarantee that I'm going to continue to be," Lucky said, only half joking.

In a little more than four months, Lucky's group had already lost nearly 90 percent of its original crews. The fact he was on his twenty-second mission was noteworthy and quite out of the ordinary. He'd proven over twenty-one missions he knew how to do the job and to survive. Beatty didn't say it, but it had to be reassuring to have Lucky in the right seat.

"You know what we should expect up there?" Beatty said, articulating what the whole table was thinking. "What do you think we'll face?"

Without knowing the target, Lucky had little to offer in specifics. But if he could impart any advice to them over fresh eggs and bacon, it was about the cold. The Germans and flak were issues, but a constant threat was the subzero temperatures.

"You'll be colder than you've ever been in your lives," Lucky said. "It will affect your ability to function."

Especially since they'd only flown one deep-penetration mission. They hadn't had to endure the subzero temperatures for hours on end yet. Lucky cautioned them to stay focused on their tasks and not dwell on their chattering teeth. Talking about the cold made Lucky flex his toes, remembering his frostbitten feet.

As they ate and made small talk, Lucky thought how fortunate they were. He knew they had no idea what they were going to be confronted with and what they should do to cope with it. Sometimes, he wished he didn't know either.

After breakfast, Lucky joined the stream of airmen heading into the massive group briefing hut. It was big enough to hold 250 men. Just inside the door was the chaplain's office and the Red Cross station. Three women were handing out coffee and doughnuts.

Lucky took one of each as he passed from the foyer into the main room. Rows of benches led up to a small stage. Easels were set up on the stage in front of a massive map covered by a black curtain.

The room smelled of leather, tobacco, and sweat. Officers took the front rows. The enlisted gunners—all sergeants
of one kind—sat in the back. Everyone's jacket was open.
Some guys, mostly the replacements, were sweating in their
fleece-lined jackets in the packed room. When the crews were
assembled, planners and commanders entered the room.

"A-ten-hut!"

Everyone popped to attention as Colonel Chick Harding, commander of the 100th Bomb Group, strode down the
aisle followed by Turner, Barker, Cleven, and Kidd. Ground
officers—intelligence, weather, ordnance—filled in the other
seats. Once the head honchos were settled in the first rows,
the briefing started.

The intelligence officer, Major Minor Shaw, stepped up to
the map and pulled the curtain back. A red ribbon showed the
flight path to the target. Lucky's eyes tracked from Thorpe Abbotts across the North Sea to Bremen, a city along the Weser
River in northwest Germany. The mission stats were next.

Flight time: five and a half hours.

Altitude: twenty-six thousand feet. They'd be on oxygen
for four hours.

The briefing went on in an orderly manner. Each officer
got up to talk through his part. Operations laid out the schedule. Crews to their aircraft by 10:30 a.m. Start engines an hour
later with takeoff set for five minutes before noon. The whole
group of twenty-six aircraft would depart the base by just after
1:00 p.m.

Lucky opened his notebook and started to take down
the details. Kidd was leading the Thirteenth Combat Wing

of sixty-three B-17s. Lucky's squadron was led by Barker and Captain Tom Murphy in *Piccadilly Lily*. Cleven, the commander of the 350th Bomb Squadron, was leading the high squadron in *Our Baby*. His best friend, Bucky Egan, was in London on leave.

This was a big mission.

All three divisions were on. The B-17s—Third Division— would go northeast over the North Sea. The Second Division, made up of B-24s, would follow the third division. B-17 bombers from the First Division would fly straight through Holland. British Mosquitoes would fly in advance of the formations and saturate the area with "carpet," or "chaff" as the Americans called it. It fouled up the German radar, using clouds of small pieces of aluminum, glass fiber, or plastic that appeared as targets on radar screens or flooded the radar screen with multiple returns.

The 100th Bomb Group was part of the Third Air Division formation. The group was in the low position. Bombers from the 390th Bomb Group were leading. They were the high group at twenty-six thousand feet. The 100th bombers were the middle group at twenty-three thousand feet. The 100th's formation would fly to the left of the high group. The 95th Bomb Group was the last group flying at twenty-five thousand feet. All three groups were about two miles apart. Three groups of P-47 Thunderbolts would rendezvous over the Netherlands coast and escort all three formations into Germany to the extent of their range.

Lucky's ship was in the low squadron's last element. The Luftwaffe's first targets were usually in the low squadron. It was the worst spot, known as the Purple Heart Corner, because it was also closer to antiaircraft fire.

Lucky hated the position, but took some solace in knowing his ship would be one of nearly seven hundred planes hitting Bremen. He was flying directly underneath *Piccadilly Lily.* On his right wing was *Sunny II,* his old ship, flown by Second Lieutenant John Griffin. Griffin was Lucky's classmate. He had been checked out as a first pilot and was finally leading his own crew. Second Lieutenant Raymond Gormley was on his left wing in *Marie Helena.*

The primary target was the submarine pens outside of Bremen on the Weser River. The more than 1,300-foot-long and more than 300-foot-wide concrete factory was the largest fortified U-boat facility in Germany and second only to La Pallice in France—which Lucky hit with Dye on his old crew's last mission.

The roof was constructed using dozens of large, reinforced concrete arches, manufactured on-site and individually lifted into place. Most of the roof was fifteen feet thick, but some parts were more than twenty feet thick to protect against bombs. The factory was built using more than ten thousand laborers from nearby concentration camps. If the sub pen was covered over, the secondary target was the center of town.

The group ordnance officer went over the payloads. Each bomber had a dozen five-hundred-pound bombs—a mix that day of both general purpose as well as incendiary bombs. The armament officer told the gunners how much ammunition they had and reminded them tracers didn't really show where the bullets were going.

Lucky perked up when the weather officer strode to the stage. It was a key piece of the briefing because American bombers were not allowed to bomb unless they could visually identify the target. Oftentimes, they would fight their way all the way into Germany or deep into France and find the target obscured by clouds. That meant they had to go to a designated secondary target. If that was closed in, then they had to bring their bombs back and drop them in the English Channel so they wouldn't be landing with them. They got credit for a mission, but the crews knew they'd still have to go back and get it another day.

Weather, for the most part, was hard to predict. They didn't have as accurate forecasts as modern weather forecasters, but the weather officer was confident they'd have a clear line of sight on the submarine pens. Lucky smiled. He had gotten to the point where he'd assume the weather was the opposite of what was briefed.

Colonel Harding, the group commander, got up last. He stressed the importance of flying tight formations and keeping alert. When he was done, the crews were dismissed. The navigators and bombardiers held their own meetings to go over the details of their specific duties. Only pilots and co-pilots stayed in the main briefing room. They went over call signs and radio channels.

The series of briefings just reinforced for Lucky how he and his crew were small cogs in a big war machine. Lucky was told where to go, how to form up, and to not drop bombs unless they could visually identify the target. But only a fool didn't understand the toll the war was taking on everyone.

By October 1943, the losses had built up.

The Luftwaffe was on the cusp of stopping the Eighth Air Force's daylight offensive. The commanders and planners didn't have to say it. There were rumors of a massive offensive, and it was obvious this was the first mission of the campaign. It was a max effort to turn the tide and shatter the Luftwaffe's ability to fight.

When the briefing was over, Beatty and Lucky met the rest of the crew at the supply hut. He drew a parachute, a Mae West life preserver, and flak vests with metal plates to protect him from shrapnel. He packed away his escape kit and pulled on his leather, fleece-lined pants and jacket. Nearby, he saw the gunners drawing .50-caliber guns and ammunition.

Grabbing fleece-lined gloves and a leather helmet, he headed for the flight line in the crew truck. On the way, they passed the group headquarters with the American flag waving above and the tech site where the damaged planes were repaired.

The gunners were already at *King Bee* cleaning and oiling their machine guns one more time when Lucky reached the hardstand. While the gunners finished, Lucky walked around the aircraft. He might be the command pilot on this mission, but it was still his duty to carry out the copilot role and inspect *King Bee* during preflight. About two hundred feet away, Lucky spotted *Sunny II* and smiled. He'd checked out there on several missions and wished he were doing one more with her.

The crews were very conscious of the fact that individual airplanes had individual personalities. He'd flown most of his missions in *Sunny* and *Sunny II*, so he knew how she flew. Part of the regular banter at Silver Wings was about the different aircraft. When Lucky got into an unfamiliar airplane, he was conscious of what kind of idiosyncrasies it had. Some were prone to manifold pressure loss, or the oxygen system was faulty, or the radio equipment didn't function efficiently.

King Bee was a relatively new plane. It was accepted in the Air Corps' inventory in July 1943. The pilot of *King Bee*'s first crew was a guy named King. The B-17 was nicknamed the *Queen B*. For lack of a better name, they mashed the names into *King Bee*. The nose art came next, painted by one of the ground crew. The practice wasn't condoned by the squadron commanders, just tolerated for morale purposes. It was a distraction. It kept their minds off the horror of what they were facing every day.

If Lucky had one gripe, it was that the B-17 burned a lot of fuel because of the way the carburetors on the engines functioned. The pilots couldn't lean out the mixture enough to stretch the fuel supply. But he'd take a fuel hog if it could take the kind of beating a B-17 could. The bomber was able to withstand more battle damage than most aircraft. He'd seen ships return with shredded tails, missing plexiglass nose cones, and holes punched in the fuselage. The B-17 earned its "Flying Fortress" nickname every time it brought a crew home safe. That was its reputation, and Lucky, from his experience flying, knew it was absolutely true.

And when they brought home a wounded ship, it was the ground crew that brought the bomber back to life. The real heroes were the ground crews in Lucky's eyes. They often worked all night outside in the cold, rain, and fog to keep the planes combat ready. In the morning, the crew chief would report what was repaired and let the pilots know if there were any trouble areas. After takeoff, the ground crews hit the sack for a couple of hours before sweating out the missions waiting for the aircrews to return. Lucky always had a hunch they were as worried about the planes as they were the aircrews.

With his attention back on *King Bee,* Lucky checked the maintenance record to see what had been done to it since it was last flown. He walked around the aircraft to make sure that everything, as far as he could visually inspect, was proper.

King Bee looked tip-top.

Once in the cockpit, Lucky grabbed the checklist from the pouch underneath his window and started to tick off the steps to start the engines.

When the B-17 was first produced, the checklist was absent. During a test flight in Dayton, Ohio, to prove the airplane's capabilities to the Army, the pilot (the chief pilot of the Air Corps) and the copilot (the chief pilot of Boeing) failed to remove the locks on the control surfaces before takeoff. They managed to get the B-17 about fifty feet in the air when the pilots figured out they couldn't maneuver. The bomber stalled out and crashed. It was the best heavy bomber invented to that date, far superior to anything else that was flying. And yet because they didn't have a checklist, they crashed.

That was the birth of the checklist. It didn't matter if the pilots had memorized the start-up procedure. Everyone consulted the checklist.

Lucky read out a step, and Beatty executed it. Lucky smiled. So far, Beatty was crisp and efficient going through each step. Of course, Lucky didn't know how Beatty was going to react under fire. Lucky didn't have any misgivings about his ability to uphold his end of the bargain. The lives of eight other people rested on his and Beatty's shoulders, and that was a pretty heavy responsibility.

While they waited for the signal to taxi to the runway, Lucky took a moment to make sure Beatty knew his role. They reviewed the mission details. How long the mission would be. The critical rendezvous points and the timing needed to get in formation. There was comfort in the plan. It brought order to the chaos of combat. It was the best-case scenario. But deep down, Lucky knew no plan survived first contact with the enemy.

The Luftwaffe always had a vote.

TWELVE O'CLOCK HIGH

As *King Bee* climbed, Lucky keyed his mic. "Copilot to crew," he said over the interphone. "Take your positions."

Tech Sergeant Alfred Loguidice, the radio operator, gave the gunners the signal, and they all headed to their positions. Staff Sergeant John Rupnick crawled into the rear bicycle-style seat in the tail compartment and manned the two machine guns. Staff Sergeants Angelo Licato and Edward Karamol stood behind the single .50-caliber machine guns sticking out of each side of the fuselage behind the wings. Tech Sergeant George Burgess, the crew chief and senior sergeant, left his perch behind the pilot seats and took his position in the top turret, swinging it around in a 360-degree arc before facing forward so he could protect the ship's twelve o'clock. Staff Sergeant Morton Levine crawled into his position in the ball turret.

In the nose, Lieutenant Grady Moyle, the navigator, checked the cheek gun on his side, working the action and laying a belt of ammunition in the tray. Second Lieutenant Griffiths, the bombardier, crawled into the bomb bay and armed the two-ton payload of bombs by removing the arming wires from the fuses and sliding them into the pocket of his leather jacket. He was required to turn them in at the end of the mission to prove that he had removed them.

Over the English Channel, Lucky spotted the formation. The lead ship, *Just-a-Snappin'*—flown by Captain Blakely and Major Kidd—fired an orange flare. It arced into the sky. That was the signal to form up. The bombers fell in behind the lead in a staggered formation. Up ahead, Lucky saw *Piccadilly Lily*. He closed on her, taking a position just off center and slightly lower and behind. Off his left wing was *Marie Helena* flying slightly behind and above him. *Sunny II* was flying off his right wing, slightly behind and below Lucky.

Beatty was on the controls as the bombers closed in. Lucky kept one eye on the gauges and one eye on Beatty. So far so good. The young pilot was doing a good job flying formation, keeping his nerve as the bombers packed together for protection. Flying almost wingtip to wingtip frayed the nerves, but the closer the better was the creed for mutual protection and a better bomb pattern. But too close meant a slight mistake and one bomber was liable to take out another one.

As soon as the bombers packed in close, Lucky started to sweat. To calm his nerves, he scanned the other ships through the windshield. The contrails swept off the wings like the wake of a speedboat. He was so close just behind and below *Piccadilly Lily* he saw the ball turret gunner in the plexiglass ball and the waist gunners prepping their guns.

An hour into the flight, Lucky keyed his mic. Pilots and copilots usually used hand signals in the cockpit so they didn't clog the airwaves. But this was the first time Beatty and Lucky had flown together in combat. He wanted to make sure Beatty knew what he was doing.

"I'll take it," Lucky said over the interphone, meaning he was taking control of *King Bee*.

Pilots and copilots often swapped control because flying the B-17, especially in formation, was like grappling with a bear. The pilots wrestled the massive planes more than flew them, all while fighting the elements in unpressurized cockpits. But on the flip side, the ruggedness and ability to fly after taking tremendous damage from fighters and antiaircraft made up for it.

The sky was crowded with four-engine bombers as the 100th merged with other groups coming from bases scattered around eastern England. The air armada started to climb so that when they hit the enemy coast, they would be at about their bombing altitude of twenty-five thousand feet.

As *King Bee* climbed, Lucky wiggled his toes in his fleece-lined booties. Ever since he'd suffered the frostbite injury on the mission in July, he'd developed the twitch. Sort of a signal to his mind that his feet were still functioning. He did it unconsciously, a ritual every time the cockpit started to get cold.

The formation was rapidly approaching the point where crews could abort. There were several alternate crews flying with them. They'd either continue on the mission in the event of another bomber aborting or return to base.

Lucky scanned the dials. Everything looked good. The

engines were running efficiently. Each engine on the B-17 had a turbo supercharger, which boosted manifold pressure at takeoff and provided sea-level air pressure at high altitudes. Without them, high-altitude bombing was impossible. The radio was functioning. No issue with the electrical or oxygen systems. *King Bee* was ready to fight. There was no reason to abort.

Some of the aborting bombers flew back through the formation, breaking up some of the groups and making the flight a game of chicken. But soon, the coast of Europe appeared on the horizon. It was almost 3:00 p.m. when the formation crossed the coast northwest of Groningen in the Netherlands and turned 118 degrees toward Bremen. Contrails stretched as far as ten miles behind the bombers as the formation churned forward.

"Navigator to crew. Over the enemy coast. Look out for fighters."

The formation was observing radio silence as they crossed over the Dutch coastline. But the Germans knew where the bombers were. It was hard to hide a formation of several hundred B-17s with miles of streaming contrails.

Lucky saw specks on the horizon soon after the navigator updated their position. This time, as he gazed out of the windshield, he knew what the specks were. From the copilot seat, it looked like tiny black specks dancing against a blue sky as American P-47s—the formation's fighter escort—tangled with Fw 190s. The German fighters were staying out ahead of the bombers waiting to turn in for a frontal attack.

German pilots knew the range of the P-47 escort fighters

was limited, so they waited until the American fighters exhausted their fuel. It wasn't until the escort fighters got drop tanks that they were able to go deep into Germany, and that made a big difference. But in October 1943, the P-47s only had the gas in their main tanks, meaning when it was gone, the bombers were on their own.

As long as the specks continued to swirl in his windshield up ahead, they were safe. It was only when the specks became fixed dots that the bombers were finally in the Luftwaffe fighter's crosshairs. With dwindling gas, the American fighters finally peeled off and headed back to refuel. The dots became fixed in Lucky's windshield. He wouldn't call seeing the German fighters a relief. He'd been sweating them out since they'd gotten close to the coast.

At least now he was no longer dealing with the unknown.

As the American bomber formation crossed the coastline, the German stations triangulated its course and knew the bombers were headed to Bremen. They ordered the fighters to defend the city with "great intensity," per Hermann Goering's instructions.

Hermann Goering, a World War I fighter ace turned commander in chief of the Luftwaffe, was struggling to defend the Reich. After the fall of France in 1940, Hitler promoted Goering to Reichsmarschall, which gave him seniority over all officers in Germany's armed forces. But by 1943, his standing with Hitler had slipped because of his inability to stop the Allied bombing campaign.

"The chief thing I'm to blame for is not having given the

Jagdwaffe [Luftwaffe's fighter] heavy-caliber defensive weapons early enough and having failed to grasp the importance of the Flying Fortress," Goering admitted later.

But in October 1943, all the blame fell on his pilots. Goering feared his men had "lost their nerve." The Luftwaffe was still light-years ahead of the Eighth Air Force in skill and experience, but they could not win a war of attrition. At an October 7, 1943, meeting, Goering issued new orders to his fighter pilots. He was through watching the Reich get pounded by the Flying Fortresses during the day and the Royal Air Force at night. His fighters were going to defend the fatherland to the last man.

"If it does not, it can go and join the infantry," Goering ordered after a meeting at Hitler's alpine retreat. "The German people doesn't [sic] give a damn about the Jagdwaffe's losses."

None of the Luftwaffe fighter pilots wanted to spend the rest of the war in the mud. Spotting the formation crossing the Dutch coast, they bore down on the formation of Flying Fortresses at twenty-five thousand feet.

In his headphones, Lucky heard the gunners calling out incoming fighters as they prepared for the German attack. The chatter helped bleed off some of the adrenaline as they prepared to open fire, but the fighters were still a way off. Lucky keyed the mic strapped around his throat.

"Get off the intercom," Lucky said, cutting through the gunners' chatter. "Settle down and man your guns."

Lucky was tense but calm as the specks started to grow

into planes in his windshield. Focused on his job. He felt the pulsating vibration of the four Cyclone engines. His eyes danced across the gauges, not reading them as much as looking for trouble. None of the needles were in the red.

Lucky heard a burst of fire. The fighters were still well out of range. He keyed his mic again.

"Hold your fire," he said. "Make sure they're in range. Don't waste ammo."

Lucky knew having ammo could be the difference between living and dying. But he didn't blame them for being trigger-happy. They were all scared to death. It didn't matter how many times he was under attack, it was scary when someone was shooting at you.

The gray German fighters were starting to attack the high squadron in the formation. Lucky saw the lead planes taking fire as the fighters worked their way down to his formation. *King Bee*'s gunners swung their guns into position and racked back the charging handles.

The fighters were coming in on a line.

"OK, here they are," Lucky said. "Eleven o'clock level. Enemy fighters."

Coming in level allowed the Fw 190s to stay out of range of the gunners in the high squadron. As they closed, Lucky saw small orange balls flashing from cannons in the fighters' red noses.

Lucky felt the sweat roll down his face even though the temperature was forty below zero. He took the stick from Beatty, who'd spent the better part of the last hour keeping them in formation. In a few seconds, the German fighters would be in range, and Lucky wanted the controls.

"Hold your fire until they get close," Lucky said to the gunners again.

Shooting down a fighter was no easy feat, and many inexperienced gunners wasted a lot of ammunition firing when the fighters were out of range. The German fighters were closing at five hundred miles per hour, or two hundred yards a second. Both the fighter pilot and gunner had less than three seconds to engage. After that, both men were just wasting ammunition.

A fighter shot past *King Bee*. It was just a gray streak to Lucky. It passed so close he ducked his head and turned away, anticipating a collision. The interphone exploded with agitated voices as the gunners—the attacking fighters now in range—called out vectors and equipment status. Soon, the attacking Germans were plunging through a maelstrom of .50-caliber bullets as they closed.

Lucky tried to imagine the battle in his head just by listening to the chatter.

"Watch out. Fighter six o'clock low."

"Bogeys coming in from nine o'clock level."

The whoosh of wind and the drone of the bomber's four engines was punctuated by short bursts from the guns—German cannons and American .50-caliber machine guns answering back. The fighters took turns diving at the bombers, slicing through the formation like missiles. Out of the corner of his eye, Lucky saw a flight of Fw 190s barreling into the squadron. It looked like the fighters were aiming for the bombers like Japanese kamikazes.

"More fighters. Eleven o'clock level."

The Fw 190s flashed in front of the cockpit for only a few seconds. But those four seconds seemed like four years to Lucky. It was an interminable period of time. They'd just crossed the European coast, and the fighters were pressing the attack as if they were over Berlin. Lucky had never seen them so aggressive, and it appeared his formation was the target of their fury.

The Germans attacked just as the formation was in a flat turn. It was no easy task for three hundred bombers to turn at the same time to avoid collisions and to keep the integrity of the formation. If they broke up, they were vulnerable to the fighters. Lucky concentrated on *Piccadilly Lily,* the squadron's lead ship, as the next wave of German fighters started their attack.

Oberleutnant Erich Hondt of the Jagdwaffe Gruppe Eleven turned his Fw 190 toward the bomber formation and bore in on *Marie Helena* for another pass. The twenty-nine-year-old's heart was pounding as the B-17 grew in his windshield. Hondt had a reputation of recklessness and medal-chasing. He'd already claimed four B-17 kills in his career. The first was shot down near Spiekeroog. Another was *Captain's Ball,* which Hondt sent down in flames near Hamburg, Germany. He shot down his last one six days before the attack on Bremen.

Marie Helena was the next target in his sights as he lined up his Fw 190, which had red stripes from the top of the engine cover to the back of the wings, for another run. Hondt knifed through the formation, spraying the bombers before climbing above the formation and coming in for another pass. He knew his orders. Knock down the bombers at all costs.

Hondt shot past *Piccadilly Lily* as he zeroed in on *Marie Helena*. When he was in range, Hondt pushed his trigger and opened fire. The guns in the Fw 190s nose spit out 13 mm rounds at nine hundred rounds per minute as he closed on *Marie Helena*'s wing. He was about to attack again when his aircraft was rocked by .50-caliber fire from one of *Piccadilly Lily*'s gunners.

Hondt wasn't sure if he'd be able to make another pass. Goering's order to fight to the last man echoed in his mind. He opened fire again, ignoring the stream of tracer rounds from the twin .50-caliber guns in *Marie Helena*'s top turret. The rounds smashed into his fuselage as he continued to pour fire into the bomber. Out of ammunition, Hondt aimed his fighter at the bomber's left-wing root.

Lucky spotted Hondt's Fw 190 flash past *King Bee*'s left wing. One second, the German fighter was closing. The next, blue sky turned to a fiery orange where *Marie Helena* had been flying.

"Was that the Fw?" someone said over the radio.

"That was a Fortress."

The whole battle seemed to pause for a second. Everything went quiet.

"My god," Lucky said. "He rammed *Marie Helena*."

Lucky had no idea why. Was it a mistake? Was the German pilot dead? Did he misjudge his pass?

Deep down, Lucky understood the math. It was better

for the Germans to trade one pilot in a fighter to take down ten men in a B-17 bomber. But it was something to see it in practice, and it sent chills up his spine.

Marie Helena turned into a fireball falling just off *King Bee*'s wing. Lucky slid to the right to avoid the flaming wreckage tumbling through the air above him. His windshield filled with black smoke from the fire as the wreckage passed overhead. A few seconds later and it would have taken down *King Bee* too.

"Any parachutes?" Beatty said over the interphone.

"No," Rupnick said from his tail gun position.

Lucky was sure no one got out.

Below them, the wreckage landed near Bellingwolde in the Netherlands. Hondt, the German pilot, was thrown from his fighter and survived, but he was severely burned.

Losing *Marie Helena* threw the formation into chaos. *Heaven Can Wait* took evasive action and slid across the face of *King Bee*. Lucky's windshield filled with the tail of the olive-drab bomber.

"Jesus," Lucky said. "Look out!"

He pushed the controls forward to dip the nose, putting some blue sky between the two bombers. Lucky heard metal on plexiglass scraping together. Burgess—manning the twin .50-caliber machine guns in the top turret—ducked below the turret's cupola as the wing smashed the plexiglass panels. His screams cut through the chatter on the interphone. "I'm hit! I'm hit!"

With Lucky on the controls, Beatty called up to Burgess. "Pilot to top turret. Report in. You OK?"

Burgess regained his wits after he realized he was unhurt. He keyed his mic. "I'm OK. I'm OK. That was close."

"Any damage?"

Burgess took a second to inspect the turret. "A couple of cracks. Nothing serious. Everything is functioning."

Lucky exhaled.

Had he reacted a second later, *King Bee* and *Heaven Can Wait* would be two more fireballs tumbling to the ground. All around them, bombers in the formation were smoking. The whole formation was just being splintered, especially the low squadron, which was taking a beating.

German fighters kept pressing the attack. Another group of German fighters sliced through Lucky's group. A second Fw 190 passed over *King Bee* and was stitched up by a gunner in the *Zoot Suiters* from the 95th Bomb Group. Two minutes later, flames shot out of *Phartzac*'s bomb bay seconds before the bomber exploded, sending the tail and one wing in different directions.

In his headphones, Lucky heard the gunners doing their best to keep the fighters at bay. In a matter of minutes, he'd seen wings sheared off. Engines on fire.

The scene shocked Lucky.

He'd never seen the Luftwaffe so determined. It took everything for Lucky to focus on his job and not the carnage all around him. The stress just flashed through his mind long enough for him to take it into account, solve the problem, and move on. There was no reckoning with the trauma at twenty-five thousand feet. That came later, in the darkness of the barracks, when he was alone with his demons and nightmares. That was a problem he wanted to have because that meant he'd survived another mission.

As fighters buzzed *King Bee*'s cockpit, Lucky saw a storm on the horizon.

13

BOMBS AWAY

OCTOBER 1943

The cobalt sky was black with flak.

Small, black, ominous clouds spread out right before Lucky's eyes. It looked harmless—like a mini summer thunderstorm—but Lucky knew better. Inside that puff of black smoke was a maelstrom of shrapnel.

Flak petrified Lucky. He pulled on his flak apron and his helmet to shield his head. None of which was going to protect him from a direct hit, but it could stop shrapnel. It had proven effective when it stopped the shrapnel that had creased the Bible in his jacket pocket on an earlier mission, giving him one of his lucky charms.

Lucky knew if you saw the burst, the shell missed. But the smoke and fire were so thick it didn't alleviate the anxiety. A direct hit from an antiaircraft shell took off a wing or exploded the gas tanks or bomb bay. Like a hand grenade, you didn't have to hit the target to do damage. The shrapnel exploded in all directions.

The horizon was dark. The sky in front of Lucky was a mosaic of black smoke, white sparks, and the orange fire of exploding shells. A steady guttural boom reverberated up from the ground as the German guns sent up shell after shell. The German gunners five miles below were filling the cube of airspace over Bremen with fire and forcing the bombers to fly through it.

The concussion from the explosions battered the thin fuselages of the bombers. Lucky felt it in his chest as they flew through it. But the concussion was the least of his worries. Each explosion sent shrapnel slicing through the fuselage, punching holes in the skin of the aircraft, mangling systems, shredding fuel lines, and smashing control surfaces, making it nearly impossible to fly the bomber.

The shrapnel sounded like hail cascading off a metal roof. Lucky cringed each time it rattled the fuselage, waiting to hear if the shell crippled the hydraulic system or shot out the oxygen system or, worse, injured a crew member.

It was like flying in the middle of a Fourth of July fireworks finale. He looked over at Beatty. His eyes were bugging out as they pierced the black smoke wall. The pilot's natural instinct was to try to jig or jag when the German guns started to fire, but over time, the crews learned that made things worse. There was nothing to do, which was hard for a pilot, who was trained to mitigate risk and control everything. At the end of the day, surviving flak came down to the odds, which was a pretty hopeless feeling.

Lucky sent up a solemn prayer, in part asking the Almighty to let him slip through the flak screen one more time. The one consolation, Lucky thought, was the fighters usually hung back and picked off the bombers damaged by the flak when they fell out of the formation. The first wave of fighter attacks had already downed three planes. At least now, with flak exploding up ahead, the pressure of fighting off fighter attacks would wane.

Just then, a gray Fw 190 slashed through the formation, its nose guns stitching up the fuselages of the bombers above *King Bee*. Lucky keyed his mic. "Was that a fighter?" he asked.

Burgess in the ship's top turret came back. "Roger," he said. "A 190. More coming. Eleven o'clock level."

"Fighters?" Lucky said in disbelief. "Through the flak?"

"Yeah," Burgess said. "German fighters."

Flying through the flak defied logic. Lucky was aghast. He'd never seen them do that. How do you fight an enemy that was willing to kill himself to kill you? The German fighter pilots were ramming bombers and willing to risk being killed by their own countrymen to down the American bomber crews.

It was insanity. There was no relief.

The explosions cut through the wind and drone of the engines. The smoke and shrapnel from the flak was so heavy, some of the crews felt like they could have landed on it. In the cockpit, Lucky hadn't felt this hopeless since he was stuck in the tail gun with no training and broken guns. All he could do was concentrate on flying, but each explosion forced him to question how he ever let himself get in that spot. He was the poor son of a bitch worrying about his survival.

Well, you know, I'm in this spot, he thought as he scanned the dials in front of him. *I've got to do the best I can to see it through, and we've got to get through this bomb run and drop our bombs.*

All around the formation, German fighters continued to slice through the flak barrage to attack the bombers in crazy, wheeling courses, only to be confronted by streams of .50-caliber fire. The interphone was clogged with gunners calling out the fallen bombers and attacks from the fighters that braved the vortex of shrapnel and explosions to press the attack. The 100th formation had arrived with eighteen bombers. By Lucky's count, the German fighters and gunners had knocked out eight already.

Up ahead, the other B-17s were taking fire. Damaged B-17s slipped past the cockpit window. Lucky wasn't sure if they were just leaving the formation or crashing into the German countryside.

At the front of the formation in *Just-a-Snappin'*, a flak shell exploded near the plane's waist, and shrapnel slashed the stomach of Lester Saunders, a waist gunner from Chicago. In the tail, fragments hit Lieutenant Charles Via, of Clifton Forge, Virginia, who manned the tail gun as the formation control officer. The shrapnel sliced through the fuselage and hit him in the pelvis. Despite the wound, he stayed at his guns, keeping watch on the rest of the formation and battling the fighters. In the ball turret, a flak burst sheared off a piece of Bill McClelland's scalp, but he kept fighting.

Messie Bessie's rudder was smashed by another shell.

The bomber, under command of Walter Moreno, left the formation. German 190s swarmed the ship, attacking a dozen times, while flak kept exploding underneath.

In *Sunny II*, Lucky's old plane, Technical Sergeant Raymond Harjo, of Wewoka, Oklahoma, was thrown from the top turret to the gangway when a 20 mm shell blew away the top of his turret. Blood from a head wound, now freezing on the gun handles, covered his gloves as he climbed into the freezing slipstream and continued to fire. An Me 109 vectored in to attack. Harjo met it with a stream of .50-caliber rounds, exploding the fighter.

As they approached Bremen, the volume of flak picked up.

Over and over again, the shells battered the B-17. One second, the plane was flying level. The next, Lucky's world was shaken up. The concussions rattled the cockpit. Lucky felt as if he were catching a flurry of blows from Max Schmeling, the German heavyweight champion in 1930 and 1932. Lucky had to wrestle the controls to keep the plane level and in formation.

A shell exploded near the rear of the bomber. Lucky felt the jolt in his control surfaces. No doubt the waist and tail gunner got peppered. Beatty keyed his mic. "Pilot to waist gunners. You guys OK?"

Both waist gunners radioed back they were. Nothing from the tail.

"Pilot to tail gunner. You OK?"

Nothing. Beatty tried again. No answer. Beatty shot a look of concern over at Lucky, but there was nothing they could do but carry on. Once they cleared the target and were over the Channel, one of the waist gunners could go and check on Rupnick. Everyone went back to braving the barrage when the navigator got on the interphone.

"Navigator to pilot. Turning on the IP."

When the formation reached Wildeshausen—the initial point—it turned to forty-six degrees magnetic north. Lucky focused on keeping the *King Bee* level. He wanted to give his bombardier a level platform to drop the bombs. Lead bombardier James Douglass opened the bomb bay doors, and the rest of the ships followed.

"We're on the IP," Lucky said over the interphone. "She's yours."

Stationed underneath and forward of Lucky's cockpit, Griffiths, the bombardier, watched the German landscape roll past the bombsight in the plexiglass nose. He reached over to a small panel that controlled the bomb bay doors and displayed the ship's airspeed and altitude and flipped an electric switch. Behind him, the electrohydraulic mechanism opened the doors of the bomb bay.

"Bomb bay doors open," Griffiths said into the interphone.

Lucky felt the bomber shudder as the doors opened, breaking up the aerodynamic flow of the wind along the belly of the plane. A tremendous updraft shot through the aircraft, dropping the temperature even more. Everyone on the crew wanted to get the bombs dropped and the doors closed as soon as possible.

Griffiths clicked on the Norden bombsight in the nose of the plane and took control of the *King Bee*. It was up to him to pilot the ship to the target.

"Make a good run now," Lucky said, taking his hands off the controls.

The rest of the crew was trained to stay off the interphone during the entire bomb run. Only Lucky, Moyle, the navigator, and Griffiths, the bombardier, would do any talking, and even then, only in an emergency so they didn't distract the bombardier.

Lucky slowly let go of the controls and rested his hands in his lap. His arms were tired and his nerves were shot, but instead of relaxing now that Griffiths had control, Lucky felt anxiety building up in his chest.

It was clinch time.

This was the worst part of any run for a bomber pilot because when they reached the IP, an identifiable landmark about twenty miles more or less from the target, the bombardier took control and flew the bomber straight and level—no evasive action—to the target by means of the interconnection between the bombsight and the autopilot.

Despite the forty-degree-below temperature, Lucky felt beads of sweat roll off his brow. This part of every mission scared Lucky more than anything else. He was no longer in control of the aircraft. All he could do was sit and watch the gauges and the other bombers flying nearby. He concentrated on how the engines were running. What the instruments were telling him. He concentrated on where other ships in the formation were located in relation to *King Bee*. His eyes scanned from the dials to the windshield as the Luftwaffe kept attacking. His hands hovered by the stick each time a fighter shot past, ready to take it so they didn't have a midair collision. If the slightest deviation cropped up or another 190 was bearing down on the *King Bee,* he had to be willing to—or ready to—disengage the autopilot. Staying focused was his only recourse. If he didn't do that, he'd lose it completely.

The Thirteenth Combat Wing hit Bremen ahead of Lucky's formation. From the IP to the rally point northeast of Bremen, the formations followed the same path. Over the next five minutes, each plane flew a straight line to the target, giving the Germans the altitude and speed of the formations, meaning they had a good firing solution. When Lucky's formation came into range, the German gunners hammered them.

In the distance, Lucky saw thick black smoke rising from smoke pots—used to cloak Bremen—and fires from the bombs dropped by the Thirteenth Wing. *King Bee* fell in behind *Piccadilly Lily* on the approach. The smoke grew thicker and darker in his windshield as Lucky approached the shattered city.

Up ahead, a barrage of flak engulfed *Piccadilly Lily,* smashing into the bomber's nose and radio compartment. Shrapnel from the barrage slashed through the waist gunners' windows, killing Dickerson, the gunner on Lucky's old crew. He was flying his last mission. Dickerson died on the deck plates, now covered in spent shell casings. *Piccadilly Lily*'s oxygen system was damaged, and for a second, Murphy, the pilot, considered aborting the mission and flying back to England. But he figured the bomber was still airborne and safer in the formation than alone.

Piccadilly Lily stayed.

The automatic pilot was engaged when Lucky saw *Piccadilly Lily* get rocked by flak. He had seen enough. Without thinking, he grabbed the controls.

"I'm taking over," Lucky said into the interphone.

It was an automatic reaction. Because of the intensity of the antiaircraft fire and because his wingmen were going down so close to him, there was no way he could leave the flying to a machine. They were in such close formation, colliding with his wingman and taking both ships out was a very real possibility.

Up ahead, *Just-a-Snappin'*, in the lead, took a direct hit to the nose, shattering a window and throwing shrapnel into the navigator and bombardier compartments. The formation's lead bombardier—Douglass—shook off the shock. Unfazed by the damage or his torn leather flight jacket, he returned to the Norden bombsight.

Thirty seconds out.

Griffiths keyed his mic. "Target located. Leave airspeed and altitude exactly as is."

Griffiths waited for the lead bombardier. Lucky saw a red flare fire from *Just-a-Snappin'* as it salvoed its two tons of bombs. Edmund Forkner, the radio operator in *Just-a-Snappin'*, typed out a message in Morse code back to Thorpe Abbotts.

"Bombs away at 1525."

Griffiths saw it too and pressed a toggle switch to release *King Bee*'s bombs. It signaled to a solenoid that automatically released the bombs at a millisecond interval. Hundreds of light gray bombs fell onto Bremen. It felt like hours over the city before Griffiths keyed his mic. "Bombs away. Bombs away."

Levine, in the ball turret, watched the bombs drop from the belly of *King Bee* and confirmed the release. When the last one cleared, Griffiths closed the bomb bay doors.

Lucky felt *King Bee* jerk up as it was relieved of all that weight. As the bombs tumbled down, he made an abrupt turn and headed back toward the North Sea and England as the flak continued to explode all around them. "Let's get the hell out of here," he said as he and Beatty put *King Bee* in a sharp bank.

After the drop, the whole formation made a turn to the left and descended a thousand feet as they headed for the rally point. With the bombs gone, *Just-a-Snappin'* closed its bomb bay doors as the crew surveyed the damage. Engine four was hit.

Control cables to the stabilizer and ailerons were severed, and the horizontal elevator was in shreds.

The propeller dome on the number-four engine was punctured and the crankshaft destroyed. The prop just windmilled, dragging down the bomber's already dwindling airspeed.

But the most pressing problem was that the number-three engine on *Just-a-Snappin'* was on fire.

Kidd and Blakely pushed the controls forward, forcing the bomber into a dive to put out the flames. The bomber screamed toward the German countryside as the wind blew the fire out. Pulling back on the controls, Kidd and Blakely leveled out.

Problem one solved.

Bombers usually traveled at over two hundred miles per

hour, but *Just-a-Snappin'* was limping along at barely one hundred miles per hour. It was damn near stalling speed. They were sitting ducks for the fighters circling above.

German fighters didn't hesitate. They pounced as *Just-a-Snappin'* headed for Holland and hopefully the safety of the English Channel.

The flak was still hammering them from all sides, scattering the formation. Up ahead in *Piccadilly Lily,* the pings of shrapnel were replaced with a sickening, deep thunk. A collision. It sounded like trouble to all on board. The airframe started to vibrate, and the pilots, Murphy and Barker, struggled with the controls.

Lucky saw the *Piccadilly Lily* in front of him with its right main landing gear extended, the linkage damaged by shrapnel. He'd just watched *Just-a-Snappin'* disappear into the smoke with one of its engines on fire.

The lead plane was down, and he broke out in a cold sweat, which crystallized in his mask and blocked the flow of oxygen. Lucky slid his right hand off the controls and squeezed his oxygen mask to break up the ice. Now was not the time to be deprived of oxygen. Just then, a pair of Me 109s came out of the sun and sheared off part of *Piccadilly Lily*'s tail and set the number-three engine ablaze. Flames shot out of the engine from either a ruptured oil or fuel line. Black smoke trailed the bomber. The flames, fed by the wind, burned a bright orange and trembled in the prop wash.

Piccadilly Lily slipped out of formation as a black line of smoke trailed the bomber. Captain Tom Murphy spotted the flames and followed the lead of *Just-a-Snappin'*, diving in an attempt to put the flames out. But the fire burned through the wing. The plane was doomed.

"Let's get the hell out of this crate," Barker said over the interphone. "She's going to blow!"

Second Lieutenant Floyd Peterson, the bombardier, saw the flames too. With Barker's order, he hit two buttons that set off a charge, destroying the Norden bombsight and related equipment, and then fired a single shot into it from his 1911 pistol.

Murphy steered the bomber away from the formation so the surviving crew wouldn't have to bail out through Lucky's low squadron and the wreckage didn't take out another ship.

Staff Sergeant Aaron David—one of the waist gunners—bailed out first, but his parachute didn't deploy. It's unclear if he jumped or was blown out. Marshall Lee, the crew's usual copilot, was flying in the tail gun position. He climbed out and got his parachute. Before bailing out, he went to try to help Murphy and Barker in the cockpit.

Second Lieutenant Charles Sarabun, the navigator, opened the nose hatch. The slipstream blew the hatch away. At the edge of the door, he looked back through the passageway to the cockpit and saw Lee adjusting his parachute. For a second, he considered going to help, but was shoved out the door by Peterson, the bombardier. Technical Sergeant John Ehlen, the crew chief, helped Barker get his parachute and then exited through the bomb bay. Barker and Murphy struggled to get free of the damaged cockpit.

Lucky tracked the *Piccadilly Lily* as it disappeared from

the formation. One second, the bomber was limping along, trailing a line of thick black smoke. The next, a flash and then an orange explosion filled *King Bee*'s windshield. A cloud of debris tumbled through the clouds. Lucky spotted two men fly out of the wreckage as the front of the plane plummeted toward the German countryside. Lucky wasn't sure if the ship was rammed by a German fighter or took a hit in the bomb bay.

It didn't matter now.

Things were happening so rapidly it was hard to keep track. Lucky didn't register the shock of losing Barker—his operations officer and the leader of his formation—and the *Piccadilly Lily*. He just sat in silence. Chatter on the interphone in the *King Bee* stopped despite the relentless fighter attacks.

There was nothing to say or do but continue to fight.

Up in the high squadron, the flak scattered Major Buck Cleven's formation. Up ahead, he spotted *Just-a-Snappin'* make a violent turn to the right after dropping its bombs. The bomber's number-three engine was smoking.

Cleven ordered his crew to fire assembly flares in hopes of getting the high squadron back together, but the remaining ships descended toward Lucky and the low squadron after dropping.

The crew of *Our Baby* was alone after dropping its bombs.

Cleven and Captain Bernard DeMarco, the ship's pilot, turned to the right and continued to follow the flight plan when a trio of fighters came out of the sun at ten o'clock high. The fighters opened fire, raking the bomber with their machine guns and shattering engine two. Oil shot all over the left side of the plane as the engine froze. Gas spilled out of the left wing. Cleven and DeMarco scrambled to keep *Our Baby* in the air, but the controls to engine three were shot away, and both it and engine four were lost when the cowling and lower cylinders were shot away.

"Radio to pilot. The dorsal fin and rudder are split," the radio operator told Cleven and DeMarco, as if they didn't have enough to contend with in the cockpit. "Air is widening the opening rapidly."

The stick was mush as the flak and attacking fighters shredded the control and trim tab cables. Some of the lines were hanging in front of the waist gunners' windows, fouling up the guns. DeMarco looked out of his window at the left wing. About ten feet was gone, blown off, and the nose was peppered with machine-gun shells, which started a small fire in the blankets stowed under the copilot seat.

Cleven ordered the crew to dump ammunition and loose articles in hopes of lightening the load so they could make it back to Holland. But it was futile, as engine one burst into flames after the fighters made another pass on the crippled bomber.

The crew of *Our Baby* had no choice but to bail out. DeMarco gave the order, and he and Cleven made their way to the nose hatch. The bomber was at two thousand feet when they jumped. Cleven waited to pull his rip cord until the tail passed over his head for fear of entangling his parachute on the dying bomber.

One second, Cleven was in a maelstrom of fire, explosions, and the fading drone of dying engines. The next second, he was in the wind. The silence lasted a moment until Cleven realized he was headed for a German farmhouse. But there was no avoiding it. He crashed through the front door and slammed into the kitchen. The woman of the house started to scream at him while the man pressed a pitchfork into his chest.

Cleven did his best to calm them using his college German. It must have worked, as Cleven and DeMarco, who landed nearby, were marched to a Luftwaffe station just west of Osnabrück, surrounded by irate farmers.

When the smoke cleared, there was no lead crew left but Lucky.

The *King Bee* was still airborne and keeping its airspeed. With the *Piccadilly Lily* and *Our Baby* down, he was the only leader left.

When the 100th turned on the initial point, the formation had eighteen airplanes. Only six remained. The gunners and fighters had shot out two-thirds of the formation. It was up to him to bring the other five ships and the fifty souls in them home. Lucky was calm despite bombers going down in every direction. It was as if the chaos brought clarity. He had been conditioned to survive. Now headed toward Holland and home, it was up to him to bring everyone together.

The remaining five ships formed up behind *King Bee* when another flak barrage showered the bombers with shrapnel. Lucky heard a crash. Suddenly, his ship went from flying smoothly to sluggish. He looked out his window. His number-three engine sputtered as smoke poured out of it. Lucky saw where flak had shattered the engine housing. For a second, everything became still as Lucky went right into the emergency checklist and triaged the engine.

The number-three engine was still going, but the prop revolution was severely hampered. Lucky checked the gauges. He couldn't get full power out of the engine, and the manifold pressure was falling. Without all four engines, it was going to be difficult to maintain their airspeed. They were at twenty-three thousand feet, and at that altitude, the ship's props were just hanging on. He was hesitant to feather the prop and shut down the engine because it would cost him airspeed. The alternative was to increase power in the other engines and try to make up for the loss. But that only worked if he didn't burn out the other three.

On the interphone, Lucky heard the gunners desperately fending off fighters. His airspeed was lagging, and the flak was still exploding outside of his windshield. The Germans were not going to let them escape.

Lucky could only hope his earlier prayers had not fallen on deaf ears because for the first time since he arrived in England, Lucky didn't think he was going to make it.

He felt like his luck had run out.

Luckadoo during stateside training in Florida.

[Courtesy of John Luckadoo Collection]

Luckadoo at Basic Flight Training in South Carolina. During this phase of flight school, Luckadoo acquired a silk stocking from a local girlfriend. The stocking would become a good luck charm during his tour in England.

[Courtesy of John Luckadoo Collection]

Luckadoo poses with his parents in 1943. Lucky's father, L.V., was an honorary Kentucky Colonel who loved horses. He lost the family's fortune in the stock market crash of 1929, but clawed his way back by the start of World War II.

[Courtesy of John Luckadoo Collection]

Luckadoo poses with his mother, Rowena Angeline Sauls. He described her as a beautiful petit woman who was nicknamed "Winks" by the family.

[Courtesy of John Luckadoo Collection]

Shot of Crew 25, the first 100th Bomb Group crew to complete twenty-five missions. Standing from left: George E. Flanagan, Elder D. Dickerson, Richard B. Cooke, John Parmentier—Ground Crew Chief, Victor R. Combs, Leroy E. Baker, and Donald O. Ellis. Kneeling from left: Francis C. Chaney, Timothy J. Cavanaugh, "Ollie" Turner, Glenn Dye, and John Luckadoo.

[Courtesy of 100th Bomb Group Foundation Collection]

Major Jack Kidd, the 100th Bomb Group's operation officer, standing on the tower at Thorpe Abbotts. Luckadoo admired Kidd and tried to emulate him both in the cockpit and around the base.

[Courtesy of 100th Bomb Group Foundation Collection]

Maj. Gale W. "Buck" Cleven, 350th Bomb Squadron Commander, was shot down over Bremen on October 8, 1943. He was taken prisoner, but escaped and returned to Thorpe Abbotts in April 1945.

[Courtesy of 100th Bomb Group Foundation Collection]

Bombers from the 100th Bomb Group flying in formation. The square "D" on the tail was the designation for the group.

[Courtesy of 100th Bomb Group Foundation Collection]

Bombers from the 100th Bomb Group flying in formation as German anti-aircraft shells explode around them. Each shell was fired 45 seconds before it got to the bomber's altitude. The explosion had a blast radius of about 100 to 150 feet. The shrapnel easily punctured the very thin aluminum skin of the bombers.

[Courtesy of 100th Bomb Group Foundation Collection]

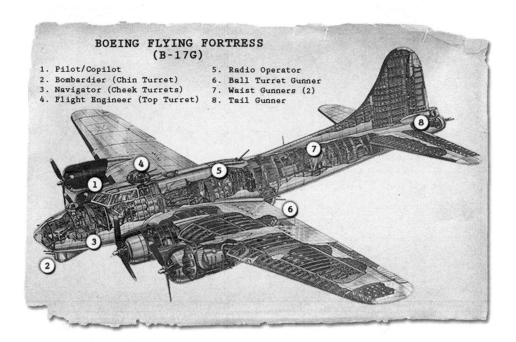

BOEING FLYING FORTRESS
(B-17G)

1. Pilot/Copilot
2. Bombardier (Chin Turret)
3. Navigator (Cheek Turrets)
4. Flight Engineer (Top Turret)
5. Radio Operator
6. Ball Turret Gunner
7. Waist Gunners (2)
8. Tail Gunner

This diagram shows crew alignment for a B-17G. In the B-17F, there is no chin turret under the nose so the bombardier mans one of the cheek guns.

[Courtesy of Sarah Sundin]

Midshipman Robert Luckadoo *(right)* visited his brother John *(left)* at Thorpe Abbotts. They are standing next to the rear door of a B-17.

[Courtesy of John Luckadoo Collection]

Crew 25 *(Luckadoo is on the far right)* posing in front of the nose of *Sunny II,* the bomber they flew their twenty-fifth mission in on September 16, 1943.

[Courtesy of 100th Bomb Group Foundation Collection]

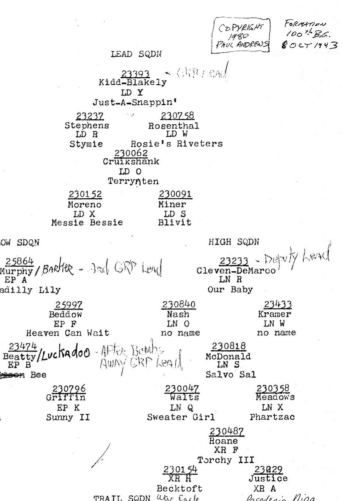

FORMATION
100th B.G.
8 OCT 1943

LEAD SQDN

23393 – GRP LEAD
Kidd-Blakely
LD Y
Just-A-Snappin'

23237   230758
Stephens   Rosenthal
LD R   LD W
Stymie   Rosie's Riveters

230062
Cruikshank
LD O
Terrynten

230152   230091
Moreno   Miner
LD X   LD S
Messie Bessie   Blivit

LOW SDQN   HIGH SQDN

25864/BARKER – 3rd GRP Lead   23233 – Deputy Lead
Murphy   Cleven-DeMarco
EP A   LN R
Piccadilly Lily   Our Baby

230723   25997   230840   23433
Keel   Beddow   Nash   Kramer
EP D   EP F   LN O   LN W
no name   Heaven Can Wait no name   no name

23474/Luckadoo – After Bombs   230818
Beatty   Away GRP Lead   McDonald
EP B   LN S
King Olson Bee   Salvo Sal

23386   230796   230047   230358
Gormley   Griffin   Walts   Meadows
EP H   EP K   LN Q   LN X
Marie Helena   Sunny II   Sweater Girl   Phartzac

230487
Roane
XR F
Torchy III

230154   23029
XR H   Justice
Becktoft   XR A
TRAIL SQDN War Eagle   Pasedenia Nina

25957
Hennington
XR D
Horny

230170   230088
Stork   Lohof
XR G   XR E
Hot Spit   Squawkin Hawk

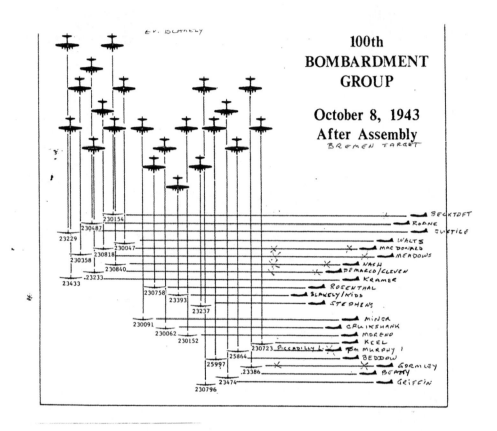

The 100th Bomb Group formation for the October 8, 1943, mission to Bremen. Lucky's *King Bee* is in the low squadron, led by the *Piccadilly Lily*.

[Courtesy of 100th Bomb Group Foundation Collection]

Capt. Alvin Barker *(left)* and Capt. Thomas Murphy *(right)*. Both men were flying in *Piccadilly Lily* when it was shot down by flak over Bremen on October 8, 1943. *[Courtesy of John Luckadoo Collection]*

Maj. John B. "Jack" Kidd and Capt. Ev Blakely crash-landed *Just-a-Snappin'* at Ludham, England, after the Bremen mission on October 8, 1943. The aircraft had over 800 holes in its fuselage from German fighters and anti-aircraft fire.

[Courtesy of 100th Bomb Group Foundation Collection]

14

THREE AND A HALF ENGINES AND A PRAYER

OCTOBER 1943

Engine number three struggled to keep up.

Lucky's heart sank as he watched the manifold pressure wane. Without it, he couldn't get full thrust, and that meant falling out of formation and losing the security of the pack. If they had to leave the formation, Lucky was convinced his war would be over. They would be shot down for sure, and they'd end up as either POWs or corpses.

Lucky called George Burgess in the top turret. He sat high enough to see all four engines. "Can you see the damage in number-three engine?"

Burgess glanced down to his right. A mist of oil was spraying out of the engine, covering the fuselage. "Oil leak," he said into the interphone. "I can see it coming out of the engine housing."

"Pilot," Lucky said, keying the interphone.

Beatty looked over at Lucky, who motioned to the throttles. Their only hope was to firewall the three undamaged engines.

"We need to throttle up the other engines," Lucky said.

Lucky reached for the throttle levers between the two pilot seats and pushed engines two and four to the max. Beatty reached over and pushed engine number one to full power to make up for engine three.

The oil pressure gauge for engine number three was Lucky's main concern now. He was getting enough power, if just barely. Lucky adjusted the engine three throttle, goosing it up slowly but not to the max, for fear of burning it out. He was still getting some power. Not full power. But enough to help keep up *King Bee*'s airspeed. If it dipped any more, he'd have to feather engine number three's prop to reduce the drag, which affected the way the airplane handled and lowered its airspeed.

Across the cockpit, Beatty shot a glance over at Lucky. He knew what losing engine number three meant and seemed to be hoping Lucky could get them through it. The weight of what was happening started to strain Lucky's shoulders, but you wouldn't know it looking at him. Head down and focused, Lucky wasn't going to show the strain to the rest of the crew, especially Beatty, whose job, like Lucky's, was to get everyone home.

But watching engine number three struggle, Lucky wasn't so sure he was going to live up to his nickname. A few weeks before, he'd watched his old crew relish their twenty-fifth and final mission. He'd watched them pack their stuff and head for the boat home. Now, as he looked out the window, all he saw was German fighters and flak. Around him, what remained of his formation was in tatters. Even if he could keep up, Lucky wasn't sure there was going to be much of a formation to protect him.

As they reached the rally point, the fighter attacks slacked off. Out of fuel, ammunition, or both, the fighters headed back to base to refuel and reload. The few remaining harassed the bombers, but didn't attack through the formation any longer. Instead, the fighters were waiting for the damaged bombers to leave the herd. Second Lieutenant Moyle, the navigator, keyed his mic and gave Lucky and Beatty the new bearing as the formation turned for home.

With a brief lull in the attacks, Lucky did the math. They had taken off with twenty-one airplanes. Three were spares who went back to the base before ever getting to the enemy coast. Eighteen bombers attacked Bremen. Only six planes were left. If they were going to make it, they needed more firepower. Strength came in numbers, but that strength was all but gone.

As they swung about for the flight home, Burgess spotted another formation of bombers above them from the top turret. He studied the formation, counting the planes before he came over the interphone.

"Top turret to pilot," he said. "The 95th is behind us."

That got Lucky's eyes off the gauges. He looked up through the clear plexiglass panes on the roof of the cockpit and spotted the formation above and slightly behind him.

Salvation.

The 95th were slated to hit Bremen behind the 100th based on the mission brief. If he could latch his formation onto the 95th's formation, they might all get back to England.

Lucky switched to the command frequency and tried to raise the 95th's leader. The seconds between each attempt felt like an eternity. Lucky checked engine three's gauges between attempts, willing the wounded prop to keep turning. Anything to keep his mind from focusing on the static in his headphones.

Come on. Someone from the 95th call me back, Lucky thought.

Finally, through the static, Lucky heard an unfamiliar voice. It was the leader of the 95th's high group. The voice cut through the static in Lucky's headphones. It was like manna from heaven. Literally, an angel above.

Lucky identified himself as the leader of the 100th's formation below them.

"We've been shot to pieces down here," Lucky said. "I've got what's left. We're gonna tack onto you."

The 95th's leader didn't hesitate. "We'd be glad to have you."

Lucky smiled underneath his oxygen mask. He relayed his airspeed and direction so the two groups could form up into one formation. "I've taken flak in one of my engines. I don't have full power in engine three. Don't have full airspeed."

"Roger," the 95th lead pilot said. "We'll slow up a bit."

They only needed to slow a few miles an hour, so it wasn't like the bombers were going to stall. Slowing down was for the mutual benefit of every airplane in the formation because Lucky's low squadron added needed protection to the rest of the ships.

One problem solved. Lucky keyed his mic. "Top turret, copilot. Fire an assembly flare."

Each bomber carried an array of flares to signal other bombers. The formations normally flew in radio silence for fear of the Germans intercepting their transmissions. Each color flare represented a different message. A red flare meant wounded on board. An orange flare signaled the other bombers to assemble on the lead plane.

Sergeant Loguidice loaded an orange flare into the launcher. He opened a small port and stuck the 37 mm M8 flare pistol out of the fuselage and fired. The flare shot from the barrel and arced behind *King Bee,* exploding into a bright orange star.

The rest of the pilots got the message. Lucky was the lead ship, and they fell in behind him. As the groups merged for the flight home, the German fighters kept their distance. Now in formation, Lucky turned over control to Beatty.

With Beatty focused on flying, Lucky worked the fuel mixture and the throttle to keep engine three going. He just had to get them to the coast, where American and British fighter cover would protect them the rest of the way.

After he triaged the engine, he keyed his mic. "All stations, check in," he said over the interphone.

One of his jobs as copilot was to manage the crew, and he wanted to make sure everyone was OK after flying through the maelstrom of flak and fighters. Slowly, all the gunners chimed in with an OK except Sergeant Rupnick in the tail gun position.

"Copilot, tail gun. You OK?"

Nothing.

Lucky tried again and didn't get an answer. He ordered the waist gunners to check on him.

The waist gunner returned to his station and plugged back into the interphone. "Waist to copilot. He's been hit," the gunner said.

"Roger, waist. Can you get him up to the radio room?" Lucky said, turning his attention to the number-three engine again.

The waist gunners hauled Sergeant Rupnick to the radio room to give him first aid.

As *King Bee* reached the Dutch coast, the Luftwaffe fighters pursuing them peeled back to their bases to prepare to fight tomorrow. Lucky let out a sigh of relief as the crippled bomber formation limped back over the dark, cold gray waters of the English Channel. As the formation descended, engine three started to respond better. The lower altitude helped. With every minute, he became more confident. Soon, he saw the hazy dark line of land.

England.

Home.

Lucky smiled. It was a joyful sight. He'd had doubts they'd make it, now he knew if he had to bail out or ditch, it was over friendlies. He wasn't going to be a prisoner.

The next hurdle: landing the crippled ship.

Not long after they crossed the English coastline, *King Bee* was circling Thorpe Abbotts. While they could see the landing field, they still weren't out of danger. Lucky had no idea how damaged the ship was. He knew engine three was malfunctioning, but he had no idea if the same flak barrage had punctured the tires or damaged the landing flaps. There was no way to tell until they put *King Bee* down on the runway.

Lucky called down to Griffiths, the bombardier. He wanted the bombardier to poke his head into the bomb bay and check the landing gear and tires. If the hydraulics were damaged, Griffiths could lower the landing gear with a crank. If the tires were shredded, he wanted to know.

Griffiths left the nose and worked his way back to the bomb bay while Lucky got the checklist, and he and Beatty started ticking off the steps to land the bomber. When it was time to lower the two landing gears, Griffiths confirmed the tires were inflated and the hydraulics worked.

King Bee was damaged, but not enough that she couldn't get Lucky and crew home. Beatty brought the bomber down. Lucky felt the tire rubber hit the concrete runway. He applied the brakes with Beatty, and the bomber slowed. Beatty taxied her to the hardstand where a crowd had gathered. *King Bee* was the first ship to land.

Lucky pulled off his headphones and his helmet. He unbuckled his seat belt and took off his gloves. Beatty sat stoically next to him. He had impressed Lucky with his coolness under fire. Nobody had panicked. His crew had performed admirably. They'd delivered their payload over the target and gotten the crew back safely. The mission was a success, but neither man felt successful. They felt like survivors.

Behind them, they heard the gunners getting out and medics coming on board to get Rupnick, who was still in the radio room. He was wounded but would live. Beatty got up first and climbed between the seats and out of the hatch behind Griffiths and Moyle. He checked on Rupnick, who was being carried by medics to a waiting ambulance, before heading toward the crew truck.

Lucky climbed out last.

When his boots hit the hardstand, Lucky knelt and kissed the ground. He walked around the nose and peered up at engine number three. The engine's housing looked like it had been hit by buckshot. The housing was slick with oil. He shook his head and thanked God for bringing his crew home.

Beatty and the rest of the crew shuffled toward the trucks that would take them back to the debrief. Their shoulders were slumped. Their heads were down, and their bodies were on autopilot.

No one spoke.

No one celebrated.

Survival was enough.

Lucky trailed the group, getting to the truck last. No one wanted to relive what they'd seen over Bremen again, but it was the last box to check before they could start putting the horror of the mission behind them.

When Lucky got to the truck, Beatty extended his hand. "Thank you for bringing us home," he said.

The pilots shook hands. Lucky smiled and then shrugged. "Thank the Lord," he said. "He brought us all home."

Lucky was about to climb into the truck when Major Turner arrived. The 351st Bomb Squadron commander was making the rounds and greeting the returning crews after sweating out the mission.

Lucky was his first stop. He wanted to know what happened over Bremen. There were rumors that Cleven, commander of the 350th Bomb Squadron, was lost and no one had heard from *Just-a-Snappin'*, flown by Blakely and Kidd, the group operations officer.

Turner knew Lucky was flying right behind *Piccadilly Lily*.

"Where's the lead plane? What in the world happened to the rest of the formation?" Turner said. "Where is Barker?"

"I saw their ship blow up," Lucky said. "They aren't coming back."

"You don't mean it," Turner said. "That was Murphy's next-to-last mission, and Barker was with him."

"I know," said Lucky, "but I think they got rammed by an Fw 190 and exploded. I don't think anybody got out."

Turner looked down at his feet. He looked toward the horizon, now growing dark as the late-afternoon sun started to set. Reality was sinking in. He'd just lost fifty men, including his operations officer, in the attack. The group lost its operations officer, lead bombardier, and navigator in *Just-a-Snappin'* and Cleven, the commander of the 350th Bomb Squadron.

Losses weren't unusual, particularly in the Bloody Hundredth. They had numerous occasions where they'd been shot up badly and very few came home. That's how they got their moniker—the Bloody Hundredth—because when they lost, they usually lost big, and this was one of the big losses. Bremen was just the first mission in a week's worth of high-profile targets. But they'd lost a number of senior pilots. At this rate, the whole group would be replacements with no one with experience to lead it.

Turner looked at Lucky. "OK, that makes you the squadron operations officer," he said.

Turner told Lucky to meet at the squadron headquarters the next morning to assume his new duties.

Lucky didn't know what to say. He was still a second lieutenant—the first rank you get upon commissioning. Officers and enlisted alike nicknamed it the "butter bar" because of the rank's gold color. There wasn't an outfit in the United States Army Air Corps with a second lieutenant in charge of operations. Most second lieutenants were still learning their jobs, but Lucky was twenty-two missions into his tour. His experience alone made him one of the most senior and seasoned pilots on the base, rank be damned. Lucky knew what it took to complete the mission and return. That was valuable to Turner and the rest of the pilots.

"I'm going to order captains and majors around," Lucky said. "I don't have any rank."

Turner was still in shock. "We'll promote you as fast as we can," he said. "You'll have the authority, and I'll back you up."

"Yes, sir," Lucky said as he gathered up his gear and joined the rest of the crew.

There was no use arguing. He'd sort it out later. Right now, the driver was waiting to take him to the debrief. Met by officers from the intelligence department, each man took a shot of rum to calm their nerves before starting the debrief. Gathered around a table, the crew and intelligence officers went over the mission in detail.

Which planes went down?

Where did they crash?

Did they see any parachutes?

What kind of opposition from the Luftwaffe?

What about the flak?

When did they drop their bombs?

Did they hit the target?

Much of the information was tenuous. It changed so drastically from one mission to the next, mainly because of the Luftwaffe's ability to move their antiaircraft batteries so a heavily defended target one day was left undefended the next. They could also move their fighter groups from Northern Germany clear down through Southern France depending upon where the bombers' targets were. By the time the bombers got to the target or were flying their approach routes, the Luftwaffe was there to meet them.

The most important nuggets of information—like how the Luftwaffe flew through their own flak—were immediately sent up to the high headquarters and factored into planning for the next mission.

Lucky and the crew relived every moment of the mission over again in the debriefing first as a crew and then individually. Lucky's mind wandered back over Bremen. He saw the bombers in flames tumbling out of the clouds. The puffs of black smoke as flak rounds tried to knock him out of the sky. He knew the men whose hardstands were now empty, their bombers smashed along the flight path from the Dutch coast to Germany and back. All he could do was rationalize that he'd survived for a reason. Lucky knew someone was going to die and someone was going to survive on every mission. So far, he'd been a survivor.

As they debriefed, the other bombers trickled in. Everyone was fortunate to get back. Five more bombers made it back besides the ones who came with Lucky, including *Just-a-Snappin'*.

Just-a-Snappin' was down to three thousand feet over Holland when the fighters finally peeled off. Kidd grabbed the controls and banked left. Next to him, Blakely, the pilot, turned right.

Kidd swore into the interphone, getting Blakely's attention.

"Let's go one way or the other," Kidd said.

Soon, they were over water. Blakely gave the crew the order to dump excess weight. Gun barrels. Ammunition. Even the bombsight, which was one of the few self-correcting models in the bomb group, went out the hatch. The bomber finally leveled off at less than a thousand feet. The last two functioning engines on the left wing kept *Just-a-Snappin'* over the waves.

Using the sun to navigate, Kidd and Blakely tilted the

plane fifteen degrees to the left to hold course. While Blakely flew, Kidd transferred fuel to the left-wing tank. As they crossed the coast of England, they spotted the first airfield and lined up to land. As the runway got closer, Kidd realized it was a dummy field near Ludham. Fake aircraft designed to trick German bombers were lined up along the runway. *Just-a-Snappin'* was barely airborne. They didn't have time to be choosy.

The pilots lowered the landing gear, but when the wheels touched down, the rudder cable snapped and the tail wheel didn't extend, meaning the back of the airplane was dragging along the ground. The flak had shot out the hydraulics, making the brakes inoperable. The bomber was thundering across the field straight at an ancient oak, one of two trees on the whole base.

Kidd and Blakely killed the engines to prevent a fire. Engine four's windmilling prop flew off as the bomber careened toward the tree. Kidd heard the fuselage crumple against the ancient oak as the bomber slammed to a stop.

Everything was silent in the cockpit except the hiss of smashed oxygen lines. Kidd looked over at Blakely. They were fine. A miracle. Looking out of the cockpit windows, he didn't see any fires. Kidd slid open his side window and eyeballed it, but it was too small to exit. He'd have to find another way out until he realized the nose was smashed too. Crawling through the nose compartment, Kidd jumped the few feet to the ground, where he joined First Lieutenant Harry Crosby, the group navigator, and First Lieutenant James Douglass, the group bombardier. Both men miraculously survived the crash unharmed.

The crew helped the wounded out of the wreckage. Via, the crew's usual copilot, was wounded in the pelvis while manning the tail gun. Staff Sergeants Lester Saunders and Edward Yevich, the waist gunners, and Staff Sergeant Bill McClelland, the ball turret gunner, were wounded. Some of the able-bodied gunners were sent for help.

Hours later, help arrived. The wounded were taken to a hospital in Norwich, where Saunders passed away. Via recovered from his wounds but would never fly again. The rest returned to duty.

The *Just-a-Snappin'* crew returned to Thorpe Abbotts to a joyous homecoming later that night and had called ahead to say they were alive, but the mission haunted Kidd. Going over what happened, his survival was because a few things broke his way. Kidd found out after the crash that, had they ditched in the North Sea, they would have drowned because the life rafts were shredded by shrapnel. If the fuel didn't transfer to the left wing, the last two operable engines would have starved, or if the rudder cable was severed over the sea, they would have crashed.

It was a matter of luck, faith, or a little of both.

After a shower and some chow, Lucky went to the officers' club for a drink. There was no way he was going to sleep without a stiff one to calm his nerves. The officers' club three weeks earlier had been packed with men celebrating the first crew to complete twenty-five missions. On the ceiling, he saw their names written by candle smoke right alongside those who were dead or prisoners.

Now a sparse crowd drank in silence or huddled in small groups, swapping stories about what happened, who got knocked out of formation, and about how the German fighters flew through their own flak.

The traffic light on the mantel was on green.

They faced their mortality over Bremen and would have to face it again over another German city the next day. No one thought it would get easier, especially Lucky, who knew now he would not only have to fly again into harm's way, but he'd also be responsible for sending other crews.

Lucky drank his first glass of bourbon in a few gulps and ordered another. It was almost too much to take. Nearly all the guys he had come over with had been shot down. He didn't know the replacement crews and didn't make fast friends. The guys who did make it back were relieved to have another day upright.

After the mission and debrief, Lucky realized if he'd been aware of the danger and chances of survival as he fought to keep the number-three engine turning, he would have cracked. But for some reason, when the battle was at its highest as Fw 190s buzzed the cockpit and the sound of wind and the hum of the engines was punctuated by the staccato bursts of machine-gun fire, Lucky found peace in the work. He focused on the task at hand and shut everything else out. But standing in the solemn officers' club, there was nothing to focus on except the memory. Reliving the mission in his head, the aftermath was far worse.

Lucky knew some pilots who went on every mission convinced it was their last and made peace with their God. That way when they made it back, they were amazed. Lucky tried to be practical about it, because if he allowed himself to really wallow in self-pity, he was inviting it. He was brought up in the Baptist church. He went to Sunday school and church regularly. Before leaving for England, he believed his destiny was controlled by a higher power, but he wasn't privy to knowing exactly what his destiny was going to be.

From the day you're born, you're fast approaching your expiration date. For the aircrews in the Eighth Air Force, it came at the blink of an eye. Lucky found himself fighting for his country five miles above continental Europe, facing nearly insurmountable odds, and the only explanation he could accept was sheer luck. It didn't matter if he prayed—he did often—or if he was good at his job. It was just luck if he came home or not. Nothing else mattered.

That didn't mean he was a robot. He felt it in his guts every time another B-17 went down. He mourned the loss of his squadron mates and hated himself every time he was relieved it wasn't him. But his only motivation was staying alive one more day, one more hour, one more minute. And so far, luck of the draw favored him time and again.

Lucky had no idea why he was spared while others were not. He made no apology that he prayed fervently that he'd be successful and live through each mission. But if he were honest, he had no real basis for believing he would come back.

Lucky just reminded himself he volunteered, and all he could do was his job to the best of his ability.

He owed his crew that at least.

But late at night, when it was just Lucky and his nightmares over Bremen, he knew his survival was just a matter of pure luck.

15

BLACK WEEK

OCTOBER 1943

The mission to Bremen was just the start.

It kicked off a week of maximum effort missions that would later be called Black Week. The Eighth Air Force was still licking its wounds from the brutal raid on Bremen.

The air war was at a critical stage in October 1943. The Luftwaffe was on the cusp of stopping the daylight offensive, so the Eighth Air Force ramped up attacks. For Lucky, now the operations officer for the 351st, it was another case of having to learn on the job, just like when he'd taken over the copilot seat on Dye's crew.

Operations officer was arguably one of the most important jobs in the squadron. It carried more responsibility than any other, with the exception of the commander, because that's where the buck stopped. The operations officer was at the nexus of everything. Lucky went from being just a combatant to a staff officer and combatant.

Instead of waiting for the next mission, he went to numerous meetings to keep the group functioning as a unit. Lucky spent the next several weeks going over maintenance reports, overseeing repairs on the squadron's planes, and tracking the crews as they prepared for upcoming missions. New crews were arriving daily to fill in for the ones lost over Germany. It was his job to make sure the squadron could answer the bell when it was time to fly missions.

One of his first acts was to get acquainted with the staff. Eight sergeants ran the operations office in the 351st squadron headquarters building. The sergeants did the paperwork—a lot of it—while Lucky met with staff officers and managed the squadron's planes and personnel. He was still only a second lieutenant, but he was working with captains, majors, and lieutenant colonels now. His promotion to first lieutenant wouldn't come until the first of November, but Lucky was too busy to think about it. Despite his low rank, he was respected because of his experience and was eventually promoted to first lieutenant in November and captain in February 1944.

Fulfilling the responsibilities of a staff officer, in addition to being an aircrewman, was quite a change. But Lucky enjoyed being the operations officer. It was more satisfying than just flying a single mission with a single crew. Now he was in charge of a dozen crews and their aircraft.

On a big board in the operations shop, he kept track of what was available, both from crews and equipment, what stages of repair the damaged bombers were in, and how long it would take for them to be ready for a mission. He also worked closely with group operations to make sure his squadron met mission requirements.

Lucky scanned the squadron's roster and didn't recognize a lot of names. Most of the people he knew in the group had been lost. When replacement crews arrived, Lucky did a check ride with them to make sure they were capable of flying combat missions. Some crews arrived in the afternoon, got assigned to a barracks, went to dinner, and he'd send them up the next day without any practice, without any introduction at all, and they would be lost.

The veteran fliers said those crews "just came to dinner."

When a mission came in, it meant Lucky was working overtime. He had a long list of things that had to be done before the first prop started to spin. Mission planning started with the warning order alerting the crews they were flying the next day. As the green light came on in Silver Wings, Lucky studied the requirements, determining who was going to fly in what position and if any substitutes needed to be made to fill out a crew. He also assigned the three spare ships in case one of the primary bombers couldn't make the mission. When they got to the enemy coast, and if no ships aborted, the spares flew home.

With the formation fixed, he made sure the different bomb loads were set. The armorers completed the loading overnight, and it was Lucky's job to follow the field orders from headquarters to determine what kind of bombs the ships carried and make them available at the hardstands.

After Bremen and the raid on Marienburg, the 100th received another mission order. The new target was Münster, and the 100th was the low squadron again. This was a max-effort mission to bomb workers' housing. Lucky read over the operations order and let out a short whistle. Since Lucky arrived in England, the targets were always industrial or military targets—ball bearing factories, submarine pens, and marshaling yards. But October 10 was different.

The target was the city center of Münster.

The bombers didn't target civilians. That didn't mean they didn't hit them. But they never flew a mission with non-combatants in their sights. Only the RAF in their night raids conducted "city busting" missions. American crews were supposed to be precision bombers.

But the aiming point in the order was the steps of Münster's medieval cathedral. The Eighth Air Force justified the target because a large portion of German rail workers lived in the city. Killing the workers would cripple the railroad and limit the Germans' ability to move material from its factories to the front. The bombers would arrive at noon when Sunday mass was letting out.

After a sleepless night making operational plans, Lucky rose again before dawn and marched to the operations office. He reviewed the order, made sure the formation was set, and then went to the preflight briefing, fueled by an endless flow of coffee.

Egan, the 418th Bomb Squadron's commander, was flying as the group's command pilot. When he heard the target, he let out a cheer. The ranks were depleted by losses sustained in the previous two raids. This was a chance to take the war to the German people.

"It was a dream mission to avenge the death of a buddy," he said, referring to Cleven, who he believed was dead.

Egan was on leave and missed the Bremen mission, when Cleven, who was his flight school roommate and wingman at Silver Wings, was shot down. Egan didn't know Cleven was a prisoner of war after being shot down over Bremen two days before.

Lucky, sitting in on the briefing, didn't need any justification for the target. He gave little thought to where the bombs went, but the topic came up now and then at Silver Wings, especially from new crews who were still wrestling with knowing every mission they were killing combatants and noncombatants alike.

Even noncombatants were enemy to American aircrews. They were supporting the German military. They were making it possible for the Germans to kill Americans. No one under an American bomber was innocent, and this target gave the 100th a real chance to avenge the airmen lost battling the Nazis.

Also in the briefing was Robert "Rosie" Rosenthal— who enlisted fresh out of law school in 1941. Rosenthal and his crew arrived in September just in time to fly his first combat mission to Bremen with Lucky. He was now on his third mission.

Prior to the war, Rosenthal worked in one of the largest law firms in New York City. He was playing basketball with his best friend in the park on December 7, 1941—the day Pearl Harbor was attacked—and enlisted the next day because he knew democracy was under attack. He'd be the pilot of *Royal Flush*, flying in the low squadron with the rest of the 100th's bombers.

When the briefing was over, Lucky stood on the balcony of the control tower as the olive-green bombers once again rumbled down the runway headed into harm's way.

The flight across the Channel was routine. Sporadic attacks by German fighters dogged the formation, but didn't yield heavy losses. When the formation crossed into the Ruhr River valley they ran into more than 350 German fighters. Even the most veteran crews were shocked at the sheer number of planes attacking them.

Wave after wave made head-on passes at the low group in the formation. The 100th B-17s poured defensive fire into their attackers, seemingly to no avail, as one wave of fighters broke away, another slashed through the formation, and then another and another. The fighters passed the gunners in a flash with the noses of their planes winking and glittering as they fired. Twenty-millimeter shells exploded, punching holes in wings and fuselages. The Germans passed so close that the Americans could see the scarves around their necks.

Smoking B-17s were falling out of formation, some in a death spiral as the crews attempted to bail out of the doomed aircraft. Egan's lead ship was badly damaged by the fighter attacks. There was no choice but to bail out. First Lieutenant John Brady, who was flying the aircraft, gave the order and then followed Egan to the bomb bay.

"Go ahead, Brady, as I'm senior man," Egan said.

"No, you go ahead," Brady said, as he was the pilot and it was his crew.

Before they could say another word, machine-gun bullets punched through the entire length of the bomb bay.

There was no more discussion.

"I'll be seeing you, Brady," Egan said, stepping into the wind.

Egan pulled the rip cord as soon as he cleared the ball turret. Brady followed.

The rest of the bomber formation limped along. As they neared the city center, Münster's antiaircraft defenses threw up a flurry of fire. The volume wasn't like Bremen, but the guns were more accurate. They zeroed in on the bombers and peppered them with shrapnel, taking out engines and shredding wings.

The bombers fought through the flak and finally dropped. First to release was the 95th Bomb Group, then the 390th and finally the remnants of the 100th at the rear of the Thirteenth Combat Wing formation. The attack devastated the city center, heavily damaging the cathedral and starting fires that burned for days. Hundreds of civilians were killed.

But at a terrible cost.

The low formation started with thirteen bombers. By the time the bombs dropped, all but one of the 100th's bombers were shot down. As they turned for home, 120 men either died or were prisoners.

Royal Flush was the lone 100th bomber left.

Alone, Rosenthal was struggling to keep up with the 95th Bomb Group's formation. His crew was shot up—one of his waist gunners was wounded—and flak knocked out one engine on his left wing. When Rosenthal feathered the prop, it damaged the engine next to it. Both engines on his left wing were damaged and one on the right wing was failing. There was no way he was going to catch up. He gunned the last two engines, but the formation slipped away, leaving *Royal Flush* to the mercy of the German fighters, bent on destroying what was left.

Four Fw 190 fighters attacked in line abreast from six o'clock. They closed to eight hundred yards and opened fire. Staff Sergeant Bill DeBlasio, the tail gunner, waited until the fighters got into range and fired three short bursts from his twin .50-caliber machine guns.

One burst cut the wing off a fighter on the left, sending it into his wingman. Both planes spiraled down in flames. DeBlasio tracked his guns over to the fighters on the right and fired again. The inside plane jerked as the rounds tore into the fuselage. Smoke poured out of the engine and cockpit. DeBlasio watched the pilot bail out. He turned the pair of guns on the last plane just in time to see it peel off.

For about five minutes, there was just the wind and the struggling engines. Rosenthal only had two engines on the right wing and had to feather them intermittently to keep the props spinning. The bomber was at fifteen thousand feet when a pair of Ju 88s joined four more Fw 190s. The planes were staggered. The two Junkers Ju 88s—a multi-engine fighter-bomber—were on each end with the fighters in the middle.

DeBlasio zeroed in on the lead Ju 88 first. He got off a few bursts before he spotted the rockets hanging off the Junkers's wings. The Ju 88s lowered their flaps and fired. The volley of rockets shot out—a trail of smoke obscuring the fighters—and sailed over *Royal Flush*.

The German pilots missed.

DeBlasio didn't hesitate. He opened fire on the lead Ju 88. The bursts hit, and soon the German bomber was on fire. It slid off to the right as DeBlasio shifted fire to the Fw 190s coming in at six o'clock. They were within six hundred yards when he raked them with .50-caliber bullets. He swung the twin guns from left to right. Two Fw 190s crashed into one another, trying to evade the machine-gun bursts.

Rosenthal heard the machine-gun fire, but he knew they couldn't shoot their way home. Since they weren't in formation, Rosenthal banked hard and then dived toward the ground. He wasn't going to make *Royal Flush* an easy target.

"Rosie—hold a stable platform so we can shoot them," one of the gunners said over the interphone.

Rosenthal shook his head before he keyed his microphone. "So we can shoot them?"

He kept dodging, throwing *Royal Flush* into banks and dives until the German fighters gave up and went looking for easier prey.

"Tail gunner, pilot," Rosenthal said. "Fire off remaining ammo and come out of the tail."

DeBlasio unleashed several long bursts at the departing fighters, expending what little ammo he had left. With the twin .50-caliber guns spent, he crawled out of the tail gun position and through the waist toward the radio compartment. The crew was gathered there. The plane was below ten thousand feet, and Rosenthal warned them they might have to ditch.

When the bomber made it to the Dutch coast, they spotted American fighters and knew they were safe. *Royal Flush* kept on toward England. When they crossed the English coast, Rosenthal let out a sigh of relief, but that was short-lived. A third engine died. Only one left. *Royal Flush* hobbled toward Thorpe Abbotts and circled for a while in thick cloud cover looking for the airfield. They found it just before the bomber ran out of fuel. Rosenthal lined up on the runway as the last engine failed.

Lucky waited for his planes to return. Everyone was late. Updates were sporadic, but what little news they heard wasn't good. The drop was successful, but they'd faced furious fighter attacks and accurate antiaircraft fire. Lucky scanned the horizon with his field glasses when he spotted the *Royal Flush* on final approach. None of the bomber's props were turning.

The *Royal Flush* slammed onto the runway and came to a skidding halt. The bomber was smoking. The wings and fuselage were stitched with machine-gun fire. Basketball-size holes from rockets and flak shrapnel were punched in the wings and fuselage.

Ambulances raced to the crippled bomber to retrieve the wounded crew. Those who could fell out of the plane in relief. Some kissed the tarmac. DeBlasio crawled to the grass and vomited for what seemed like an eternity.

Rosenthal jumped out of the aircraft and headed for the ambulances to check on his crew.

"Are they all this rough?" he asked another officer who didn't fly that day about all the 100th's missions.

Rosenthal climbed into a waiting ambulance with Staff Sergeant John Shaffer, who was wounded, and headed to the hospital.

Lucky watched the ambulance leave the hardstand with his field glasses before turning his gaze back to the horizon. When no one else returned, he went back to his office. The debrief was over, and Lucky was still wrapping his head around the losses. He looked over the list of crews lost over Münster. Beatty's crew was on the list. Their aircraft was hit by flak while under attack and exploded in midair. There were no survivors. The same crew that had been on the brink over Bremen had finally run out of luck.

The shock of losing Beatty's crew hung over Lucky. Two days before, they'd just survived the Bremen mission, and he was confident in their abilities. Now they were gone.

Lucky sent his sergeants to the barracks to police up the lost crew's personal effects. The sergeants lined up the boxes on the floor of the operations office. One by one, Lucky went through them to make sure there was nothing embarrassing for the next of kin. After the inspection, the sergeants taped up the boxes and addressed them. While the boxes were prepared, Lucky sat down at his desk. It was his job to notify the next of kin for those who didn't come back.

In most cases, Lucky didn't learn till quite a while after the mission if someone was killed or on the Red Cross POW list. For those poor bastards, the war was over, but the misery had just begun.

But the telegrams were a stark reminder of what his chances were when he went out every day and how sad it was to have to collect that guy's belongings and ship them off. If he were being honest, Lucky was sure his chances of finishing all twenty-five missions were zero. That was in the back of his head as he wrote telegram after telegram, delivering the worst news to someone's mother, father, brother, or sister.

Lucky had more missions. More rolls of the dice. If he lived up to his nickname, he'd be headed home. If he didn't, someone else would be in his chair writing the same telegram to his mother.

The next day, Rosenthal reported on the day's activities to the Third Air Division's headquarters. Everyone was in shock as he described the fighter attacks and flak. The room was absolutely silent when Rosenthal was done. For a half minute, you could hear a pin drop as the officers grappled with the fact the 100th Bomb Group was destroyed over Münster.

Eighty-eight B-17s had been lost in the last three days, nearly nine hundred men. Bad weather forced the Eighth Air Force to stand down for several days. On October 14, the bombers returned to the air. Those who had lived through the first half of Black Week survived only to face out-and-out destruction over Schweinfurt, the single bloodiest day in the air war of 1943.

The 100th had only eight operational B-17s, four planes each joining the 390th and 95th as composite groups. They suffered zero losses.

16

FRIENDLY INVASION

OCTOBER 1943

Lucky arrived in London at noon on a Friday, knowing for the next forty-eight hours only his liver was in harm's way.

He'd gotten the weekend pass a week after the Bremen mission to visit Sully, his childhood best friend, in the English capital. Sully, now a fighter pilot in the Royal Canadian Air Force, was flying Hawker Typhoons against Luftwaffe bomber attacks.

They'd reunited a couple of weeks before at Thorpe Abbotts. Sully, having learned Lucky was nearby from gossip among his old classmates, arrived at Thorpe Abbotts in a Spitfire, his old plane. He found Lucky in the operations office reviewing maintenance schedules and aircraft readiness reports. Lucky's squadron mates were taken aback by a Royal Canadian Air Force fighter pilot with a Tennessee accent.

Sully's visit was a welcome break from the drudgery of staff work. While he still had missions to complete, Lucky was no longer dodging fighter attacks and flak on a daily basis.

Most days, he powered through a stack of reports, writing mission orders and making sure the squadron ran smoothly. It was thankless work, devoid of the romance of flying, but an integral part of an operations officer's job.

After catching up in the office, Lucky found a B-17 in need of a check flight and smuggled Sully aboard with a skeleton crew. He and a copilot taxied the bomber to the end of the runway and took off, turning away from the coast so they wouldn't attract any German fighters. Sully, who was standing behind the pilot seats, swapped out with the copilot. Flying over the green countryside of England, Lucky showed Sully all the workings of the bomber. Finally, Lucky let Sully take over. Once he put his hand on the controls, Sully banked the bomber hard to the left. He leveled out and banked to the right, trying to get a feel for the airplane. For a few minutes, Sully put the bomber through its paces. Climbing, diving, and banking. Lucky alternated between making sure the airplane was operating efficiently and watching the smirk creep across Sully's lips as he flew. He already knew what his best friend was going to say when Sully tapped Lucky on the shoulder and leaned over so he could yell into his ear.

"Buster, this ain't flying," he said. "You're just a truck driver."

Lucky laughed. Compared to a Spitfire, the B-17 was slow and lumbering.

"I guess you got a point!" Lucky yelled back over the engine noise. "You're having all the fun in a fighter. But I've got nine other guys hanging on my shoulders, and we're just delivering the bombs to the target." Lucky had learned firsthand the value of a crew and the responsibility of getting every man home.

Sully pointed to the deck. "Let's land, and I'll let you fly a real plane," he said. "You'll know what flying really is about."

Lucky landed the bomber and taxied it back to the hardstand. Sully deplaned and cajoled Lucky over to the Spitfire, begging him to climb aboard and fire it up. Lucky stood by the wing of the fighter, which looked like a toy next to the massive B-17s, and shook his head.

"That's a stupid thing to do because I'm not a fighter pilot and I'd kill myself," Lucky said.

His reasoning fell on deaf ears. Sully wasn't taking no for an answer, as young men, they'd both dreamed of being fighter pilots. Now Sully was giving Lucky a chance to at least get a taste of it before he returned to the lumbering bombers.

"No, no, no," Sully said. "It's a piece of cake. I'll show you how to fly."

Sully turned on all his charm. The same charm that made him the class president, the ROTC regimental colonel, and the star member of their fraternity in college.

Lucky couldn't resist. He climbed up the wing and folded his lanky, six-foot-two-inch frame into the cramped cockpit. It felt like he was flying in a bathtub. Sully replaced him on the wing and went over all the instruments, pointing out how to start the engine, the airspeed indicator, and how to work the flaps and landing gear.

"All set?" Sully said.

Lucky nodded and smiled. The principals of flying a plane were universal, and at least this time, he didn't have to worry about more than one engine and a crew. His only concern was himself.

"Take her up," Sully said.

Lucky fired up the Rolls-Royce Merlin engine and felt every one of the thousand horses. He let off the brakes and started to taxi to the end of the runway. The controls felt strange. A stick versus the larger half-moon wheel of the B-17, but the power scared him. It was like being strapped to an engine with wings. It was so sensitive and so different from flying a B-17 that he was super careful as he passed the 100th Bomb Group Flying Fortresses on their hardstands. The Spitfire had a narrow carriage and was prone to tip to one side while on the ground—called a *ground loop*—especially on uneven ground. The pilot had to fly it every second of the time, and it was a handful.

At the end of the runway, Lucky gunned the engine, and the fighter shot down the concrete track and into the blue sky. Everything was coming at him quickly. Lucky knew immediately he was out of his element. The reality of being airborne in a British fighter hit him. He didn't have any business doing it and could be court-martialed. Lucky aborted the flight. Instead of flying off, he returned to the pattern and landed.

He was airborne less than ten minutes. His Spitfire flight turned into a touch-and-no-go with a short taxi. As the roar of the engine waned, Lucky climbed out of the cockpit and met Sully, who was waiting nearby.

"See, that's what flying is all about," Sully said. "Now you're really a pilot."

Lucky shook his head. "This is all right for you," Lucky

said, his heart rate still thumping like he'd just flown to Bremen and back. "But it's not for me."

Sully let out a laugh and patted his friend on the back. "OK," Sully said. "OK. I guess we need truck drivers too."

Sully was due back to his base, so they agreed to meet in London.

A few weeks later, Lucky made good on the agreement. His train arrived at Liverpool Street Station. Dressed in his pinks and greens, Lucky pulled on his wool service cap with a russet-brown leather visor and eagle insignia on the front—crushed down the way fliers liked to wear it. The American aircrews removed the grommet that kept the wool service cap rigid so a headset fit over it, but the crews usually didn't wear the hat in the cockpit. They really took it out so the hat had a crushed, worn look. Dubbed a "fifty mission crusher," the hat became a signature piece of an airman's uniform.

Lucky shouldered his leather overnight bag and joined the crowd getting off the train. There were English civilians, but the majority of passengers were American servicemen. Lucky spotted patches and uniforms from not only fellow airmen but soldiers, all coming to London for a good time.

All over England, American forces were building bases and training areas in anticipation of the invasion of France. The Americans' arrival was known as the "friendly invasion."

Tens of thousands of U.S. servicemen flooded England beginning in 1942. Yanks were everywhere, the British thought, complaining about warm beer and British weather: rain, fog, and mud.

For American service members headed to England, the
War Department issued a handbook to lessen the culture
shock since many had never traveled abroad. The tips ranged
from common sense (e.g., don't mock the English accent) to
the practical (e.g., eat a small portion when invited into an
English home so as not to eat all the family's weekly rations).
The main point of the handbook was to remind the American
soldiers and airmen England had been at war for four years.

"Britain may look a little shop-worn and grimy to you,"
the handbook said. "The British are anxious to have you
know that you are not seeing their country at its best. There's
been a war on since 1939."

The handbook warned Britons are reserved, not unfriendly, and tough, adding that more than sixty thousand
British civilians—men, women, and children—died in Luftwaffe bombing attacks.

"So, if Britons sit in trains or busses without striking up
conversation with you, it doesn't mean they are being haughty
and unfriendly," the handbook said. "Probably they are paying more attention to you than you think. But they don't speak
to you because they don't want to appear intrusive or rude."

When the Americans weren't training, they were drinking,
chasing girls, and finding themselves surrounded by English
children. Kenneth Pullen was fourteen when the Americans
arrived in London. Seeing them in the streets was a shock
because most Britons had no idea "what an American looked
like face to face." He'd only seen them in the movies "shooting
Indians in a cowboy hat or at policemen in Chicago."

Paid five times as much as British soldiers, American

soldiers and airmen spent freely, including leaving bills and coins on pub counters (a no-no in Britain), and charming British girls. As many as nine thousand babies were born in Britain out of wedlock.

"Overpaid, oversexed, and over here," became a popular British gripe.

At the front of Liverpool Street Station, Lucky climbed into a black taxi. The driver gunned the engine, merging with the traffic. Sully had gotten Lucky booked into Claridge's, a five-star hotel at the corner of Brook Street and Davies Street in Mayfair. The hotel was in an affluent area in the West End of London toward the eastern edge of Hyde Park. It served as headquarters of the Kingdom of Yugoslavia's forces in exile and home of Peter II of Yugoslavia.

The hotel was a series of redbrick terraced town houses with a grand lobby. A doorman opened Lucky's door as he paid the driver. Lucky was impressed. The whole place smacked of royalty. This was what he imagined England to be like before he arrived. Even during a war, London could still impress.

Strolling into the main lobby, Lucky spotted Sully. His friend was dressed in his Royal Air Force azure-blue uniform with his silver wings pinned to his chest. Sully's uniform was the color of the sky on a clear day and in sharp contrast to Lucky's pinks and greens—his brownish-green blouse with lighter-colored pants with a pink hue.

The friends shook hands and retired to their adjoining rooms. For the rest of the afternoon, they told stories about missions, talked aircraft, and compared gossip about friends in Chattanooga over a bottle of bourbon.

Sully talked about his new plane, the Hawker Typhoon. It was so overpowered that when it took off, the pilot had to use full opposite rudder just to keep the plane straight on the runway because the engine torque was so strong that the Hawker Typhoon tended to ground loop. Lucky couldn't imagine transitioning to another plane. He was finally comfortable in the B-17. Training to fly another bomber, in a war zone, felt like a mountain too high to climb.

Around 4:00 p.m., Sully put the top on the bottle and led Lucky—after cleaning up—back to the lobby to meet Peggy, his girlfriend and the friends' host for the weekend.

"How did you meet her?" Lucky asked.

He suspected they'd bonded over her polo ponies, but that was just a hunch. Sully didn't have time to answer because when they got to the lobby, she was there waiting.

Peggy was stunning, a petite woman with bright eyes and a disarming smile. She was elegantly dressed and coiffed, and was a bit older than either of them, but very aristocratic. Sully greeted her with a kiss. Lucky shook her hand. Both men were taken by her beauty and grace.

It was teatime for the English but happy hour for the boys from Tennessee. The trio retreated to the café. Sully and Peggy started with tea, but quickly turned to drinks, which turned into a steak dinner at the hotel restaurant. The spread was decadent and some of the best food Lucky had tasted since arriving in England. After the meal, Lucky and Sully were ready to see the town.

Despite the war, London's nightlife survived. The first few weeks of the war in the fall of 1939 saw public places deserted, but it wasn't long before Londoners returned to their pubs, nightclubs, and dance halls in droves.

Famed war correspondent Edward R. Murrow investigated nightlife in London's West End during the Blitz and concluded "business is good; has in fact improved since war came," noting an uptick in the number of bands.

"Where one could eat without musical distraction in the old days have now engaged small orchestras," Murrow reported. "Customers want to dance."

It was a sentiment shared by Peggy and the boys. She ushered them into a taxi in front of the hotel and gave the driver an address. Lucky watched London pass through the window of the cab. The whole city was dark. Unlit streetlights made the night darker. Only the shielded headlights of the cars offered any illumination, offering fleeting glimpses of the buildings or people shuffling along the sidewalk. The scene was off-putting, a reminder that the war was still on, despite the steaks and booze from dinner. Occasionally, the blackout curtains in the windows broke, allowing light to spill out like warmth in the cold, dark city.

The taxi dropped them off in front of a blacked-out building, and Peggy whisked them past naked brick walls to a grubby metal door. She knocked, and a peephole slid open. One look at Peggy and the hole shut with a snap. Behind the door, Lucky heard someone throw the locks, and the metal door creaked open.

A burst of music hit Lucky like a wave. Walking inside,

he was greeted by a gorgeous, brightly lit casino. Blue clouds of smoke hung over the tables, where men in tuxedos and American and British military uniforms from every service played cards and roulette with women in evening dresses. Sully and Lucky were in awe, blinking in the bright light after coming from the dark city.

Lucky and Sully moved into the club and stood on the edge of the dance floor smoking. It was a lot to take in. The casino was a far cry from the officers' clubs on their airfields. It was like being in a movie. Peggy didn't miss a beat. She was in her element, and Lucky lost track of her soon after entering the club. He finally spotted her as she moved through the crowd, kissing and hugging men and women alike.

Lucky was still taking it all in when Peggy arrived with three drinks. She handed one to Lucky, who inspected it. Served in a pilsner glass, it looked like a black storm cloud of beer on top of a drop of bubbly gold. Lucky shot a glance at Sully, who was taking a long drink of the concoction.

Peggy noticed Lucky's apprehension.

"It's called Black Velvet," she said.

"What on earth is that?" Lucky said, swirling around the mixture in his glass. "A black what?"

Peggy smiled and patted Lucky on his shoulder. She leaned in, her perfume filling his nostrils. "Half Guinness and half champagne," she said, a hint of mischief in her eye, like the drink was part dare and part gloating, knowing he'd like the drink.

Lucky wasn't sure. He looked down at the glass again. Lucky felt a long way from Chattanooga.

"You'll love it," Peggy said. "It's just like velvet on your tongue."

Lucky shrugged and took a sip. The concoction was slick as a whistle. The bitter of the Guinness with the sharp bite of the champagne. She was right, and Lucky polished the glass off in a few gulps. He instantly craved another one as he felt a warm buzz come over him.

The trio found a booth on the border of the dance floor, and Sully held court, ordering round after round between stories from his war days and before. Soon, they were joined by a small group of drop-dead gals. The two friends were the center of their own party. After a while, they decamped to another club. Soon the casinos all swirled into one glorious carnival of light, music, and Black Velvet. The war, for the first time since he'd arrived in June 1943, was a distant memory. The drinks mixed with the nostalgia of being with his best friend was like armor against the horror he'd suffered through for the last six months. He was no longer staring death in the face and drinking to dull his nerves and tamp down the fear.

The party. The dancing. The drinks downed in celebration, no regrets.

It was like fuel to his spirit. A reminder of what living felt like.

As the night went on, the table filled with empty glasses, cleared away by busy waiters. Lucky didn't spend a dime that night and staggered out of the last club just as the first hint of sunlight kissed the horizon. Falling into bed a half hour later was like heaven after months on a cot. The sheets were clean and smelled of spring.

Lucky fell into a dreamless slumber.

A maid woke him in the late afternoon when she came in and cleaned his room. Room service helped him battle the hangover. After resting and cleaning up, Lucky met Sully in the lobby, and they headed to Peggy's place.

Lady Peggy owned a town house on Baker Street that she'd converted into a club. She called it the American Stork Club, something of a precursor to the Playboy Club. It was five stories tall, and she populated it with beautiful British women to entertain soldiers, but only by invitation. She stocked it entirely from her own wine cellar, and each floor had its own dance floor and décor.

Five clubs in one.

More drinks. More girls. Dancing. Dinner. Lucky and Sully repeated their first night in London on their second night, starting at the American Stork Club and ending back in his room in the clean sheets that smelled of spring.

Sunday was pain.

A splitting headache. An upset stomach. A general surly disposition. Hungover and late for his train. By the time Lucky returned to Liverpool Street Station, he was nauseous, and his head felt like a piston from one of the B-17's radial engines was banging away in his skull.

Lucky and Sully sat in silence as the train rumbled east out of London. Sully's stop was first. He rose wearily, grabbed his luggage, and said his goodbyes. The friends shook hands.

"Come down and see me next chance?" Sully said.

Lucky nodded. "First chance I get, I'll fly down."

Sully smirked. "You come down and I'll show you what a Typhoon is," Sully said. "It ain't like flying a truck. Or a Spit."

It was a promise.

17

LAST POST

NOVEMBER 1943

A repaired bomber needed a check flight, and Lucky knew just where to go.

It was only a few weeks after his pass to London, and Lucky was intent on fulfilling his promise to Sully. His best friend was flying Hawker Typhoons out of RAF Martlesham Heath. The base was just thirty-five miles south of Thorpe Abbotts, near Woodbridge in Suffolk.

Like Thorpe Abbotts, RAF Martlesham Heath was cut out of the English countryside to service the air armada doing battle daily with the Luftwaffe. At the outbreak of the war, Martlesham became the northernmost station of No. 11 Group RAF, Fighter Command. Squadrons of Bristol Blenheim bombers, Hawker Hurricanes, Supermarine Spitfires, and Hawker Typhoons operated from the airfield. It was also the former home of No. 71 Squadron, formed of American volunteers. The squadron was stationed at the field in 1941.

Lucky scrounged up a crew and finished the preflight. He

cranked up the bomber, and they took off into the gloomy, cloudy, fall English sky. Lucky and the crew loitered around Thorpe Abbotts as Lucky checked to make sure the ship was tip-top. Once he was confident the B-17 wasn't going to have a catastrophic failure, he had the navigator set course for RAF Martlesham Heath.

The flight was quick.

As Lucky got into the landing pattern, he surveyed the RAF base. It was a grass field with a cluster of buildings and a tower. The runway was half the length of the one at Thorpe Abbotts. It was a fighter base and not built to accommodate heavy bombers. It wasn't as bad as Dye's stunt in Ohio, but squeezing the four-engine B-17 bomber into a fighter field was going to be a trick.

Lucky circled the runway and then brought the B-17 down. As soon as the tires hit the grass, Lucky and the copilot stood on the brakes as the tree line at the end of the runway grew in the windshield. Lucky held his breath until the bomber finally slowed to a stop. There was no runway to spare.

Heading for the tower, he spotted the wreckage of a Typhoon fighter near the runway. Its wings and airframe were smashed and charred with black scorch marks from the engine down the fuselage. The grass under the wreckage was singed. Whatever happened to the fighter ended in a fire.

Lucky taxied past the wreck and stopped in front of the control tower. He slipped out of the hatch below the pilot window and waved when he spotted an RAF officer on the balcony above him.

"Are you lost?" the RAF officer said. "Why are you landing here? Do you need petrol?"

Lucky shook his head. "I don't need any petrol or maintenance or anything on my ship," he said. "I'm on a social call. Saying hello to Flight Lieutenant Sullivan."

Lucky looked at his watch. He only had a few minutes to visit. While he was authorized to conduct the check flight, he really didn't have permission to make any stops. If he took too long, his command might think the bomber went down because of mechanical failure.

"I'm going to have to get back to my base soon," Lucky said. "I'd just like to say hi and get going. Do you know Sullivan? Could you just show me to his quarters?"

The RAF officer's shoulders slumped. "You knew Flight Lieutenant Sullivan?"

Lucky nodded. "*Knew* him? I *know* him. He's my best friend."

The RAF officer turned on his heel, heading back into the tower so he could come down. "Right, well, you've got to see the squadron leader," he said.

Lucky knew it was customary when you land in a foreign base to report to the commanding officer, but he was already short on time and didn't want to waste any of it talking with the base commander. "I know that is the protocol," he said before the RAF officer went back into the tower. "I'm really in a bit of a hurry, and I'd just like to say hi to Sully. Tell me where he is because I do have to get back."

But the RAF officer wouldn't accept Lucky's protests.

"No, you've got to see the commander," he said. "Wait there. I'll be right down."

Lucky turned to his copilot and crew and told them wait by the ship. He wouldn't be long. He followed the RAF officer across the airfield toward a cluster of buildings. The officer escorted him into the squadron leader's office.

"Go on in," the RAF officer told Lucky before returning to the tower.

Lucky knocked on the door and then entered the office. Wing Commander Gordon Leonard Sinclair was scribbling something on a sheet of paper at his desk. He was thin with wavy blond hair and boyish looks. He didn't look up when Lucky stepped into the office. Finally, Lucky cleared his throat. Sinclair put his pen down and looked up. He sized up Lucky, dressed in his flight gear, and then returned to his paperwork. It was clear Sinclair heard the massive bomber land, but he was busy and didn't have time for an American pilot sightseeing around his country.

"Yank, what the hell are you doing here?"

Lucky didn't know. He wasn't there to meet Sinclair. He was looking for Sully. All he wanted was the group commander to tell him where his friend was on the base.

He shrugged. "Well, sir, I'm just here on a social call to say hi to my best friend," he said, "Flight Lieutenant Sullivan."

Sinclair looked up and folded his hands. He then looked back down at the paper he was writing on his desk. "You knew him?"

Lucky nodded. This was the second time he'd been asked

the question in past tense since he arrived. "Sir, he's from my hometown," he said. "We are the closest friends. We're fraternity brothers. Yes, sir, I know him very well. Is he around?"

Sinclair looked out toward the runway. "Did you see the wreckage when you landed?"

"Yes, sir," Lucky said.

Sinclair didn't say anything. It took a second for Lucky to understand what he was telling him. One second, Lucky was excited to see his friend again. After meeting him in London, Lucky felt like their friendship was rekindled. They were back at university. Back to chasing girls and dreaming big. But that feeling was dashed in an instant. He had no idea the wreckage he saw near the runway was Sully's plane.

"Oh my god," Lucky said, the weight of the realization making his shoulders stoop.

Sinclair slumped in his chair. He was also feeling the weight of the loss. "We lost him yesterday afternoon."

Sinclair explained Sully was on takeoff and got up to about five hundred feet when the Typhoon's engine quit. Bluish-white smoke poured out of the exhaust stubs as he fought to keep the fighter airborne. He turned left to circle back to the airfield. The trees were coming up, and he had to lift the nose slightly to clear the top branches. The crippled Typhoon belching smoke from the sputtering engine eked over the tips of the trees. But the move cut the fighter's airspeed. It started to spin and then fell like a rock.

"He just cartwheeled in," Sinclair said.

The primary cause of this accident was engine failure,

and a forced landing was unavoidable. Later, the accident report concluded Sully made the wrong decision not going straight ahead when he realized that his engine was failing.

"No judgment can be passed on Sullivan for making such a decision, made as it was under the direct stress and difficulty," the accident report concluded.

Medics and ground crew raced to the crash site. Sinclair told Lucky that Sullivan suffered multiple injuries and burns. He died at the scene.

Lucky heard what Sinclair told him, but was still processing it. Sully was only twenty-one years old. Lucky had lost too many friends already, but losing his best friend from home too, weeks after seeing him in London, was a shock to his system. Lost in his own grief, Lucky didn't hear Sinclair until the commander repeated he was working on a message to Sully's mother.

"I'm just cabling her," Sinclair said. "I want you to do it."

It took Lucky a second to register Sinclair wanted him to notify Sully's mother that she'd lost her only son to an accident. "Sir, with all due respect, he was flying for the Canadians," Lucky said, "not for the Americans. And I think as one of your airmen, it's your responsibility to notify his next of kin."

Sinclair nodded in agreement. It was his duty. He'd done it many times, and each time likely left him hollow. Each time he delivered the worst news in the world to total strangers, but at least they were his countrymen. In this case, Sully was an American. There was comfort, Sinclair hoped, in getting the news from someone from home. Someone who knew her son so well. He pressed Lucky to do it. "I think she would appreciate hearing the news from you, rather than from me," Sinclair said.

Lucky had no choice, but he still didn't want to do it. How could he comfort Sully's mother when he needed comforting too? He was still in disbelief when he sat down at the desk and wrote out a cable to Sully's mother. He explained that her son was killed on November 7, 1943, in an aircraft accident while taking off on a mission from his base. He told her Sully would be buried in England with his comrades. Lucky also promised he'd attend the funeral.

Before Lucky left RAF Martlesham Heath, Sinclair told him the funeral location and time. Lucky vowed to be at the ceremony. As he flew back to Thorpe Abbotts, he thought back to Chattanooga. He chuckled remembering him schmoozing with the old-timers at Chattanooga's Rotary Club as the high school ROTC regimental commander. He could still taste the Black Velvet on his tongue as he and Sully partied until dawn in London. He remembered going with Sully to his mother's so he could get permission to fly fighters. Now he wished Mrs. Sullivan had said no like his own father had. Sully had achieved his dream, but it had cost him everything. Sully's short life burned bright, but fate only poured him half a life.

Landing at Thorpe Abbotts, Lucky knew he had to do one more thing for Sully. He went to his office and shut the door. He dialed Peggy. She was happy to hear from him after spending a memorable weekend in London. But the happy greeting didn't last as Peggy started to wonder why Lucky was calling her. Her surprise quickly turned to sorrow as Lucky delivered the devastating news.

After hanging up, Lucky headed for Silver Wings and a stiff drink to toast his friend, but more importantly, to dull the pain.

It was an overcast day. The weather fit Lucky's solemn mood as he flew two days later from Thorpe Abbotts to an airfield southwest of London near Brookwood Military Cemetery for Sully's funeral service.

Set aside in 1917, the cemetery was the final resting place for Commonwealth casualties of the Second World War. The Royal Air Forces section sat in the southeast corner.

Lucky joined the crowd at a small chapel on the cemetery grounds. After a short service, Sully was carried in a simple pine box by his Royal Air Force colleagues to his final resting place at grave number nine, row three, plot forty-seven. He was among the other fallen Royal Canadian Air Force pilots.

A Canadian chaplain presided over the funeral, giving Sully a final farewell. Overhead, Typhoons thundered above in tribute. Two wreaths were laid at the head of the grave— one sent by Sully's squadron and one on behalf of his mother. Written on the card was simply, "From his mother."

Lucky watched in silence as his best friend was laid to rest in foreign soil. It was only a few days after the accident, and the image of the wreckage of the Typhoon was burned into his memory.

Lucky had to steel himself against the emotion of the funeral. The Americans didn't hold them for downed airmen at Thorpe Abbotts. The friends he'd lost in his squadron were shot down and didn't return. One minute, he was sharing a drink with them in the officers' club or enjoying a pre-mission breakfast, and the next, they were gone. Their possessions packed away, sent home with their memory while the rest of the squadron continued on to the next mission.

Lucky had become a little calloused to death. He'd formed a protective crust. Emotional armor. It was the reason he kept most of the replacement crews at arm's length. He never knew when he was witnessing their last meal. That kind of grief only made it harder for him to climb into the bomber again. Any loss of focus meant death. He was required to go back out and keep flying. That needed a clear head and laser focus.

But this was different.

He'd seen the wreckage. He'd seen the exact spot where his best friend lost his life. Seeing his friend's final resting place brought up feelings he'd so far successfully suppressed. Sully's death tested his resolve more than any other. Lucky felt the grief bubbling up, threatening to break through the crust he'd formed to keep himself sane. If the mission to Bremen cracked Lucky's confidence, then losing Sully kicked in a hole. Lucky felt mortal, and completing his tour to get home safely felt insurmountable. In the back of his head, he knew he was required to keep flying. It was an exercise in futility to be constantly reminded of the chances he took in the cockpit on each mission. It took every ounce of strength for him to swallow down the pain and push it from his mind. To focus on what he could control and leave the rest to God, fate, or both.

The firing party's three volleys of seven snapped Lucky

out of his stupor. Then a Canadian trumpeter sounded the last post, the Commonwealth counterpart to taps. Lucky listened. Each note punctuated the loss of his friend. Unlike taps with its slow, mournful melody, the last post had an almost triumphant feel like it was celebrating the bravery of the fallen before becoming more solemn at the end. For Lucky, he'd already heard the bugle call too many times and didn't care to hear it ever again.

Sully was finally laid to rest at 2:30 p.m.

A white cross was erected above his casket. A squadron mate placed Sully's blue cap next to the cross. Lucky took one final moment with his best friend, saluted, and then headed back to the airfield. The notes of the last post echoed in his head as he climbed into the B-17 to fly back to Thorpe Abbotts.

Six days after the memorial, Commander Sinclair wrote Sully's mother a letter outlining the circumstances of her son's death and shared details from the funeral. He assured her Sully's death was instantaneous.

"I find it difficult to express the great sympathy which we all feel with you in the very sad loss which you have sustained," Sinclair wrote. "This feeling is intensified in the knowledge that Sully was so far from his home, which he left so very long ago to join the Royal Canadian Air Force, before the United States entered the war. Sully was one of the gallant band who knew that the cause of freedom might demand the supreme sacrifice, and he gave himself gallantly. His passing left a gap in our ranks which will hardly be filled."

18

BIG B

Silver Wings was quiet.

The green light over the mantel was on, and the crews knew they'd be up early for another mission. Only the men who weren't going on the mission or worked on the staff were having a drink.

Lucky stood by the bar alone. It was November 1943. He'd been working nonstop in the operations shop since returning from Sully's funeral. He'd finished his twenty-third mission—uneventful for the most part—leading a raid on Gelsenkirchen. He'd joined Second Lieutenant John Griffin's crew as command pilot aboard *Goin Jessies*. The mission was a success, and the squadron returned without losing a crew.

Two more missions left and he'd be on a boat home.

After Gelsenkirchen, Lucky was eager to get back in the cockpit and finish up. He just hadn't found the missions yet. He wasn't looking to replicate Bremen. With all the losses, Lucky figured he'd earned a couple of milk runs to finish out the string. Plus, being in the operations shop allowed him to pick the missions now. Lucky, still nursing his drink, was lost in his own thoughts when he felt a tap on his shoulder. It was Major Ollie Turner, the 351st Bomb Squadron commander.

"You'd better get some sleep," Turner said. "You're flying tomorrow."

That was news to Lucky. He was the operations officer and had designated all the crews for tomorrow's mission before he came over to the officers' club. He was damn sure he wasn't going on the mission. "What are you talking about?"

"We're leading the group," Turner said. "I want you to fly as command pilot."

Lucky knew the squadron was leading. It was customary for the squadron commander to fly in the lead ship when it was his unit leading the group. He'd penciled Turner in when he got the orders.

"I'll lead," Lucky said. "But if we're leading, you're supposed to fly command."

Turner shrugged and then looked away. "I know," he said, meeting Lucky's gaze again. "But I want you to take this mission."

That struck Lucky as odd. Why would Turner want him to fly? Something didn't feel right, but it wasn't like he had much of a choice. An order was an order. Lucky finished his drink and left Turner alone at the bar. He marched off to the barracks and climbed into his bed. He didn't dwell on the change of plan, instead focusing on getting as much rest as possible. Before dawn, one of his operations sergeants shook him awake. He climbed out of his cot and went through pre-mission.

A shower.

A shave.

A quick breakfast. Lucky followed the crowd to the briefing and took a seat near the front and took out his notebook.
Even though he did the planning for his squadron, headquarters
didn't reveal the target. And he didn't hang around after des-
ignating the crews because he didn't think he'd fly the mission.

The briefing officers filed into the room. Everyone popped
tall, coming to attention in front of their seat when they saw
General Curtis LeMay, commander of the Third Air Division, come in with the usual suspects. Lucky noticed everyone
stood a little straighter with "Iron Ass" LeMay around.

He felt uneasy.

It was unusual to see LeMay. He didn't come to a briefing unless something big was happening. LeMay had a stern
look on his face. He wasn't angry as much as determined. He
stood at the head of the room, in front of the map covered by
a curtain, and waited for the crews to retake their seats. Once
everyone was settled, LeMay addressed the room.

"Gentlemen, you're the only ones that are flying today,"
LeMay said. "I have to tell you that this is such an important
mission, it's one that I have pointed my whole military career to leading. But if I get into that airplane today, they will
court-martial me. So, you'll have to do the job and I have to
tell you that if we only get one plane over the target, we'll
consider it a success."

Oh, my aching back, what is coming off? Lucky thought.
Jesus. One ship over the target was a success? Hell, it felt like
they were going to bomb Hitler himself.

Lucky's hunch was close. When the curtain came down, his eyes followed the red yarn from Thorpe Abbotts across the North Sea to Berlin, the Nazi capital.

They were going to hit "Big B."

This was not the first time the Allies had attacked the Nazi capital, though. The French were the first to hit Berlin in a small raid on June 7, 1940, as French lines were collapsing under the weight of the blitzkrieg. But they hadn't been back since.

The British RAF had just started to hit Berlin at night.

"It was the target which above all the Luftwaffe was bound to defend," said Sir Arthur Travers Harris, commander of the RAF Bomber Command, about Berlin.

Harris believed attacking the Nazi capital could be the blow that would break German resistance.

"It will cost us between four hundred and five hundred aircraft," he said. "It will cost Germany the war."

Between November 1943 and March 1944, British Bomber Command made sixteen attacks on Berlin. The first raid occurred on November 18–19, 1943. Berlin was the main target, and was attacked by more than four hundred Avro Lancasters aided by four Mosquitoes. The city was under cloud and the damage was not severe.

The second major raid was on the night of November 22–23, 1943. This was the most effective raid by the RAF on Berlin. It caused extensive damage to the residential areas west of the city's center. Because of the dry weather conditions, several firestorms ignited. The Kaiser Wilhelm Memorial Church was destroyed. Several other buildings were either damaged or destroyed, including the British, French, Italian, and Japanese embassies, the Berlin Zoo, and the barracks of the Imperial Guard at Spandau.

But those were night attacks.

Goering boasted that Berlin would never be bombed by the Eighth Air Force in the daylight. LeMay vowed to make Goering eat his words.

Lucky sat in the briefing speechless. No wonder Turner didn't want to lead. Not only were they flying into the teeth of the Luftwaffe's defenses, but the 100th was the only group flying and this was the first time the Americans were going to attack Berlin—and in broad daylight.

Lucky's mouth was dry, and he felt a nervous sweat coat his skin as the briefing started in earnest. Nothing about this mission sounded good. After the curtain came down, the meteorologist got up to brief. Standing next to the map, he presented the reason for the daylight mission.

"We've got such an unusual weather condition over the continent," the weather officer said. "The entire continent is going to be covered by a thick cloud cover, so instead of the usual twenty-five-thousand to twenty-nine-thousand-feet bombing altitude, you're going to go in at twelve thousand feet, just above the cloud deck."

They'd already been forced to return to targets because of cloud cover in the past. Now the weather shop was predicting thick cloud cover over Berlin. The idea of fighting all the way to Berlin only to find the target covered was inconceivable. Lucky wasn't the only pilot thinking about it. He could feel the tension growing in the room.

Major Jack Kidd, the 100th Bomb Group operations officer, got up and briefed next. He talked through the details. The launch schedules. Time hacks. Headings. Once the formation turned on its initial point, Kidd told the pilots to dive through the clouds and break out over Berlin at six thousand feet.

"It will be high noon, and your target is the Reichstag."

Located near the center of the city, the building was built in 1894 to house the parliament of the German Empire. The building had a massive dome at the center with two rook-like façades on either end. After a fire in the 1930s, the Nazis abandoned the Reichstag for the Kroll Opera House for parliamentary sessions. But the main meeting hall of the building was still used for propaganda presentations.

Lucky tried to concentrate on the details, but he couldn't shake the feeling of dread. It started in his gut when he first spotted LeMay, but now it had grown like a cancer to take over his whole body.

This was a suicide mission.

Lucky scanned the assembled crews, looking for Turner. The squadron commander was near the front, sitting with the other commanders. Turner must have felt Lucky's eyes burning a hole in his back because he looked over his shoulder. Lucky caught his eye and shot him the middle finger. Turner looked away.

The son of a bitch knew the target the night before and went out of his way to find Lucky in the officers' club so that he could order him to go. Instead of doing his duty as a squadron commander, Turner was asking his men to risk their own lives while he sat this one out safely at Thorpe Abbotts.

Turner signed the death warrants of his men, like commanders sometimes must, but he didn't have the courage to fulfill his duty as a leader and be at the front of the formation. Lucky understood his duty and the duty of everyone climbing into a bomber that morning. But he couldn't abide someone who shirked the same duty.

Lucky wouldn't let it stand.

After the briefing, he cornered Turner at the squadron's office. Lucky towered over Turner, who had to look up at his subordinate to meet his gaze. Turner had a severe case of Napoleonic syndrome, constantly overcompensating for his lack of height. He was always trying to improve his stature by doing things or acting in a way that would demand your respect.

But Lucky had no respect for him now. What did he have to lose? This mission was sure to kill him. For the second time in his career, the first time in a frenzy of flak over Bremen, Lucky was sure he wasn't coming back to Thorpe Abbotts.

"You yellow son of a bitch," Lucky said, wagging a finger in his commander's face for emphasis. "You knew what this mission was and you put me in this spot and you're supposed to fly it."

Turner raised his hands as he tried to respond, but Lucky didn't let him. Lucky slammed his fist on the desk. He didn't want to hear a word from Turner.

"Let me tell you something," Lucky said. "LeMay said if we only get one ship over the target, it's worth it. I'm gonna be that ship. I'm coming back from this mission. And when I do, if I see your ugly face, I'll kill you."

If that wasn't rank insubordination, Lucky didn't know what was. But if Turner court-martialed Lucky, he'd have to fly the mission in his place. Turner's face was red with anger, but he never opened his mouth. He just turned away.

Lucky stormed out of the squadron office. He followed the rest of the crews to the equipment shed and drew his flight gear. Lucky rode out to the hardstand in silence. He was seething. The rest of the crew was at the ship, and Lucky went about his duties, focusing on each entry on the checklist to suppress the rage.

With everything checked out, Lucky taxied the ship to the end of the runway. The cloud deck was low, and Lucky could barely make out the tower. It was like taking off in a cloud. Lucky throttled up to full power and waited for the flare. When it finally shot into the gloom, Lucky let off the brakes, and the ship rocketed down the runway and climbed into the gray.

After a steady forty-five-minute climb, Lucky broke through the overcast clouds around ten thousand feet into a spectacular blue sky. Behind him, almost twenty ships followed. Lucky formed up the three squadrons and turned for the enemy coast. There was no fighter escort. The idea was to sneak in over the cloud cover and catch them by surprise. It was radio silence as the formation headed for the Nazi capital.

As they approached the enemy coast, Lucky noticed the blanket of pillowy gray clouds below started to thin and then scatter. Lucky spotted the green fields of the Netherlands below.

So much for the element of surprise.

The pit in Lucky's stomach—which he'd been able to ignore by focusing on the task at hand—grew. Even with the clouds, the mission was suicide. Now they didn't have any cover. If the Luftwaffe flew into flak to defend Bremen, what would they do to defend Berlin? The odds of even one ship making it was slim now.

The thought of flying to his death was a reality on each mission, but going to Berlin with one group surrounded by blue skies felt less like a mission and more like an execution.

And for what?

So LeMay and the Bomber Mafia could prove the value of high-altitude strategic bombing? So America could send a message that even Berlin was touchable? Lucky never resented his commanders more than when he was flying at twelve thousand feet to certain death over Berlin. His only solace was if he had to bail out and survived, he'd spend the rest of the war in a prison camp. Lucky was resigned to his fate, sending a little prayer heavenward while hoping his luck held enough to at least survive, when he heard the radio operator come over the interphone.

"Radio operator to pilot. Abort. Abort. Abort. Return to base."

Lucky exhaled.

A sense of relief washed over him. It was as if he were on death row and heading for the electric chair when the governor called just in time to stay an execution. Word went out to the rest of the formation, and Lucky turned for home. The Eighth Air Force wouldn't hit Berlin that day. It took four more months before American bombs hit the German capital. The first American daylight raid on Berlin was not until March 1944.

Now that the mission no longer hung over his head, the fact Lucky was even leading the formation turned from resignation to rage. It welled up in his chest the more he thought about Turner and his decision to send Lucky instead of himself. Lucky couldn't serve under a man unwilling to do what he was asking his men to do.

Turner was a coward.

Lucky landed and caught a jeep to the 100th Bomb Group's operations shop instead of the debriefing. He found Major Kidd, the group's operations officer, and asked to speak with him. Kidd led the Bremen mission, and Lucky admired him more than he did any other officer in the group.

Lucky sat down in Kidd's office and told him how Turner weaseled out of the mission to Berlin. Lucky was clear. He had no respect for his commander. Kidd nodded along with Lucky as he told his story. He had led his share of missions and understood the importance of a commander to be in the front.

"I cannot serve under that guy one more minute," Lucky said. "Please, whatever you have to do, give me a transfer."

"I don't blame you," Kidd said, taking a second to think.

As luck would have it, there was an opening in another squadron Kidd needed to fill.

"I desperately need another operations officer in the 350th," Kidd said. "Would you take that job?"

Lucky didn't hesitate. "You betcha," he said.

From left to right: Howard Keel—Pilot; William Carleton—351st Engineering Officer; Alvin Barker—351st Operations Officer, killed during the Bremen mission; E. C. "Doc" Kinder—Flight Surgeon; and Luckadoo *(far right)* singing at Silver Wings, the officers' club at Thorpe Abbotts.

Luckadoo *(middle facing the camera)* attends Sully's funeral on November 11, 1943, at Brookwood Military Cemetery. Notice Sully's cap on his grave. Before his death, Sully wrote this in the event he was killed: "If I should die, think only this of me: That there's some corner of a foreign field that is forever Tennessee."

[Library and Archives Canada; Ottawa, Canada; Service Files of the Second World War - War Dead, 1939-1947; Series: RG 24]

A series of clippings and a portrait of Leroy "Sully" Sullivan, Luckadoo's childhood best friend from Chattanooga, Tennessee. He served with the RAF. Sully was killed in a take-off accident. "Words cannot express the grief of a loss such as this, but one cannot help but feel the joy of having known him," Luckadoo writes below. "And I know he was happy in what he was so gallantly doing."

[Courtesy of John Luckadoo Collection]

The wreckage of *Sunny II,* the aircraft used by Luckadoo and his crew to complete several missions, including their twenty-fifth. The bomber crash-landed in Harleston, England, on December 30, 1943, after a mission to Ludwigshaven.

[Courtesy of 100th Bomb Group Foundation Collection]

John H. Luckadoo and William D. DeSanders shake hands on February 13, 1944, moments after landing at Thorpe Abbotts. They had just completed their twenty-fifth mission to Livossart and Bois Rempre in *Alice from Dallas II*.

[Courtesy of 100th Bomb Group Foundation Collection]

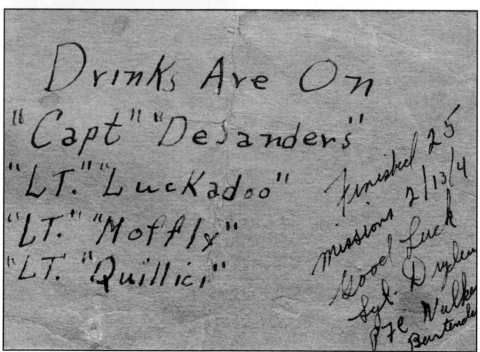

Card from Silver Wings, the officers' club at Thorpe Abbotts, noting the completion of Lucky's twenty-fifth mission. He was happy to pay for the drinks. *[Courtesy of John Luckadoo Collection]*

20 February 1944

SUBJECT: Tour of Operational Missions performed by John H Luckadoo,
Captain, AC.

TO   : Whom it may concern.

1. The following is a list of operational missions performed by
John H. Luckadoo, Captain, AC, while assigned to the 100th Bombardment
Group (H), AAF Station # 139:

#	Date	Target	Time
1	June 26, 1943	Le Mans	4:45
2	" 28, 1943	St. Nazaire	10:05
3	July 4, 1943	La. Pallice	10:30
4	July 10, 1943	Le. Bourget	5:15
5	" 14, 1943	Le. Bourget	4:15
6	" 17, 1943	Hamburg	5:30
7	" 25, 1943	Warnemunde	7:45
8	" 26, 1943	Hanover	5:45
9	" 28, 1943	Oscherleben	5:30
10	" 29, 1943	Warnemunde	7:15
11	" 30, 1943	Kassel	6:00
12	August 12, 1943	Bonn	5:00
13	" 19, 1943	Woensdrecht	4:00
14	" 24, 1943	Bordeaux Gireaux	4:00
15	" 27, 1943	Watten	3:30
16	" 31, 1943	Le. Mureaux	5:30
17	September 6, 1943	Conches	9:15
18	" 7, 1943	Watten	3:30
19	" 9, 1943	Beauvais-Tille	4:15
20	" 15, 1943	Paris (Renault)	5:45
21	" 16, 1943	La. Pallice	11:00
22	October 8, 1943	Bremen	5:30
23	November 19, 1943	Gelsenkirchen	6:00
24	" 26, 1943	Bremen	6:20
25	February 13, 1944	Noball # 120	4:00
		25	150:10

ALBERT M. ELTON,
Major, Air Corps,
Commanding.

The list of missions completed by Luckadoo while assigned to the 100th
Bomb Group.

Luckadoo, pictured with his Air Medal and Distinguished Service Cross. He was part of the original 100th Bomb Group cadre to arrive in England. His crew was the first to reach twenty-five missions.

[Courtesy of John Luckadoo Collection]

From left to right, Luckadoo, his wife Barbara, his sister Nancy, and brother Bob pose in front of his Maroon Buick in 1945.

[Courtesy of John Luckadoo Collection]

Lucky and his wife Bobby in 2016 at a 100th Bomb Group Foundation reunion.

[Courtesy of John Luckadoo Collection]

Kidd started the paperwork as Lucky went back to debrief. By the time he was done, Lucky had a new job. He transferred that day and moved across the base from the 351st's operations shop to the 350th's. Lucky became the first officer in the 100th Bomb Group to be an operations officer for two squadrons.

As Lucky settled into his new job—same as the old one—he was relieved. Being the first to bomb Berlin would have been an accomplishment, but only if he survived.

Lucky wasn't looking for notoriety. He just wanted to go home.

19

HIS BEST DAY

FEBRUARY 1944

Lucky climbed into the copilot seat of *Alice from Dallas II* and pulled the preflight checklist out of the pocket under the window.

Last one. Number twenty-five.

But sitting in his seat in front of the wall of dials felt strange. Before becoming the operations officer, he was flying constantly. Daily, even. Since his promotion to operations officer—first with the 351st and then 350th—he hadn't flown much. With winter came foul weather, and his ground duties kept him from flying another mission. Lucky spent the holidays doing paperwork and staying warm until another mission to Bremen and the aborted Berlin mission. The raid on the Nazi capital would have been his second to last mission had they dropped.

But it got scrubbed.

The November mission to Bremen had not. Lucky was pretty apprehensive when he found out the target. The October mission there was costly, but Lucky knew not to expect the same thing. German defenses were fluid. One time, they might fly through flak to down bombers, but the next time was a milk run. This time, Bremen was just that. They faced lighter resistance, and he made it back with relative ease compared to his twenty-second mission.

It was now February 13, 1944, and Lucky cherry-picked his last mission. Being the operations officer had its perks. When the mission came down from Eighth Air Force headquarters, Lucky knew it was the one. The 350th was designated to lead the group on a raid to bomb a V-1 emplacement on the French coast just across the English Channel. The British had urged the Eighth Air Force to go after the V-1 rocket launching sites.

The V-1 flying bomb, also known to the Allies as the *buzz bomb*, was an early cruise missile that used a pulse jet for power. The V-1 was the first of the so-called vengeance weapons developed to terrorize London. Ground-launched V-1s were propelled up an inclined launch ramp by an apparatus known as a Dampferzeuger, a steam generator. A piston in the tube, connected underneath the missile, was launched forward by the steam. This enabled the missile to become airborne with a strong enough airflow, allowing the pulse-jet engine to operate. The launch rail was 160 feet long, consisting of eight modular sections and a muzzle brake. Because of its limited range, the thousands of V-1 missiles launched into England were fired from facilities along the French and Dutch coasts.

Lucky's last mission was to lead a raid to knock out as many of the missiles' launching pads as they could, specifically to silence the launch site in Livossart, a few miles inland near the Belgium border. It was less dangerous than trying to penetrate all of Europe and gave Lucky the best chance to survive.

When the mission came down, Lucky was the acting squadron commander. Major Albert Elton took over the 350th after Cleven was lost over Münster on October 10, 1943. But the stress of command took its toll, and by February 1944, Elton was suffering from combat fatigue. His weight had dropped to 103 pounds because of stress and too many sleepless nights. He was sent to recoup at a flak house, leaving Lucky in command.

When Lucky heard about the mission, he notified the squadron they'd be flying lead in the morning and then called Captain Bill DeSanders, one of the 100th Bomb Group's original pilots from Texas. Like Lucky, DeSanders was also sitting on twenty-four missions. About as tall as Lucky, DeSanders was thicker and wore a thin mustache. Lucky selected DeSanders's crew to lead the formation.

"Bill, you've only got one left, one mission to go, and so do I, and this mission is for us," Lucky said. "I'll lead it with your crew, and I'll be the command pilot."

DeSanders was short on missions because of a hospital stay. On July 25, 1943, he fell ill with the flu and was hospitalized. Captain Richard Carey, the operations officer of the 350th before Lucky, flew with DeSanders's crew instead.

Unable to bomb Warnemunde, the primary target, the group flew to Kiel, where intense flak damaged Carey's plane. He decided to ditch in the sea. All the crew except for the pilot and copilot were in the radio room when the ship hit the water. Two wounded crew members got out of the overhead hatch, but the others were trapped in the radio room and went down with the bomber. Carey and the other survivors were picked up by a fishing boat. When they got to shore, the Germans were waiting.

The crew was taken prisoner, but he was spared because of his illness. Assigned a new crew, he'd survived long enough to fly his last mission. But on this mission, Lucky and DeSanders were flying with a crew made up of senior enlisted soldiers and command personnel. This wasn't a regular crew.

Both Lucky and DeSanders were some of the last crews grandfathered into the twenty-five-mission goal. Lieutenant General Jimmy Doolittle was now commanding the Eighth Air Force and raised the mission quota by five, to thirty missions.

Doolittle made the change in March 1944 because the tide had turned and now the American crews were the veterans. The crews weren't fighting German aces any longer. The ranks of the Luftwaffe had thinned, and unlike the American crews, they couldn't be replaced with the same frequency.

Hundreds of B-17s and B-24s had arrived from the United States. The Eighth Air Force was also sending waves of bombers. It sometimes took more than two hours for every bomber in the formation to hit a target. The bombing raids crippled Nazi Germany's ability to manufacture synthetic fuel, meaning fewer fighters in the air.

But leading a group wasn't easy.

Doolittle needed veteran pilots to lead these massive formations because the command pilot had to be mindful of the fact there were hundreds of planes mimicking his every move. A slight course adjustment meant hundreds of adjustments in the trailing aircraft. Abrupt turns could spread the formation out and break it up, making everyone vulnerable to fighter attack. There weren't many pilots who could be good lead crews or command pilots because of the responsibility.

Doolittle also changed up his fighter strategy. He unleashed the fighter pilots on the Luftwaffe instead of trying to stave off the attacks on the bomber formation. American fighters targeted German bases, hitting the Luftwaffe fighters before they even got in the air.

That made a hell of a big difference.

But that didn't mean the Luftwaffe wasn't still aggressive when they did attack. The German pilots still gave no quarter.

Lucky barely slept the night before. He was awake before the sergeant from the operations shop shone a light in his face to wake him. After showering and dressing, he went by the operations office on the way to breakfast. Weather was the issue. It was raining, and the target was fogged in, the weather officer told him. But there was a chance it would burn off.

Lucky nodded and headed off to breakfast. The mission was still on, barely. After a half hour of bad coffee and pushing his breakfast around his tray, Lucky headed for the briefing, where the plan was laid out in detail. Lucky knew it already, but dutifully took notes and prepared to fly it.

In the back of his head, he felt the pressure of his last mission. Everyone in the squadron knew this was his last hurrah. He'd seen the younger pilots staring at him. He'd caught some of the veterans—men with ten or more missions—give him a knowing nod. No one made an overt deal. It was like talking to a pitcher during a no-hitter.

Don't be the jinx.

But as Lucky went through the briefing, he couldn't shake the weight of the mission. Lucky was proud of what he'd accomplished, but he couldn't imagine sticking out his chest because he had twenty-four missions under his belt. He was grateful to be still walking or standing upright, but he knew the last one was the most important.

Lucky had experienced the excitement of a twenty-fifth mission with Dye. He saw the euphoria on the faces of his crewmates as they returned to Thorpe Abbotts for the last time.

He wanted it for himself.

Despite the thorough briefing, Lucky had a hunch the mission would get scrubbed. He was proven correct after the pilots and gunners drew their flight gear. Before they could board the crew jeeps to the hardstands, the weather officer appeared and informed Lucky the mission was off. He'd have to fly his last mission another day. Everyone returned to the barracks. Lucky went to the operations shop.

It was a day off for the aircrews but not for the administrative duties of the acting commander and operations officer. Just as he settled into the day's paperwork, the weather officer was at the door.

The mission was back on.

The cloud deck over the coast was breaking up. Headquarters wanted the bombers in the air before noon. Lucky sent out the order, and the operations sergeants policed up the crews. Everyone hit the equipment shed before heading to the hardstand.

DeSanders and the crew met Lucky at *Alice from Dallas II*. By now, the crews got through preflight without a hiccup, but Lucky felt stale in the cockpit. He had to think about what he was doing versus before when he just knew. The whole process of flying the massive four-engine bomber was instinctive. Now it felt robotic as he tried to shake off the rust.

As he read off the checklist, the fate of so many others crept into the back of his head. He thought of Charlie Via, his classmate wounded over Bremen, who was recouping from his injuries. He left Thorpe Abbotts and would likely never fly again. He was lucky to have his life, but so many others had given theirs. Sully. Countless squadron mates, many who were anonymous to Lucky because he didn't have a chance to get to know them.

Lucky said a little prayer, part of his own preflight checklist, and made sure he had his creased Bible in his jacket pocket and lucky stocking scarf around his neck. Each step gave him confidence. By the time the engines started to turn, he was comfortable again. The familiar rhythm of the propellers gave him confidence. The vibration in the stick. The static on the interphone. He was back in his office and ready to accomplish his mission.

Mission twenty-five.

His best day.

DeSanders throttled the B-17's four engines and took off. Four more hours and they'd be done.

This was going to be a milk run.

By 11:30, Lucky, in *Alice from Dallas II,* was climbing to eighteen thousand feet at the front of the air armada headed for the French coast. The formation was halfway across the English Channel when Lucky spotted the Luftwaffe fighters on the horizon. A mix of Me 109s and Me 110s. They weren't waiting for the bombers, meeting the formation over the English Channel. Lucky watched as the fighters rocketed past his lead ship, the twin .50-caliber machine guns mounted under the plexiglass bombardier compartment in the nose firing as they passed. *Alice from Dallas II* was a G-model B-17, meaning it had a chin gun turret. Now when Luftwaffe fighters attacked from twelve o'clock high, the B-17 crews answered.

The first fighter passes were focused on Lucky's ship. The Germans attacked the leader, hoping to throw the whole formation into chaos. But as they shot past, they went after any target of opportunity, hoping to knock a ship out of formation.

The interphone exploded with chatter as the gunners called out the approaching fighters. It was like flying through a swarm of bugs. Lucky felt his heart rate tick up. He'd faced this kind of onslaught in the past, but usually over Germany. The cacophony of the engines mixed with the buzzing fighters and the staccato burst of machine-gun fire soon blended into one continuous roar. It was almost overwhelming. All his ground time had dulled his nerves. His breathing came out ragged. Sweat rolled off his brow. His heart pounded against his chest. This was supposed to be a milk run, not a fight for his life.

He shot a glance over to DeSanders. He was calm, unfazed by the flurry of fighters. On the interphone, the gunners calmly called out fighter locations. Below his feet, the bombardier and navigator prepared to drop the payload.

Lucky closed his eyes and refocused. All he had to do was his job. He relaxed, his instincts taking over as he and DeSanders set the formation on the initial point and gave the bombardier control.

Just after passing over the French coast, Lucky spotted the target. The Germans had concealed the concrete launch ramps with camouflage netting. But the ramps were so large, it was impossible to cover them up on the flat coastal plain. Next to the giant ramps were three squat supply buildings on the edge of the massive concrete pad.

Smoke wafted from the launch site in an attempt to screen the complex, but an offshore breeze blew it away from the oncoming bombers. Lucky checked the gauges and heading. They were lined up precisely.

Flak exploded around Lucky's ship as the formation got closer to the target. It paled in comparison to Bremen, but they were still taking fire. With the Norden bombsight flying the airplane, there was nothing for Lucky to do but wait for the bombs to fall. Soon, he heard the bombardier on the interphone getting ready to drop. It felt like hours until he finally heard the two words that told him his mission was almost over.

"Bombs away."

Lucky didn't realize he was holding his breath in anticipation. He exhaled as the bomber rose up in the air. He felt weightless for a second before reaching out to take control. Below, two tons of five-hundred-pound bombs rained down on the German launch site. Behind them, more than three hundred bombers unloaded as Lucky and DeSanders made the turn for home.

As they circled back, the bombardier reported in. "We hit it right on the nose," he said.

That didn't often happen. In most instances, the bombs missed by miles, which meant they'd have to come back. *Not this time,* Lucky thought. Hopefully his twenty-fifth mission would be the last time the Eighth Air Force would have to hit this target. A few minutes later, *Alice from Dallas II* was back over the English Channel.

They were home free.

DeSanders was flying, leaving Lucky to look out of the windshield at the gray water and the hazy, brown coastline of England. Even in the winter, she looked glorious as the formation slowly descended. When the bomber crossed over the shoreline, Lucky leaned over and slapped DeSanders on the shoulder.

"Boy, oh boy, congratulations," Lucky said in the interphone.

DeSanders, his oxygen mask pulled down, smiled and stuck out his hand. The pilots shook on it. On their interphones, the rest of the crew congratulated the pilots. If they'd had a bottle, they would have cracked it right then.

When Thorpe Abbotts came into view, DeSanders took a victory lap around the tower. The crew fired off flares as they passed. They were done and hadn't lost a ship on the mission. Lucky spotted a crowd forming at *Alice from Dallas II*'s hardstand. DeSanders lined up for landing. The bomber touched down, and Lucky and DeSanders swung it around and headed for the hardstand for the last time.

As they taxied, the top turret gunner, Technical Sergeant Albert DeGregorio, patted DeSanders and Lucky on the shoulders. His smile was as large as the pilots'.

Lucky and DeSanders shut down the engines for the last time. DeSanders left the cockpit first. Lucky waited for the rest of the crew to climb out. He took a second in the cockpit to savor the moment, surveying the dials and remembering how far he'd come from his first hours next to Dye in Nebraska. He'd vowed to be the best bomber pilot he could be and felt like he'd accomplished the goal. The propellers were still when Lucky finally climbed out. He knelt near the landing gear and kissed the ground.

Twenty-five.

Lucky's war was over.

As he stood with DeSanders and took pictures, he felt light. A weight lifted from his shoulders. For the first time in almost a year, he was living with a future again. Death was no longer lurking over the horizon. He'd done his part, and it was up to somebody else to take it from there.

From the hardstand, DeSanders and Lucky debriefed—after a few shots of rum—and then cleaned up and hit the officers' club. It wasn't long until both were roaring drunk. Before the end of the night, Lucky added his name to the ceiling tiles next to Dye's and the rest of his old crew. Better late than never, he figured.

Over the next few days, Lucky finished up his duties as operations officer as he waited for his boat home. His flying days weren't over, he just didn't know where and what he'd be doing. The Eighth Air Force offered him a slot in a program where pilots who completed their allotted missions flew Mosquito bombers to survey bomb damage. The twin-engine bombers could outrun the German fighters during the reconnaissance missions. Lucky considered the slot, but turned it down because flying over Germany in an unarmed bomber didn't appeal to him. He had pressed his luck too many times already. He also turned down command of a squadron because he'd have to fly additional bombing missions. He could never have the operations officer fly in his place.

Finally, the Army Air Corps offered him an instructor position training replacement crews in the United States. There was no hesitation. He told headquarters to cut the orders.

Lucky was going home.

20

HOME

Lucky checked his uniform and took a deep breath before knocking on Nell Louise Sullivan's door in Chattanooga.

He'd come to Tennessee soon after returning to the United States on the USS *George Washington*. Lucky played poker every day during the twelve-day crossing, arriving in New York with a fat bankroll and thirty days of leave.

He'd spent a few days with his parents in Chattanooga. Since arriving, he'd been lauded and applauded and paraded around as the returning war hero. The Sunday before, he'd been asked by the pastor of his family's church to say a few words about his service in Europe. The church fell silent waiting, but Lucky declined. He didn't want to talk about what he'd survived. Those memories were better left overseas.

But there was no getting around calling on Mrs. Sullivan. Memories of the last time he'd been at the house with Sully flooded back. They'd arrived with plans to join the Royal Canadian Air Force and become fighter pilots. The memory brought a slight smile to his face because of how naive they'd been. Both he and Sully thought there was glory to be won in war. They imagined returning to Chattanooga heroes.

Lucky now knew that was a myth. He understood as only a man who had lost everything that war was folly. It took his best friend's life. It took his idealism and left him with nothing but the trauma of losing friends and nightmares sparked by hours in the cold blue, battling fighters, teeth-rattling flak, and frostbite.

And for what?

Even fighting one of the world's greatest evils wasn't enough for Lucky. He didn't regret his service. He'd answered the call and was proud to have done so. Lucky only wished it were for something other than war.

After Lucky knocked, Sully's mother opened the door in shock. She didn't expect to see Lucky on her stoop again. Mrs. Sullivan looked thin and older, like the stress of losing her only son was weighing on her. She offered Lucky the best smile she could muster and invited him inside.

Lucky sat on the couch in the living room. His head hurt. He'd suppressed the memory of Sully's funeral for so long, and now it was bubbling up to the surface again. After small talk about his return home and his arrival in Chattanooga, Lucky told Mrs. Sullivan about his visits with Sully, the funeral, and how highly regarded her son was among his fellow pilots.

"He was doing what he wanted to do, and he was at rest," Lucky said.

Mrs. Sullivan listened quietly, a stoic look on her face.

Tears welled up in her eyes as Lucky finished. She was proud of her son and his sacrifice, but she was not happy with his final resting place. She wanted him home.

"You buried him among strangers," Mrs. Sullivan told Lucky. "I want you to bring his remains home."

Lucky looked down at his crushed, olive-green hat in his lap. He had no answer. What she was asking was beyond his abilities.

"Mrs. Sullivan, I'm very, very sorry, but he was flying for the British, not for the Americans, and I have no influence with the Royal Canadian Air Force," Lucky said, pausing for a second to find the right words, if they even existed. "I'm just a captain in the Eighth Air Force. I didn't have any control over what they did with his remains."

Mrs. Sullivan shook her head. She didn't want to hear what couldn't be done. She wanted her son home, and she thought Lucky was the man to do it. "You were his best friend, and he's over there among all those strangers and I want his remains brought home and I want you to do it," she said again, this time not as a request but a demand.

Lucky didn't know what to say to her. He'd do anything to comfort her and by extension Sully, but what she was asking him to do was impossible. Lucky might be home, but he was not free of obligations. He was still in the Army, awaiting orders to his next duty station. Even if he could get back overseas, there was no way he could have Sully's remains transported home. The world was at war.

Lucky looked Mrs. Sullivan in the eye. There was no use in keeping her hopes up. "Mrs. Sullivan, I'm very, very sorry, but there's nothing I can do," he said. "I'm powerless to do anything. He was flying for the Canadians, and I have no connection with them or any influence with them at all. This is wartime; maybe after the war, there would be some opportunity to repatriate his remains, but during wartime, I'm not sure that it could be even approached."

Mrs. Sullivan shook her head as she dabbed away tears. Lucky knew she heard him, but she refused to accept it. It was clear there was nothing left to talk about if Lucky couldn't bring her son home.

Mrs. Sullivan saw Lucky to the door. When he'd left two years before, Lucky hoped he'd follow his friend on a great adventure. There was no hope this time. Just the hollow feeling left by the absence of Sully and the trauma felt by his mother, who'd now lost a husband and son to war. His heart ached for her. All he wanted to do was make it right, but was helpless to do so. He felt nothing but despair.

At the door, Lucky tried to thank Mrs. Sullivan for seeing him. She gave him a nod and closed the door without saying another word.

Mrs. Sullivan never spoke to Lucky again.

After thirty days' leave, Lucky begged the Air Corps to make him a trainer, but they sent him to a redistribution center down in Miami Beach instead. His billet was at the Cadillac Hotel, which overlooked the shoreline. His only duty was to show up for morning roll call. Otherwise, he spent his days on the beach or at the pool. Each man was rationed whiskey through coupons redeemable at the local liquor stores, but for Lucky and the others, the coupons were currency swapped, traded, and hoarded so they could drink all they could hold. Lucky stayed pretty boozed up in part because the inactivity was taking a terrific toll on his mental health.

Since arriving home, he'd been bored and stressed. Overseas, he'd been too busy to process the trauma. In Miami, Lucky was visiting Bremen in his nightmares, and survivor's guilt hung over him like the English fog.

Sully.

Via, his flight school classmate who flew with Major Kidd over Bremen, was recovering from his wounds but would never fly again.

Even Cavanaugh, whom Lucky heard transitioned to B-29s and joined a crew with Major White, the man who'd yanked out his chair during a poker game. Both men were killed when their plane hit a mountain during training.

Soon after arriving in Miami, Lucky got a letter from Eleanor. She was coming to South Florida on the train expecting a diamond ring and a lifelong commitment.

But that was not in Lucky's plans.

He'd loved her in South Carolina, and she'd kept his spirits up in England, even providing him with a lucky stocking. But Lucky wasn't in love with her any longer and didn't want to get married. The man who almost washed out of flight school was replaced with a seasoned pilot who understood life was fleeting. He planned to enjoy every second of it.

Lucky broke it off soon after she arrived in Miami and put her back on the train to South Carolina.

"Honey, I'm just really sorry," Lucky told her. "You've been lovely to me all these months. But it is over. I'm not the person I was when you first met me."

Eleanor got back on the train heartbroken. It was heartless, and Lucky felt terrible doing it, but knew he wasn't a catch. It was better to break it off and not string her along while he drank away the trauma of war.

After a full day and night at the bars chasing the bottom of a bottle, Lucky and some of the others waiting for assignments returned to the hotel. It was five in the morning. Lucky was headed for his room and a couple of hours of sleep when a friend tapped him on the shoulder.

"You'd better look at the bulletin board, Lucky."

Lucky waved him off. "What the heck for?" he said.

"You'd better look at the bulletin board."

Lucky reluctantly stopped in the lobby and through a drunken haze made out his name on the list for physicals. Damn it. Lucky checked his watch. He had about an hour. He hit the sack and then, between cups of coffee, cleaned up and headed for the hospital.

The first step was a fourteen-page questionnaire about his mental health. Lucky's hangover had a hangover, and he was in no mood for the whole exercise. He checked yes for everything and headed to the dental clinic intent on checking the boxes as fast as possible so he could get back to his bed.

Lucky was dozing in the dentist chair when he heard a corporal coming down the hall.

"Captain Luckadoo, Captain Luckadoo! Where in the world is Captain Luckadoo?"

The dentist stopped. "Hey, that's you."

Lucky shrugged. The dentist flagged down the corporal.

"Sir, would you please come with me?" he said.

"Why?" Lucky said.

He noticed the corporal had the questionnaire in his hand. And across the front of it in great big red letters was stamped STOP PROCESSING. The corporal took Lucky to the office of a wizened, little major. His nameplate said he was a psychiatrist. The office was spartan with a metal desk and three chairs. The major met Lucky at the door. He had thick glasses and only came to Lucky's chest. They shook hands, and Lucky took a chair in front of his desk. The major sat down behind it and reviewed Lucky's questionnaire.

When he was done, he looked up at Lucky. "Well, based on your answers to the questionnaire, we're gonna send you over to the recovery hospital in Saint Petersburg," the major told him.

"I don't want to go to a rest home in Saint Petersburg," Lucky said. "For crying out loud, I want an assignment. I want something to do because I haven't flown for three months, and I haven't had any responsibility, and you know, I ought to be imparting some experience to somebody that's gonna be facing what I did who hasn't done so yet."

The major glanced down at Lucky's answers and then

shook his head. "No, you're due a rest," he said. "You turned in this kind of report. We think you're ready for the rest home."

Lucky had to swallow down the rage. Send him to a hospital to recover? From what? Boredom. He'd never gone to or needed a rest, even when he was facing fighters and flak on a daily basis. Now the Air Corps was going to send him for a rest after he was safe and bored in the United States.

"No, goddamn it, I need an assignment," Lucky said. "I don't need to go to this rest hospital."

The major shook his head as he filled out Lucky's orders. "Well, if we deem that you are a candidate for this hospital, you have to go for six weeks," he said. "You be on the train at five o'clock this afternoon to Saint Petersburg or you're gonna be court-martialed."

Lucky went back to the hotel and packed. He had no choice. The next day, now sobered up, Lucky was standing in front of the commandant of the hospital. Lucky's file was on the colonel's desk. When Lucky arrived, he'd requested the meeting hoping to get an assignment, not a rest.

"Why are you here?" the colonel asked him.

"Well, I'll be damned if I know, Colonel."

"Well, I'm sorry that they sent you here, but as long as you're here, of course, the Air Force says you've got to stay for six weeks. You can lie on the beach, or you can go down to the bar on the corner, or you can do whatever you want to, but you just have to report to roll call every morning at eight o'clock."

Lucky had already found the bar, called the Sundowner. He'd joined some others there after arriving the night before.

"OK, you can find me, sir, down at the Sundowner," Lucky said.

The colonel nodded. He was flipping through Lucky's file. "I see you're a pilot," the colonel said.

"Yes, sir."

"Well, you know, I'm entitled to my own airplane, but I'm not a pilot. And I wondered if you'd be willing to stay here and be my personal pilot if I get an airplane."

Lucky did not want to be a flying taxi driver. "Well, sir, with all due respect, I appreciate the offer, but I think I'd be much more useful to the service if I were in an instructor position somewhere and had a chance to instruct crews that are being replaced going overseas, because I was one of the first returnees to the States."

Six weeks later, Lucky got orders to Bryan, Texas, to learn how to fly instruments, a skill he needed in England flying through the fog. But the training was excellent, and Lucky discovered that Bill McKenzie, a fraternity brother from Chattanooga, was an instructor.

Bill was madly in love with one of the local girls and roped Lucky in as his wingman. Bill's girlfriend had a houseguest who needed a date. Lucky agreed to the blind date, and they all met at a wedding reception before retreating to the officers' club for dinner, dancing, and drinks. Bill's girlfriend's sister—Bobby—was also part of the group.

It was dusk, and everyone was in the shadows when they got acquainted. When they got to the club, everyone was in the light. Lucky took one look at Bobby and fell in love.

Oh my god, I've got the wrong date, he thought.

Toward the end of the night, Lucky pulled Bobby aside. "Could I have your phone number? I'd like to call you, and we'll go out to dinner or something."

Bobby offered a coy smile. "I'm not sure I can fit you into my pattern," she said. "I'm dated up for the next two weeks."

Lucky knew how to fly a pattern. "OK," he said. "Put me down for two weeks from now."

Two weeks later, Lucky took Bobby out for dinner. She was the middle daughter of a U.S. ambassador from Bryan. Her father hoped for a boy, so Barbara became Bobby. Bobby grew up in Europe with her sisters, and while her parents were fulfilling their diplomatic duties, Bobby was shunted off to either France or Switzerland, where she and her sisters were homeschooled. When they studied Rome, they went there. Same with Egypt and Italy. Lucky knew she was too smart to have hooked up with him. Bobby was the luckiest thing that ever happened to him, and it was because the Air Corps decided to train him to fly instruments.

After that first date, he was in the front of the pattern, even after he finished instrument training and B-17 instructor school in Ohio. Lucky and Bobby wrote letters back and forth, and the romance blossomed.

She was the one. Lucky knew it. He just had to get back to Texas to seal the deal. After graduating from B-17 Flight Instructor School in Ohio, he went through Texas on his way to Florida. He and Bobby went out a couple of times. On his last date before he had to leave, Lucky showed her an engagement ring.

"What do you think of this?"

"Well, it's beautiful," she said. "Gorgeous."

"Well, I just want to know your opinion about it," Lucky said and put it back in his pocket.

Bobby folded her hands across her chest. He was teasing her, that she knew, but she wasn't sure why.

"Well, if you like it well enough, why don't you put it on?" Lucky said.

"What for?" she said.

"Because I want to marry you."

"You what?" Bobby was stunned.

"Yeah, we need to get married."

Lucky returned from England searching for peace. He found it with Bobby. That was when he knew she was forever because she allowed him to think of something he'd forgotten since England. A future. He no longer lived moment to moment. He now thought about what building a life might look like starting with the love of his life.

They were engaged in Texas just before he headed to Mac-Dill Field in Tampa, Florida. Bobby saying yes was one thing. The next step was getting the approval of her father, Bill.

"We have to go to New York and tell my father that we're going to be married," Bobby said.

Junior and Bobby's mother were divorced, and he had an apartment in New York City's Plaza Hotel. Lucky arranged to meet there so he could ask for Bobby's hand. They met for tea at the hotel and announced that they were going to be married.

"I don't approve," Bill said.

Lucky found out later her father envisioned his daughter would marry an aristocrat or royalty, and a captain in the Air Force wasn't aristocratic enough.

"I beg your pardon?" Lucky said.

"No," he said. "It won't last. It won't last six months. You'll be in here begging for a divorce within six months. I don't approve."

Bobby wasn't hearing it. "Well, Dad, we're going to be married because we're in love, on February 2 in Bryan, Texas, at Saint Andrews Episcopal Church, and if you'd care to be there, you'll be welcome, but otherwise, we're going to be married anyway."

Lucky and Bobby left together. Will Jr., as his family called him, knew General Hap Arnold, the Chief of Staff of the Air Force, and called in a favor. Lucky found out later how the call went down.

"Hap, I want you to court-martial Captain John Luckadoo."

Arnold was perplexed. "My goodness, Bill, what for?"

"He wants to marry my daughter," Bill said.

The general wasn't going to play along and shut it down immediately. "Well, you know, Bill, that's hardly grounds for a court-martial," Arnold told Bill.

"Well, it certainly is in my book," Bill said before hanging up.

Despite Will Jr.'s protest, Lucky and Bobby were married in Bryan, Texas, in February 1946. He did show up and agreed to escort his daughter down the aisle. As they walked, he made sure every guest heard him talking to his daughter.

"You know, you still don't have to go through with this."

Bobby continued to the altar, where Lucky was waiting. When he got to the pulpit, the rector asked him who gives this woman to be married. Will Jr. didn't say a word. Bobby's grandmother finally stood up and escorted him by his coattails like a child back to his seat. He never agreed, but the ceremony continued on without his consent.

And he never, never approved.

A little more than a year later, Will Jr., on his way to take over as ambassador of Uruguay, passed away from a heart attack. He was fifty-three.

Lucky was in his office at MacDill Field when his phone rang. He was part of a combat crew inspection team. It was his job to certify crews for combat, but one of his crews was about to mutiny.

Lucky was puzzled. Mutiny? Over what?

"The crew is so scared of the pilot and they're so mad at him, they're going to mutiny," the operations officer said. "And you've got to check him out."

Lucky went down to the flight line as the crew was about to take a check flight. When he got to the B-17, he spotted the pilot. It was Blackie, the flight instructor from South Carolina who had saved Lucky's career during flight school. He'd joined the Air Corps and was preparing to head overseas. Blackie had trained thousands of students and didn't recognize Lucky, but there was no mistaking it. Lucky motioned to Blackie, now a captain, to come over so they could talk before the flight.

"Captain, what's the problem here with your crew?"

"They're a bunch of goddamn idiots," he said. "They don't know what they're doing, and we've got to get to combat."

Lucky wasn't so sure. He wanted to see how the crew performed, but it was up to the pilot—the crew's commander—to lead the way. Lucky grabbed his gear and started toward the plane.

"Let's see how you do," Lucky said. "I'm going to take you up on a test flight, and I'm going to pull a prop on you or an engine or drop the wheels or flaps or something and see how you react to emergencies."

Lucky could feel the animosity between Blackie and the crew as they went through preflight. At the end of the runway, Lucky, sitting in the copilot seat, instructed Blackie to take off and climb to fifteen hundred feet.

"I'll tell you what to do from there," Lucky said.

They started down the runway, and Blackie froze on the controls. Lucky grabbed the controls and pulled up. The bomber went through the trees at the end of the runway, but stayed airborne. Lucky's heart was pounding in his chest. He figured that was his twenty-sixth mission right there.

When the bomber got to altitude, Blackie took over. It was clear to Lucky he could no more fly the airplane than beans. He was an excellent pilot on the Vultee BT-13 Valiant trainer but failed in every respect as a bomber pilot. Lucky didn't even let him land. After the flight, as the crew was getting out, Lucky stopped Blackie in the cockpit.

"Captain, I'm very sorry," he said. "You're not combat ready, and I will not under any circumstances certify you for an airplane commander."

Blackie was deflated. He begged Lucky to pass him. "I've got to get to combat," he said.

But Lucky knew better. It wasn't about him.

"Not with nine men on your shoulders, you don't. You might be all right to fly cargo or transports, but you've got the responsibility of nine other lives every time you take off. And that's a heavy responsibility, and you can't handle it."

Lucky left Blackie in the cockpit, the irony not lost on him that he'd just ended the bomber career of the man who'd saved his flying career. That night, there was a knock at Lucky's door. It was Blackie. Tears were streaming down his face.

"Captain, I've got to get to combat," he said when Lucky opened the door.

"Why?" Lucky asked.

Lucky knew what was in store for the crews he was training. Combat wasn't something anyone wanted. Lucky sensed this wasn't a macho move. There was something driving Blackie. After a few minutes of asking him why in different ways, Blackie finally revealed the truth. "I've been divorced and have some domestic problems," he said, looking down at his boots. "I want to go to combat."

Lucky knew what that meant. This was a death wish. He didn't care whether he took nine other people with him. Lucky wasn't going to let him go to combat just to get back at his wife.

"I'm awful sorry, Captain, I can't be responsible for letting you do that," Lucky told him. "I'll recommend you for transport or cargo, but not as an airplane commander of a B-17."

Blackie left defeated.

Lucky never told him how he'd gotten him through flight school.

21

LAST FLIGHT

The sky over Fort Worth was clear as Lucky took off in a B-25, one of the executive planes assigned to the Eighth Air Force. In the pocket of his flight suit, he had two letters. One was from the commanding general of the Eighth Air Force, and the other was his resignation.

If all went well, this was his last flight as an air force officer.

Three years before, Lucky was still at MacDill when the Allies defeated Nazi Germany. With no need for more B-17 crews in Europe, Lucky transitioned to B-29s and was preparing to deploy to the Pacific when the United States dropped the atomic bomb and ended the war with Japan.

World War II was over, and Lucky was offered an opportunity to join the regular Air Force. The Air Corps split from the Army and needed capable officers.

Now that the war was over, Lucky let himself think about a future. He was newly married, and for the first time since

1942, he had designs on building a life with Bobby. Military service appealed to him, and he was good at it. He'd found a home in the Air Force and didn't have a burning ambition to return to college, so he and Bobby figured the military would be his career.

After taking the exam and getting accepted, Lucky found out the Air Force allowed newly integrated officers to go to any college in America under full pay and allowances, including flying pay, which in those days was a 50 percent bonus above the base salary. Lucky could get his degree and let Uncle Sam pay for it. If the Air Force was going to let him go to college, he'd be a fool not to do it. He set his sights on a bachelor's degree and a law degree if he could swing it. He figured some legal training would be helpful regardless of his profession.

Lucky was accepted to Stanford University and was eyeing the fall of 1948 to start, but his orders never came. He was based at Carswell Air Force Base in Fort Worth as an air inspector for operations and training for the Eighth Air Force. Unsure why his orders were delayed, he got a plane and flew down to Maxwell Field in Montgomery, Alabama. That is where the Air University administered the program. Lucky met with the program manager to inquire about his orders. The officer found Lucky's file and was thumbing through it as Lucky explained the reason for his visit.

"You've got this wonderful program to go back to college for the newly integrated officers. I applied and got accepted, but I have never gotten any orders. How come?"

The officer looked at Lucky's application and then back at him. "How old are you?"

"I'm twenty-six," Lucky said.

The officer nodded like he had the problem figured out. "You know we've got an age limit of thirty-two in this program," the officer said.

Lucky was aware but knew he was well under the cutoff.

"Well, we've got so many in the pipeline ahead of you that if they don't get in before they reach thirty-two, then they lose out."

It was a waiting game. Lucky understood and just needed to know how long his orders would be delayed.

"According to our calculations, just before your thirty-second birthday," the officer said.

Lucky practically fell out of his chair. "You're telling me that I've got to wait another six years," Lucky said. "I've been out of college now for six years and I'd have to wait another six to go back to school?"

The officer closed Lucky's file and folded his hands. "Sorry, but that's the situation."

Lucky left dejected. He flew back to Texas and talked to Bobby. He didn't want to wait to start school. Over dinner, Bobby and Lucky tried to figure out their future. Bobby was happy to be a military spouse, but only if it made sense for Lucky.

"Wait twelve years before I go back to college is ridiculous, and if I were a civilian, I could go to college now under the GI Bill, so I think I'll resign my commission," he said, after thinking about his options on the flight home.

"Well, I can't blame you. If you feel like that's what you want to do, I'm with you," Bobby said.

The next day, Lucky submitted his resignation. When the colonel in charge of the personnel division in the Eighth Air Force headquarters got it, he called Lucky. He'd served with Lucky previously in the air inspectors division and thought highly of him.

"Luckadoo, have you lost your mind?" the colonel said. "You're throwing out a military career just to go back to college?"

Lucky told the colonel it was what he wanted to do. He didn't want to wait more than a decade to go to school.

"I'll tell you what," the colonel said. "I'll give you just twenty-four hours, and you either withdraw this resignation or I'm going to endorse it to the effect that you are not the caliber of individual that should ever have been rendered a regular commission."

Lucky couldn't believe what he was hearing. He'd passed the exams, and the air force welcomed him with open arms. The colonel had no authority to place that endorsement on his letter.

"My record won't support it, and the regulations say it's either approved or disapproved, but if you put any kind of endorsement like that on my resignation, it's illegal."

Lucky had no idea why the colonel was giving him such a hard time. They'd worked together without this kind of rancor. The Air Force was in its infancy, and maybe the colonel wanted to keep as much institutional knowledge as he could in the service. But threatening Lucky with an illegal endorsement wasn't the answer. Lucky later found out that because the colonel was a West Pointer, he took a dim view of reservists getting a regular commission without going through the military academy.

"You try me," the colonel said.

Lucky needed more time to think and maneuver. There was no way he was staying in the Air Force. He just had to figure out a way to get out without the colonel disparaging his file. "Well, sir, this is Thursday, would you kindly give me to Monday morning to reconsider?"

The colonel took a second to think it over. "All right. You be in here at eight o'clock sharp with the right answer, or you're toast," he said before killing the line.

Lucky had no choice but to go over the colonel's head. After hanging up, he made a call to Major General Roger Ramey's office. He was the commanding general of the Eighth Air Force. Lucky got his secretary.

"I need five minutes with the general for a personal matter. Could you arrange an appointment?"

The secretary consulted the general's schedule and came back with bad news. "Well, Captain, I'm sorry, he's out on an inspection trip, and he won't be back until Sunday morning at eleven o'clock, for about an hour, and then he's going out again on another trip."

Lucky only needed five minutes with him, but there was no way to fit into his schedule until Sunday. His secretary told Lucky he would be working over the weekend.

"Why don't you call him?"

On Sunday morning, Lucky called Ramey at his office. The general was at his desk. Lucky told him he had a personal matter and needed five minutes.

"Would you grant me an audience?"

"Sure, come on out," Ramey said.

Lucky was living off base. He got into his uniform and headed to the headquarters. In Ramey's office, Lucky told the general about his desire to go to college and his reasons for resigning. Ramey agreed with Lucky. The colonel couldn't attach a recommendation to his resignation letter.

"Can you type?" Ramey asked Lucky.

"Yes, sir."

Ramey motioned toward his secretary's desk. "You go out there and get on my secretary's typewriter, and you type up an endorsement, approved for my signature."

Lucky typed a letter, and Ramey signed it.

"Now, my advice to you is that you're going to get this kind of pushback possibly all the way up through the chain of command, so my suggestion is you hand-carry this through the Pentagon."

The next morning, Lucky was headed for Washington. He spent a couple of hours at the Pentagon walking his resignation from office to office as the Air Force out-processed him. Ramey was right. Lucky got pushback, but the general's letter greased the skids.

When the day was done, Lucky was no longer going to be an active-duty officer. He'd traded his wings for a college degree. Even with his release from active duty, he missed enrollment in Stanford. But with some help from Bobby's mother, he got into the University of Denver under the GI Bill and graduated in 1950 with a bachelor of science in business administration and a bright future in real estate.

His life was finally his own, and with Bobby at his side, the future was bright. After graduation, the Luckadoos found their way back to Texas, where they built a life together that included a daughter. Lucky and Bobby were married for seventy-one years. The love of Lucky's life passed away in 2017.

When Lucky took stock of his life, he knew that it turned out in part because of his work ethic, character, and values. His childhood was hard but joyful. He'd answered the call to serve and did so without reservations. He'd led operations for two squadrons and prepared numerous crews for the crucible of combat when he returned after his tour.

But that wasn't all of it.

Lucky was close to washing out of flight school except for the good fortune of getting one more chance with an instructor that could teach him how to be a pilot. He'd led his crew and others to safety when the skies of Bremen were claiming the 100th Bomb Group's best. He had defied the odds and flown twenty-five missions and survived, a feat of which far too many others had fallen short. The war had claimed too many friends, including his best one. And when he'd returned to the United States, he'd found the love of his life by chance on a blind date with another woman and won her over even after her father disapproved.

Lucky was a lot of things. Pilot. Air Force officer. Husband. Father.

And most of all, he was just damn lucky.

AFTERWORD

I loved flying.

Still do.

But I didn't always love the memories that came with it, especially being shot at while at the controls of a B-17. Like many of my contemporaries, I didn't talk about my wartime experiences for more than fifty years because recalling them was not a pleasant exercise. Those weren't the happiest days. In fact, to be perfectly honest, I found verbalizing what transpired an agonizing chore. But over time, it has been cathartic. I've since taken part in numerous documentaries and oral histories, but this book is the first time my story has been captured in its entirety.

I want *Damn Lucky* to be an accurate and forthright documentation of that horrendous period in my life, as the losses haunt me still. Yet I am keenly aware how incredibly blessed I am to have survived it when so many did not. I lived to marry a wonderful woman, have a family, and live a productive life. My beautiful Bobby was by far the luckiest thing that happened to me in my entire lifetime, and her profound effect on me during our seventy-one years together was what made me what I am today. Without her phenomenal insight and wisdom, I would have undoubtedly floundered aimlessly about through my adulthood and never amounted to anything, but with her astute counsel and guidance, I hope my life has attained some meaning. And although I objected to the Air Force sending me to instrument pilot school in Bryan at the time, it turned out to be my luckiest day—because that is where I met her.

Now at ninety-nine years of age, I can still see the faces of those lost in their prime who were not as fortunate as I, or as lucky. The European air war was an untested battlefield, and I shall always question some of the ill-advised decisions of those in charge, including the replacement of all the original copilots in the 100th Bomb Group with newly minted graduates of my flight school class, just prior to being shipped out to combat. Similarly, relegating copilots of the Eighth Air Force to the tail gun position of the lead ships, with absolutely no training whatsoever as aerial gunners, left the B-17s vulnerable and unprotected from rear fighter attacks. Air combat was new and had no time-tested guidelines, and yet any rational person has to question the wisdom of those decisions.

We were young citizen-soldiers, terribly naive and gullible about what we would be confronted with in the air war over Europe and the profound effect it would have upon every fiber of our being for the rest of our lives. We were all afraid, but it was beyond our power to quit. We volunteered for the service and, once trained and overseas, felt we had no choice but to fulfill the mission assigned. My hope is that this book honors the men with whom I served by telling the truth about what it took to climb into the cold blue and fight for our lives over and over again. We found ourselves thrust into a world war, proudly answering the call to defend our freedoms. They dubbed us *the Greatest Generation,* but we veterans of World War II consider only those who gave the last full measure to be the true heroes.

But they weren't the only heroes.

As a result of the Japanese attack at Pearl Harbor, the United States was galvanized into action, not only in mobilizing its military manpower but also the civilian population to ratchet up its enormous production capacity. It was unlike anything the world has ever seen. Without that unfailing and unprecedented contribution and support, we would never have prevailed—and yet we have failed to acknowledge it adequately. A National Day of Recognition for our Home Front Heroes remains one of my lifetime ambitions. Every frontline veteran of war feels an eternal debt to all those civilian supporters, who not only sacrificed to outproduce the world but kept the home fires burning so we had a home to return to and fight for. Surely such recognition and expression of appreciation is long overdue.

While being terribly proud to have served my country when called upon in time of need, I now view armed conflict as a sad commentary on adversaries' failure to reach a reasonable resolution of their differences. While defeating the Nazis in Europe and the Japanese in the Pacific were noble causes, from my vantage point, I see only war's victims. War is futile and foolish. There are no victors, only victims. And sadly, if you look at history and you go back to the beginning of time, wars have not accomplished anything. I am appalled that diplomacy fails to resolve differences. Time and again, we find that wars are usually fomented by old men, but always fought by young men—and now women.

Having survived such folly, I now fear the freedoms bought with the lives and blood of my generation are being squandered by the current generation. I am appalled that we stand today on the precipice of a civil war. We are, actually, the Dis-United States of America. We are witnessing the betrayal of our cherished values from within—as well as without.

Never forget that we are all first and foremost Americans. We should look for common goals and seek compromise, rather than conquering the other side, which serves only to divide us. As private citizens, we can do something to alter our perspective. United, we've done amazing things: We defeated fascism, put a man on the moon, and created a cultural and economic empire that is the envy of the world.

Somehow, we've forgotten that. America will never be perfect. It will always have problems. But the only solution is to stay together and find common ground. Stay united. We proved that in World War II, and we can prove it again.

—John "Lucky" Luckadoo, Major, USAF
(Ret.) 100th Bomb Group (H)
Dallas, Texas

What you hold in your hands is one man's harrowing glimpse of total war from five miles high. You were a lucky bastard if you survived your training, much less your missions. Major John "Lucky" Luckadoo was just that, damn lucky.

We thank him for sharing this memoir. We cannot express enough our gratitude to all the men and women who served in World War II, especially that of the Mighty Eighth and the 100th Bombardment Group. If you enjoy the story of Lucky, then there are many more stories of the "Bloody Hundredth" for you to access at www.100thbg.com.

Our mission is simple. The 100th Bomb Group Foundation is dedicated to the preservation and dissemination of firsthand historical accounts of the men, missions, and machines that fought in the skies over Europe during World War II. The foundation's extensive archives, museum exhibits, publications, and artifacts associated with this famous B-17 bomber unit provide a worldwide platform to educate generations, keeping alive the bravery and sacrifice that ensure our freedom still today.

We hope you will join in our mission to preserve this

history and legacy of the 100th Bomb Group and the Mighty
Eighth.

—Michael P. Faley
100th Bomb Group and Eighth Air
Force Historian

A NOTE ON SOURCES

The bulk of the narrative was constructed using exclusive interviews with Lucky in 2020. Michael Faley's treasure trove of pictures and documents on www.100thbg.com were invaluable. The 100th Bomb Group Foundation's collection is unsurpassed and a real treasure for anyone interested in the European air war.

Additional background material came from the following books:

Bowman, Martin. **Castles in the Air.**
Bowman, Martin. **Clash of Eagles: USAAF 8th Air Force Bombers Versus the Luftwaffe in World War II.**
Caidin, Martin. **Black Thursday: The Story of the Schweinfurt.**
Crosby, Harry H. **A Wing and a Prayer: The "Bloody 100th" Bomb Group of the U.S. Eighth Air Force in Action over Europe in World War II.**

Friedrich, Jörg. **The Fire: The Bombing of Germany, 1940–1945.**

Galland, Adolf, Josef Kammhuber, et al. **Fighting the Bombers: The Luftwaffe's Struggle Against the Allied Bomber Offensive.**

Jackson, Robert. **Bomber!: Famous Bomber Missions of World War II.**

Miller, Donald L. **Masters of the Air: America's Bomber Boys Who Fought the Air War Against Nazi Germany.**

Morris, Rob. **Untold Valor: Forgotten Stories of American Bomber Crews over Europe in World War II.**

Murray, Williamson. **Luftwaffe.**

Nijboer, Donald. **Flak in World War II.**

Sebald, W. G. **On the Natural History of Destruction.**

Weal, John. **Focke-Wulf Fw 190 Aces of the Western Front.**

Yenne, Bill. **Big Week: Six Days that Changed the Course of World War II.**

ACKNOWLEDGMENTS

My name might be on the cover, but this book exists because of a team. First, thank you to my family for supporting me while I wrote this. I know you guys didn't always want to talk about Luftwaffe tactics or the difference between the G and F models, but you were kind enough to listen. This book exists because of your support.

Hat tip to Kelly Kennedy for reading early drafts and helping me shape it into the version you read. Her insight was instrumental in improving the manuscript. She is one of the best writers I know.

Thanks to Frank Weimann, my agent, for not only making this book a reality, but for being a friend and sounding board. He believed in the idea from the start and made sure we found it a home. But I owe Frank for more than just his sage advice. He is a friend and mentor.

Thanks also to Marc Resnick and Lily Cronig at St. Martin's Press for elevating my work one edit at a time. They both had the same comment after the first draft that pulled the whole story together. From the start they cared about the book as much as I did and that goes a long way. I look forward to working with them for a long time—and no doubt my work will be better for it.

Finally, Mike Faley and Nancy Putnam from the 100th Bomb Group Foundation read and fact-checked the manuscript for me. They caught some embarrassing errors and helped me write this extraordinary story accurately (if an error got through it is my fault). I am in their debt. Mike also found the amazing photos and helped educate me on the 100th and the air war. If you enjoyed the book, please visit and support the 100th Bomb Group Foundation. They are doing amazing work.

But most of all, thank you to Lucky for trusting me with his story. He was generous with his time and, most of all, his memories. The conversations weren't easy and I am forever grateful that he was willing to go back into his memory and experience the horror of war again for me.

We called the book *Damn Lucky*. The title was Lucky's idea from the start. Lucky understood how fortunate he was to survive, return home, and marry the love of his life. I'm fortunate to help amplify his story but, most of all, I'm damn lucky to consider him a friend.

INDEX

A-20 bombers, 36

African Front, 13, 119

Afrika Korps, 119

Air Corps Tactical School,
Montgomery, Alabama,
67

airplane(s). *See also* B-17
bombers

A-20 bomber, 36

Avro Lancaster, 240

B-17 bomber (Flying
Fortress), 1–10, 37–55,
59–63, 65–70, 71–82,
83–98, 99–112, 113–22,
123–37, 139–52,
153–65, 167–82,
183–99, 202–12,
214–16, 220, 228,
237–47, 249–60, 264?,
270, 273–76, 277,
285–86, 289

B-17G bomber, 79, 256

B-24 bomber, 68–69, 146,
252

B-25 bomber, 36, 277

B-26 bomber, 36

B-29 bomber, 265, 277

bathroom relief in, 101

Bristol Blenheim bomber,
227

Focke-Wulf Fw 190 fighter,
71, 77–80, 101–2, 120,
132–33, 156–65,
169–88, 191, 197,
206–10

Hawker Hurricane, 227

Hawker Typhoon, 213, 220,
225, 227–28, 231–32,
234

high-altitude missions in,
99–112, 144

Ju 88, 208–9

Me 109, 91, 101, 120, 171,
177, 256–57

airplane(s) (*continued*)
   Me 110, 89–91, 256–57
   Mosquito, 146, 240,
      260
   P47 Thunderbolt, 146,
      156–57
   PT-17, 24
   Supermarine Spitfire,
      213–16, 225, 227
   targeting equipment on, 69,
      75, 81, 124–25, 172,
      175, 178, 194, 257
   Vultee BT-13 Valiant
      "Vibrator," 24–33,
      274
Alice from Dallas II (B-17),
   249, 255–59
Alkire, Darr, 37–38,
   50
American Stork Club,
   224
antiaircraft fire (flak)
   88 mm, 103
   Allied, 60
   German, 3–4, 76, 80–81,
      102–7, 129–32, 143,
      147, 167–82, 183–85,
      193, 197, 207–8, 210,
      245, 257
Army Air Corps. *See also*
      Eighth Air Force, Third
      Bombardment Division;
      100th Bomb Group,
      Eighth Air Force
   Lucky's enlistment to,
      21–22

   offensive strategies of,
      67–70, 78–79, 102–5,
      124–25, 130, 145–49,
      193–94, 201, 252–53,
      286
   tour-of-duty requirements
      of, 72, 123–24, 135,
      252
   training by, 23–34, 36–50,
      62–63, 66–67, 81, 83,
      86, 92, 95–96, 136,
      260, 264, 270, 273–76
Arnold, Hap, 272
Avon Park, Florida, 24
Avro Lancaster bombers, 240

B-17 bombers (Flying
      Fortresses), 1, 3, 5,
      8–10, 53–55, 59–61,
      65, 68, 70, 71–73, 77,
      80, 82, 84–85, 87–91,
      93–94, 97–98, 99–112,
      113–22, 126–35, 137,
      139–52, 153–65,
      167–71, 173–74,
      176–77, 179–82, 183–93,
      195–99, 202–12,
      214–16, 220, 228,
      237–47, 249–56,
      258–60, 277, 285, 289
   characteristics of, 2, 6–7, 37,
      69, 75, 256
   crews of, 39–43, 75–76
   formation flying by, 4, 74–75,
      78, 102–7, 131–32,

146–47, 183, 185–87,
    252–53
G model, 79, 256
Norden bombsights on, 69,
    75, 81, 124–25, 172,
    175, 178, 194, 257
training on, 37–52, 62–63,
    66–67, 81, 83, 86, 92,
    95–96, 136, 260, 270,
    273–76, 286
B-17 Flight Instructor School,
    Ohio, 270
B-24 bombers, 68–69, 146,
    252
B-25 bombers, 36, 277
B-26 bombers, 36
B-29 bombers, 265, 277
Baker, Leroy, 42–43,
    86–88
Barker, Al, 139–40, 145–46,
    177–79, 191
Barth, Theodore H., 69
Battle of Britain (WW II), 102,
    119–20, 218
Battle of Chickamauga (US
    Civil War), 14
Battle of Missionary Ridge (US
    Civil War), 13
Beatty, Maurice, 3–4, 7–10,
    142–44, 149, 152,
    154–55, 159–60,
    163–64, 168, 171, 176,
    183–85, 187, 189–91,
    211
Berlin, bombings of, 237–47
Berlin Zoo, 241

Blackman, "Blackie"
    (instructor), 27–33, 39,
    273–76
"Black Week" (WW II),
    201–12. See also
    Bremen, Germany,
    bombing of
Bremen raid during, 1–10,
    139–52, 153–65,
    167–82, 183–99, 201,
    204–5, 235, 237, 245,
    246, 249–50, 265, 283
Münster raid during, 203–12
Schweinfurt raid during,
    212
Blakely, Everett, 9, 154, 176,
    191, 194–96
"Bomber Mafia," 68, 125, 245
Brady, John, 206–7
Bragg, Braxton, 14
Bremen, Germany, bombing of,
    1–10, 139–52, 153–65,
    167–82, 183–99, 201,
    204–5, 235, 237, 245,
    246, 249–50, 265, 283
Bristol Blenheim bombers,
    227
British Women's Auxiliary Air
    Force (WAAF), 35
Brooke, Rupert, 122
Brookwood Military
    Cemetery, England, 234
Burgess, George, 153, 163–64,
    169, 183, 185
buzz bombs (V-1 flying
    bombs), 250

Captain's Ball (B-17), 161
Carey, Richard, 251–52
Carl L. Norden Inc., 69
Carswell Air Force Base, Fort
        Worth, Texas, 278
Casablanca Conference of
        1943, 70
Cavanaugh, Timothy J., 40–45,
        52–56, 75–77, 85, 88,
        95, 105, 107, 124,
        128–30, 136, 265
Chaney, Francis C., 40–45,
        51–52, 56, 75, 80–81,
        85, 93–95, 105, 107,
        124, 129, 136
Churchill, Winston, 70
Citizens' Military Training
        Camps, US, 14
Civil War, US, 13–14
Claridge's Hotel, London, 219
Cleven, Bucky, 64–65, 145–46,
        179–81, 191–92, 205,
        251
Combs, Victor, 42, 47–49, 52,
        93
Cooke, Richard, 42, 86–87, 93
Crosby, Bing, 33
Crosby, Harry, 64, 196

David, Aaron, 178
DeBlasio, Bill, 208–10
DeGregorio, Albert, 259
Delta Chi fraternity, 16, 21,
        24, 215
DeMarco, Bernard, 179–81

DeSanders, Bill, 251–52,
        255–59
Dickerson, Elder, 42, 86–88,
        91, 123, 135–36, 174
Doolittle, Jimmy, 65, 252–53
Douglass, James, 172, 175, 196
Douhet, Giulio, 68
Dunkirk, France, 120
Dye, Glenn W., 35–36, 38–55,
        59–60, 63, 66–67,
        71–74, 80–81, 84–85,
        88, 92–93, 95–97, 99,
        101, 105–10, 123–24,
        128–30, 135–37, 228,
        254, 259

Eaker, Ira C., 70
Egan, John "Buck," 64–65,
        146, 204–7
Ehlen, John, 178
Eighth Air Force, Third
        Bombardment
        Division (US). *See also*
        100th Bomb Group,
        Eighth Air Force
    95th Bomb Group of, 62,
        115, 146, 164, 185–87,
        207–12
    100th Bomb Group of, 1–10,
        35–57, 59–70, 71–82,
        83–98, 99–112, 113–22,
        123–37, 139–52,
        153–65, 167–82,
        183–99, 201–12, 237–47,
        249–60, 289–90

390th Bomb Group of, 62,
146, 207, 212
"Black Week" and, 201–12
offensive strategies of, 67–70,
78–79, 102–5, 124–25,
130, 145–49, 193–94,
201, 252–53, 286
at Thorpe Abbots Air Base,
England, 8, 59–70,
71–82, 83–98, 99–112,
113–22, 123–37,
139–52, 153–65,
167–82, 183–99,
201–12, 227–36,
237–47, 249–60
tour-of-duty requirements
in, 72, 123–24, 135, 252
training in, 23–34, 36–50,
81, 83, 86, 92, 95–96,
136, 260, 264, 270,
273–76
Eleanor (Lucky's girlfriend),
5, 33–34, 115–16, 127,
265–66
Ellis, Donald O., 43, 83, 85, 89
Elton, Albert, 251

Fairchild, Muir, 68
flak. *See* anti-aircraft fire
Flanagan, George, 42, 75, 85–86
Focke-Wulf Fw 190 fighters,
71, 77–80, 101–2, 120,
132–33, 156–65,
169–88, 191, 197,
206–10

Forkner, Edmund, 175
Fort Oglethorpe, Georgia, 14
418th Bomb Squadron,
100th Bomb Group, 9,
37, 64, 204–7
French Resistance, 134
the "friendly invasion," 59–60,
217–19
frostbite, 105–12

Gander Lake, Newfoundland,
35–55
Germany, Nazi, 16–17, 287.
See also Luftwaffe
anti-aircraft fire by, 3–4, 76,
80–81, 102–7, 129–32,
143, 147, 167–82,
183–85, 193, 197,
207–8, 210, 245, 257
Luftwaffe forces of, 1–10,
56, 70, 71, 73, 77–81,
84, 89–93, 101–2,
119–20, 132–33, 136,
139–52, 153–65,
167–99, 201–12, 218,
252–53, 256–57
surrender of, 277
GI Bill, 279, 282
Goering, Hermann, 70,
157–58, 162, 241
Goin Jessies (B-17), 237
Gonzales, Omar, 64–65
Gormley, Raymond, 147
Grant, Ulysses S., 14
Great Depression, 11, 15–16

Griffin, John, 147, 237
Griffiths, Reid E., 142–44, 154, 172–73, 175–76, 189–90

Hamilton Standard controllable-pitch propellers, 25
Harding, Chick, 145, 148
Harjo, Raymond, 171
Harris, Arthur T., 69
Harris, Sir Arthur Travers, 240
Harry Clever Field, Steubenville, Ohio, 46–49
Hawker Hurricane fighter planes, 227
Hawker Typhoon fighter-bomber planes, 213, 220, 225, 227–28, 231–32, 234
Heaven Can Wait (B-17), 163–64
Hitler, Adolf, 70, 103, 157–58, 239
Hondt, Erich, 161–63
Howell, Williamson S., Jr., 271–73

Imperial Guard, Berlin, 241
Instrument Pilot School, Bryan, Texas, 269, 286

Japan
    atomic bombing of, 277
    Pearl Harbor bombing by, 11–13, 21–22, 24, 65, 69, 287
Ju 88 airplanes, 208–9
Just-a-Snappin' (B-17), 9, 154, 170, 175–77, 191–92, 194–96

Kaiser Wilhelm Memorial Church, Berlin, 240
Karamol, Edward, 153
Kentucky Derby, 15
Kidd, John "Jack," 9, 65, 73, 145–46, 154, 176, 191, 194–96, 242, 246–47, 265
King Bee (B-17), 1–10, 140, 149–52, 153–65, 167–82, 183–99
Knight, Clayton, 17
Kroll Opera House, Berlin, 242

Lee, Marshall, 178
LeMay, Curtis E., 67, 74, 102–4, 125–26, 239–43, 245
Levine, Morton, 153, 176
Licato, Angelo, 153
Loguidice, Alfred, 153, 187
Long, Grady, 119–22
Luckadoo, Bob (Lucky's brother), 114–17

Luckadoo, Bobby Howell
(Lucky's wife), 269–73,
278–79, 285–86
Luckadoo, John
awards to, 111–12
background of, 11–22
Bremen offensive by, 1–10,
139–52, 153–65,
167–82, 183–99, 201,
204–5, 235, 237, 245,
246, 249–50, 265, 283
brother's wartime reunion
with, 113–17
child's birth, 283
enlistment of, 11–22, 23–24
final mission of, 249–60
first combat by, 71–82
as flight instructor, 260,
264, 270, 273–76
flight training of, 23–24,
36–50, 62–63, 66–67,
81, 136
frostbite of, 105–12
good-luck charms of, 5–6
high-altitude missions by,
99–112
marriage of, 260–73,
277–79, 283, 285–86
military resignation of,
279–82
at Newfoundland station,
35–55
return from combat of,
261–76
Sullivan's death and, 227–36,
255, 261–64, 265

Sullivan's wartime reunions
with, 213–25
as tail-gunner, 83–98
at Thorpe Abbots station, 8,
59–70, 71–82, 83–98,
99–112, 113–22,
123–37, 139–52,
153–65, 167–82,
183–99, 201–12,
227–36, 237–47,
249–60
as 350th command pilot,
249–60, 285
as 350th operations officer,
246–47, 249–60
as 351st command pilot,
1–10, 137, 139–52,
153–65, 167–82,
183–99, 237–47, 285
as 351st co-pilot, 62–70,
71–82, 83–98, 99–112,
113–22, 123–37
as 351st operations officer,
192–93, 201–12,
213–14, 237–47, 249
war perspectives of, 287–88
as Wing Adjutant of cadets,
24
Luckadoo, LV (Lucky's father),
11, 15–16, 19–20
Luckadoo, Rowena Angeline
Sauls (Lucky's mother),
15, 19–20
Luftwaffe (German air force),
56, 70, 73, 81, 136. See
also Germany, Nazi

Luftwaffe (*continued*)
  Allied bombing campaigns
    on, 252–53
  Battle of Britain by, 102,
    119–20, 218
  "Black Week" offensives
    against, 201–12
  Bremen defense by, 1–10,
    139–52, 153–65,
    167–82, 183–99
  Focke-Wulf Fw 109 planes
    of, 71, 77–80, 101–2,
    120, 132–33, 156–65,
    169–88, 191, 197,
    206–10
  Ju 88 planes of, 208–9
  Me 109 planes of, 91, 101,
    120, 171, 177, 256–57
  Me 110 planes of, 89–91,
    256–57
  strategies of, 77–79, 84,
    89–93, 149, 162–63,
    169, 193–94
Lynch, Carter, 15–16

MacDill Field, Florida, 273–76,
  277
Marie Helena (B-17), 147, 154,
  161–63
Martlesham Heath Air Base,
  England (RAF), 119–20,
  227–33
Maxwell Airfield,
  Montgomery, Alabama,
  24, 67, 278–79

Mayer, Egon, 78
McClelland, Bill, 170, 196
McFarland, Stephen L., 124
McKenzie, Bill, 269
Me 109 fighter planes, 91, 101,
  120, 171, 177, 256–57
Me 110 fighter planes, 89–91,
  256–57
Merchant Marines, 114,
  116
Messie Bessie (B-17), 170–71
MG 131 machine guns, 79–80,
  84–92, 95
Mitchell, Billy, 68
Moffly, Ed, 63
Moody Field, Valdosta,
  Georgia, 34, 38
Moreno, Walter, 171
Mosquito bombers, 146, 240,
  260
Moyle, Grady, 142–44, 153,
  173, 185, 190
Münster, Germany, bombing
  of, 203–12
Murphy, Tom, 140, 146, 174,
  177–79, 191
Murrow, Edward R., 221
mustard gas, 18

National Day of Recognition
  for our Home Front
  Heroes, 287
Norden bombsight, 69, 75, 81,
  124–25, 172, 175, 178,
  194, 257

Norden, Carl, 69
No. 71 Squadron, RAF, 227–36

100th Bomb Group, Eighth Air
    Force, 35–36, 289–90
  349th Bomb Squadron of,
    37
  350th Bomb Squadron of,
    37, 64, 246–47, 249–60,
    285
  351st Bomb Squadron of,
    1–10, 139–52, 153–65,
    167–82, 183–99,
    201–12, 213–14,
    237–47, 249, 285
    Crew 25 of, 37–57, 62–70,
    71–82, 83–98, 99–112,
    113–22, 123–37
  418th Bomb Squadron of, 9,
    37, 64, 204–7
  makeup of, 37
100th Bomb Group
    Foundation, 289–90
Our Baby (B-17), 146, 179–81

P47 Thunderbolt fighter
    planes, 146, 156–57
Pearl Harbor, Hawaii, 11–13,
    21–22, 24, 65, 69, 287
Peggy (Sully's girlfriend),
    120–21, 220–24,
    233–34
Peterson, Floyd, 178
Phartzac (B-17), 164

Phillips, Fips, 78
Picadilly Lily (B-17), 146–47,
    154, 161–62, 174–79,
    181, 191
POWs (prisoners of war), 4,
    126, 134, 181, 197, 205,
    207, 211, 252
PT-17 trainer planes, 24
Pullen, Kenneth, 218
Purple Heart awards, 4, 111–12
"Purple Heart Corner," 4, 147

Queen Bee (B-17), 150

RAF. *See* Royal Air Force, UK
Ramey, Roger, 281–82
Red Cross, 144, 211
the Reichstag, Berlin, 242
Roosevelt, Franklin D., 12,
    21–22
Rosecrans, William, 14
Rosenthal, Robert "Rosie,"
    205–12
Royal Air Force, UK (RAF),
    219, 261–64
  Martlesham Heath Air Base
    of, 119–20, 227–33
  No. 56 (Punab) Squadron of,
    119–20
  offensive strategies of,
    69–70, 102, 158, 204,
    240–41
Royal Canadian Air Force, 13,
    17–20, 117, 213

Royal Flush (B-17), 205–10
Rupnick, John, 153, 163,
    171–72, 188, 190

Saint Andrews Episcopal
    Church, Bryan, Texas,
    272
Sarabun, Charles, 178
Saunders, Lester, 170, 196
Schmeling, Max, 171
Selective Training and Service
    Act, 1940 (US), 21
Shaffer, John, 211
Shaw Field, Sumter, South
    Carolina, 24–33
Shaw, Minor, 73, 145
Silver Wings officer's club
    (Thorpe Abbots Air
    Base), 61–65, 70,
    115–16, 126–127, 135,
    139–40, 150, 203, 205,
    234, 237
Sinclair, Gordon Leonard, 120,
    230–33, 236
Sioux City, Iowa, 37
"The Soldier" (Brooke),
    122
Soviet Union, 16, 73, 103
Spain, Civil War of, 70, 102
Stanford University, 278, 282
Sullivan, Leroy "Sully"
    death of, 227–36, 255,
        261–64, 265
    enlistment of, 13, 16–21,
        117–18

Lucky's wartime reunions
        with, 213–25
    station postings of, 118–20
Sullivan, Nell Louise, 18–20,
    118, 121–22, 232–34,
    236, 261–64
Sunny (B-17), 50–55, 59–60,
    80, 128, 150
Sunny II (B-17), 128, 135, 147,
    149–50, 154, 171
Supermarine Spitfire fighter
    planes, 213–16, 225, 227

Third Cavalry Division, US, 14
Thirteenth Combat Wing,
    Eighth Air Force,
    145–46, 174, 207
Thorpe Abbots Air Base,
    England (Station 139),
    8, 59–70, 71–82,
    83–98, 99–112,
    113–22, 123–37,
    139–52, 153–65,
    167–82, 183–99,
    201–12, 227–36,
    237–47, 249–60
    characteristics of, 59–62,
        66, 142
350th Bomb Squadron,
    100th Bomb Group, 37,
    64
    Lucky as command pilot of,
        249–60, 285
    Lucky as operations officer
        of, 246–47, 249–60

351st Bomb Squadron,
       100th Bomb Group
    Crew 25 of, 37–57, 62–70,
       71–82, 83–98, 99–112,
       113–22, 123–37
    Lucky as command pilot
       of, 1–10, 137, 139–52,
       153–65, 167–82,
       183–99, 237–47, 285
    Lucky as co-pilot of, 62–70,
       71–82, 83–98, 99–112,
       113–22, 123–37
    Lucky as operations officer
       of, 192–93, 201–12,
       213–14, 237–47, 249
349th Bomb Squadron,
       100th Bomb Group, 37
Townsend (pilot), 40, 44
Turner, Howard, 50–51
Turner, Ollie, 84–85, 89–92,
       95–97, 135, 145, 191–93,
       238–46

University of Chattanooga, 11,
       16, 21, 23–24
University of Denver, 282
US Civil War, 13–14
USS George Washington
       (ocean liner), 261

V-1 flying bombs (buzz
       bombs), 250
Via, Charlie, 63, 170, 196,
       255, 265

Vultee BT-13 Valiant
       "Vibrator" trainer
       planes, 24–33, 274

Walla Walla, Washington, 37,
       43
Wendover, Utah, 37
West Point, New York, 14, 16,
       25–27, 280
"White Christmas," 33
White, Robert, 43–44, 265
Wild Cargo (B-17), 128–34
Wolff, Robert, 128–34
World War I (WW I), 17–18,
       67–68
World War II (WW II). See
       also Eighth Air Force,
       Third Bombardment
       Division; Germany,
       Nazi
    African Front of, 13, 119
    Army Air Corps offensive
       strategies in, 67–70,
       78–79, 102–5, 124–25,
       130, 145–49, 193–94,
       201, 252–53, 286
    Battle of Britain in, 102,
       119–20, 218
    Berlin bombings in, 237–47
    Bremen bombings in, 1–10,
       139–52, 153–65,
       167–82, 183–99, 201,
       204–5, 235, 237, 245,
       246, 249–50, 265, 283
    end of, 277

World War II (*continued*)
 fact preservation on,
  289–90
 home-front production
  during, 287
 Luftwaffe defense strategies
  in, 77–79, 84, 89–93,
  149, 162–63, 169,
  193–94
 Pearl Harbor bombing in,
  11–13, 21–22, 24, 65,
  69, 287

 RAF offensive strategies in,
  69–70, 102, 158, 204,
  240–41
Wright R-1820-97 Cyclone
 turbo supercharged
 radial engine, 2

Yevich, Edward, 196

Zoot Suiters (B-17), 164

Chem. Fbr.
Woltmers
hausen
Stadt
BREMEN
Werder
Kirchhuchting